THE SUICIDE
OF AMERICAN CHRISTIANITY

THE SUICIDE

OF AMERICAN CHRISTIANITY

Drinking the "Cool"-Aid of Secular Humanism

MICHAEL D. LeMay

WESTBOW
PRESS
A DIVISION OF THOMAS NELSON

WestBow Press books may be ordered through booksellers or by contacting:

WestBow Press
A Division of Thomas Nelson
1663 Liberty Drive
Bloomington, IN 47403
www.westbowpress.com
1-(866) 928-1240

Because of the dynamic nature of the Internet, any web addresses or links contained in this book may have changed since publication and may no longer be valid. The views expressed in this work are solely those of the author and do not necessarily reflect the views of the publisher, and the publisher hereby disclaims any responsibility for them.

Any people depicted in stock imagery provided by Thinkstock are models, and such images are being used for illustrative purposes only.

Certain stock imagery © Thinkstock.

ISBN: 978-1-4497-5024-4 (sc)
ISBN: 978-1-4497-4963-7 (hc)
ISBN: 978-1-4497-4964-4 (e)

Library of Congress Control Number: 2012907626

Printed in the United States of America

WestBow Press rev. date: 05/08/2012

TABLE OF CONTENTS

DEDICATION

I dedicate this book to my Lord and Savior Jesus Christ, upon whom I depend for every breath I take. He called me home when I had strayed so far. He taught me how to be a true disciple, father and husband, and loved me when I was unlovable. While I see my human depravity as filthy and disgusting, he sees me as beautiful and wonderful. How does one react to such love without gratitude and joy?

I want to thank my wife Nancy. Her love and courage led me back to God and his truth. She is what Eve was created to be for Adam.

I thank my children Matt and Andrea. They endured too many years with a father who did not walk closely with God, yet they unconditionally loved me. I am overjoyed as I watch them draw nearer to God every day.

I thank the Board, staff and supporters of Q90 FM, along with my Stand Up For the Truth co-host Amy Spreeman for their dedication and passion for God. All of you have blessed me in many ways.

I thank the Watchmen on the Wall who have been sounding the alarm over the past forty years as the American Church has started to slowly die. I apologize to each of you for arriving so late to the battle. I hope what I have lacked in timeliness will be made up for with passion and courage.

FOREWORD

Mike LeMay is a true watchman on the wall. This book addresses many issues that currently plague our nation and American Christianity. As a Christian coming from a Muslim background, and a fellow watchman, I see how the culture is infecting American Christianity when just the opposite should be happening. Mike points this out accurately and clearly, challenging the church to once again be a beacon of light.

This book accurately addresses the "taboo" subject of Islam that most will not talk about. Islam is a cancer and a vicious virus that America and many of its churches seems to be having a love affair with, unaware of the destruction they are courting.

Mike reveals how our education system is indoctrinating our children into secular humanism, and how some Christian Colleges and seminaries seem to be embracing a similar agenda.

This book not only takes a hard look at these and other dangerous movements, but asks some serious questions about why many Christian leaders are silent about, or even embracing these movements. Mike questions if many of our churches are beginning to look more like IBM or Starbuck's Coffee, rather than a house of worship.

A growing number of people see an emerging pattern of "nice theology" being promoted by Christian leaders, but it comes with a very heavy price: The truth about God's perfect nature, the pure gospel, the absolute truth of scripture and moral clarity. Mike points out the severe consequences this is having on American Christianity.

Mike also challenges every Christian to take a good hard look in the mirror, questioning our own motives and behaviors as Christians. He asks if we are attempting to redefine God into an image more acceptable to our human desires of the flesh, rather than worshipping him in his entirety.

This book will challenge you as Mike asks very difficult questions ignored for too long by many. Every Christian needs to read this book and ponder its warnings.

Elijah Abraham

Founder

Living Oasis Ministries

INTRODUCTION

American Christianity as we know it is gasping for its last breath. It is slowly dying and at our current rate of degeneration it may only be a decade or two before it will be unrecognizable when held up against the Word of God. For all intent and purpose it will be dead, with only a small remnant remaining. This should come as little surprise to anyone who truly understands the teachings of Christianity and has been watching the church wither away over the past fifty years.

The church is under attack externally from a powerful enemy, Satan. He has assembled a strong, passionate army to neutralize, even destroy American Christianity. This army includes some very powerful institutions that together form a very formidable foe for Christianity in this nation.

The most obvious pawn of the enemy is a rapidly degenerating secular culture. It is being augmented by a growing progressive government, a strongly biased media, a public education system bent on indoctrinating our children into secular humanism, and a radical religion bent on destroying Christianity at every turn—Islam.

Fifty years ago a child in the womb was considered a life with a right to be born. Now the child in the womb is disposable property. Up until the day of delivery its life hangs on a thread as the mother contemplates whether she wants to be a mother or dispose of the inconvenience within her.

Fifty years ago homosexuality was considered to be sinful. Now it is accepted as normal, even celebrated. Today public schools encourage young children to explore their sexuality when they are as young as six years old. Homosexual marriage is now legal in eight states and within the next two years may become constitutionally protected as a "right" for every citizen in this nation.

Pornography used to be shunned as unacceptable behavior but now it produces more revenue than all major sports in this nation combined. Adults and children access it from their smart phones and download it at will.

Islam, clearly a religion of anti-Christ as defined in 1 John, has become the darling religion of American culture. Islam, a religion that teaches homosexuals, adulterers and abortionists should be put to death, is somehow embraced as a "religion of tolerance" in America. Islam, a religion that commands every Muslim to kill Christians, Jews and every infidel that will not convert to it, is somehow seen as a "religion of peace" in American culture.

American secular culture is disintegrating by the day, becoming increasingly hostile to Christianity. It is bolstered by a radically progressive court system that supports evil and shuns Christian values at every turn. Polls show that an increasing number of Americans find abortion and homosexuality perfectly acceptable, and a shrinking number of Americans consider themselves Christians.

In a nation where eighty-six percent of its citizens still claim to be Christians, read these passages from Romans Chapter One and see if they might apply today:

> "The wrath of God is being revealed from heaven against all the godlessness and wickedness of men who suppress the truth by their wickedness, since what may be known about God is plain to them."
>
> "For although they knew God, they neither glorified him as God nor gave thanks to him, but their thinking became futile and their foolish hearts were darkened. Although they claimed to be wise, they became fools and exchanged the glory of the immortal God for images made to look like mortal man and birds and

animals and reptiles. Therefore God gave them over to the sinful
desires of their hearts, to sexual impurity for the degrading of their
bodies with one another. They exchanged the truth of God for a
lie, and worshipped and served created things rather than the
Creator—who is forever praised. Amen."

Sound like America to you?

Make no mistake, American Christianity is at war, whether we wish it or not. At the current rate of attrition Christianity will be marginalized to the point where it will no longer be a worthy opponent for the onslaught of secular humanism taking this nation over. Our nation was founded on Judeo-Christian Law and principles and the church was seen as a force to keep the culture and the government in check, making sure they did not stray from those Judeo-Christian laws and principles. For nearly two hundred years the Church performed admirably. When the culture or government would begin to stray from Christian values, the church would rise up in unison and shout "Not on our watch!" But all that started to change in the 1960s. Suddenly the church seemed to have gone on vacation. As the secular culture made inroads with our children, the Church was suddenly not there to push back. This ushered in a gradual decay to where we are now—a secular humanist culture on the rise and a church that seems to be in rapid decline.

This external battle force put together by Satan is powerful and committed to destroying American Christianity. Yet with all its force it should be no match for the church. The church has two powerful weapons that should render the enemy obsolete—the truth of God's Word and the power of the Holy Spirit. But sometime in the past fifty years we began to leave those weapons behind and tried to fight this battle with our own strength and tactics.

Many powerful human empires of the past all came to ultimate destruction, no matter how powerful they seemed to be. On the exterior they had superior military forces and were in a position to continue domination for many more centuries, and no enemy could stand against them on the battlefield. But the demise of great empires or civilizations usually starts from the inside. Rome's status as a world empire began to wane as internal strife and corruption consumed her from within. Nazi Germany started to show the first cracks in its armor when a powerful underground was formed in Germany by its own citizens who were enlightened to the evil they previously supported. This underground movement started to secretly work with Germany's enemies to coordinate internal attacks and weaken the Nazi terror machine.

But an example worth noting for the purpose of this book is the Aztec civilization of Central America. Once a powerful empire reaching its height in the early 16th century, the Aztec civilization was decimated quickly with the arrival of the Spanish explorer Cortes. He quickly found allies within the empire who wished to gain power on their own and worked with Cortes in waging war against the Aztec leaders. They did find some early success weakening the Aztec Empire, but according to several historians Cortes brought another weapon with him that finally destroyed the Aztec leadership and culture—smallpox. This deadly disease was imported into the Aztec culture and destroyed it from within by weakening the empire and allowing the Spaniards and their allies to destroy this once powerful empire. The great Aztec empire was destroyed by an external virus introduced to it by foreigners.

I believe this is happening to American Christianity today. Satan, armed with powerful allies is waging a vicious attack on the Church—a Church that is already weakened by a foreign virus it has willfully ingested over the past fifty years—tolerance. If American Christianity does not defeat this virus immediately we will become so weakened internally that we will be easy pickings for the powerful army Satan has assembled.

This virus is being spread by two internal groups within the camp of American Christianity—weak, unprincipled leaders and those that follow them. Many of our leaders are embracing the poisonous virus of tolerance that is internally weakening the Church. We see fewer Christian leaders calling homosexuality sin; fewer leaders standing up to the murderous scourge of abortion; fewer leaders even talking about sin anymore. These leaders are less interested in a pure, holy church and more interested in popularity, fame and "nickels and noses". They are leading American Christianity to the brink of spiritual suicide—but they are only leading where we want them to lead us.

Christian followers are equally to blame for the slow death creeping into American Christianity. We no longer want leaders who preach about sin and our human depravity; we prefer teachers who make us feel good about ourselves. We no longer want leaders who challenge us to pursue righteousness and holiness; we want leaders who tell us how to have our best life now. We no longer want leaders who tell us we should fear falling into the hands of an angry God; we want leaders who coddle us and assure us that God loves us just the way we are—decrepit sinners.

Christian leaders and we who follow them are knowing or unknowing agents of the enemy sowing dissent and the virus of tolerance within our own ranks. We are weakening the Church to the point it may soon fall to the enemy pounding at the door.

We can blame the secular culture for the death of American Christianity but they are only doing what is expected of people blind to God and His nature and character. Just what leads us to expect these people to behave in a different manner? Their very nature hates or denies God and deep down they wish to be their own gods.

We can blame our Christian leaders who compromise, even support the secular culture by their cowardly leadership, but our leaders are merely a reflection of what we truly desire in our leaders. American Christians these days are more interested in feeling good about ourselves than we are in being challenged to walk away from our sins and seek righteousness and holiness. We are more interested in being seen as open minded and tolerant than we are in speaking the truth to the lost that desperately need that truth. So we appoint leaders who reflect our spiritual laziness and apathy.

The sad truth is that rank and file Christians—you and I—are ultimately responsible for the demise of American Christianity. We cry out against the evils of culture while secretly we embrace its values and behave no differently than the lost. We desire leaders who will help us feel good about ourselves instead of confronting our sinful depravity.

It is absolutely crucial that we view this battle in proper context. The death of American Christianity will not be a murder—it will be a suicide. The secular humanists have the poison to kill us but it can only happen if we willingly ingest that poison. Too many leaders are promoting the very poison which will kill us, holding it out there for us to ingest. But we alone will choose whether to reject it or continue to drink it. If death comes to American Christianity make no mistake about this: It will not be by murder, it will be by suicide.

Witnessing Suicide

My mother committed suicide. The death certificate states the cause as liver failure, but that was simply the conclusion of thirty years of abuse from addictions to cigarettes and alcohol.

A once strong, beautiful and vibrant woman, my mother withered away as she turned to cigarettes and alcohol, willingly ingesting the poison that would eventually kill her. American Christianity was also once a strong, beautiful and vibrant woman and she is drinking the poison of secular humanists.

My mother was once a rock of virtue and conviction—just like American Christianity used to be.

She was attacked externally by my father—just like American Christianity is being attacked by the culture. Under attack and abuse, she slowly began to think there was something wrong with her—that she was no longer beautiful and lovable. So she began to "medicate" herself thinking it would ease the pain. She slowly began to allow guilt and shame brought on by lies to consume and change her. She gave up—just like American Christianity is now doing.

The regular verbal abuse and physical attacks took their toll, and my mother finally gave up, accepting the attacks as normal and even acceptable. She slowly became what the lies of my father told her she was—unattractive and undesirable—just like American Christianity.

I have witnessed suicide—a slow, steady suicide and I am witnessing it again with American Christianity. My mother ignored the love and advice of those who truly loved her, choosing to remain on her self-destructive path. American Christianity is doing the same.

Christianity in America looks more like the culture these days than the Church in the Book of Acts. Compromise at every turn when Jesus warned us against compromise; seeking the love and admiration of the world when Jesus told us the world would hate us because it hated him first; and a growing embrace, even a love for American culture that is destroying the church itself.

In Isaiah 7:9 God warns us: *"If you do not stand firm in your faith, you will not stand at all."* Just what does Christianity in America stand for these days? Is it light and salt to the disintegrating culture? Or is it breathing in and embracing the culture, allowing this all consuming cancer to slowly kill us? There is time to rescue the church. But it will take courage, dedication and repentance—from our leaders and those they lead.

Christianity in America is on life support—and we are preparing to pull our own plug. Soon it will be but a remnant of what it once was. Will we sit by idly as we commit spiritual suicide? Or will we summon the courage to question the path many Christian leaders are taking us down? Will we discover the biblical meaning of true love? Or will we continue to treat "love" as never having to say "you're wrong". This battle has been clearly laid at our feet by the Lord our God. Continue to remain silent and question nothing we are taught . . . or be a good Berean and take everything to the Word of God to see if what we are being taught is truth. The second choice will lead us back to where we belong. The first option will lead to spiritual suicide.

We will look at the poison the culture is offering to us as Christians. But remember we are not forced to consume that poison; it will be our choice if we choose to drink it.

This book will be critical of some in Christian leadership who seem to be presenting the poison as acceptable and harmless. But this book is also directed at you and me--we are just as much to blame for the slow suicide of American Christianity. Every time we sin or accept sin; every time we fail to hold others accountable or do not allow them to hold us accountable; every time we turn an apathetic eye of acceptance to the virus infecting the church, we are every bit as responsible as anyone for the death of the church in America.

On November 18, 1978 in Jonestown, Guyana, nine-hundred-eighteen "Christians" drank the "cool-aid". They chose to follow a leader who was leading them away from the truth of God's Word. A man of great charisma and charm, Jim Jones convinced his followers to do the unthinkable—take their own lives. They, not the culture or their leader, were ultimately responsible for the choice they made.

The secular culture is the "cool-aid" and some of our leaders are offering it as an acceptable, even beneficial drink these days. Will we drink it?

I hope this book lights a fire in you to become a true biblical scholar. If you are solely depending on your pastor or Christian media to teach you the Word of God, I hope this book wakes you out of your sleepy, apathetic state. Whether or not American Christianity can escape its own self-inflicted demise is debatable. What is not in question is your ultimate responsibility to hold on to biblical truth no matter the fate of American Christianity. Read God's Word like your life depends on it—because my friend it does.

CHAPTER ONE

AWAKENING OUT OF A DEEP SPIRITUAL SLEEP

A Call to Battle

It was a pleasant, warm Friday in June, 2010. The previous thirteen months had been quite the journey. After maintaining our studio in the basement of a chiropractic office for fifteen years, we were ready to move in to our own, brand-new facility. As the staff members of a listener-supported station, we are very judicious with the financial support our listeners provided. We had put a fleece out before the Lord—if He wanted us to build a new facility we could own, He would have to provide a way for us to do so without increasing our budget and needing to ask for additional support from our listeners. God provided in an amazing way.

Here I sat in our brand new building with seventy percent more space, in a nearly perfect location, and we were actually paying less monthly than we had been paying when we were renting! God accomplished this through a group of individuals and businesses that donated a lot of time and flooring, cabinetry, windows and the roof. A year of sixty-to-seventy hour work weeks had finally come to an end. At the age of fifty-six I looked forward to a little less hectic pace.

I sat at my desk contemplating what Nancy and I should do for the weekend. She had talked about taking a drive to Door County, walking through the beautiful parks and catching lunch and coffee. Then I received a phone call that would rock my world.

A pastor from Appleton, a city twenty miles south of Green Bay, was on the phone. We had never met or spoken but I knew of him. He introduced himself and asked a question that would mark my future in a challenging, wonderful way.

"Mike, is Q90 FM planning on supporting Lifest with Jim Wallis scheduled as the key speaker?"

My answer showed how I had been lulled to sleep spiritually: "Uh, who the heck is Jim Wallis?"

The pastor told me he would send me some links to Web sites about Wallis and his organization, Sojourners.[1] Quite frankly my initial thought was to dismiss this offer as one coming from a legalistic pastor who would figure out some way to protest a historically successful Christian rock music event. The event features some pretty heavy Christian rock music, and draws tens of thousands of Christian youth and parents every year. The organization that holds the event is a fine Christian organization bringing the hope of Jesus Christ to youth around the country.

So I investigated the links the pastor sent me. I quickly realized it would take a lot more than a couple hours of research to determine what, if any, actions we should take. Q90 FM has been a title sponsor of this event every year and we served as close partners with Life Promotions[2], the organization putting on the event, intended to reach hurting youth for Jesus. I was not about to make a snap decision on such an important issue.

I informed my bride that we would probably have to forego our trip to Door County and that I would need her help researching sites. She responded in the way I had come to expect—God wanted some more of our time, and she was ready to join me in answering the call. Lifest was rapidly approaching and this issue required our immediate attention. We spent much of the weekend going through research, double-checking information on the web to verify or refute the opinions of many people who believed Wallis and his organization had no business speaking to Christian youth.

I informed my board of the potential conflict and continued researching, crosschecking and assessing the situation. I also texted a message to my close friend who heads up Life Promotions, informing him we were investigating opinions and information concerning Wallis and Sojourners. His response was kind and gracious.

By the following Tuesday, after sharing the information we found with our board, we decided the best thing to do was to talk with the organization and share our concerns. My research had led me to some very troubling information about both Wallis and Sojourners.

Jim Wallis is to say the least a Marxist sympathizer. He was a student chapter leader in the sixties for the Students for a Democratic Society, an anarchist organization that protested pretty much everything the United States held dear. Wallis led the cheers as the United States went down to defeat in Viet Nam and often spoke publicly and glowingly of Communist regimes around the world.

He was hired after the 2004 presidential elections by the Democratic Party to help them garner more evangelical Christian votes. To say the least, he was successful. Evangelical Christians, in my opinion, were largely responsible for the election of Barack Obama—the most pro-abortion, pro-homosexual president in the history of the United States[3]. Wallis currently sits as one of President Obama's chief spiritual advisors.

An important disclaimer here: I consider myself a conservative--both politically and spiritually. Politically, I believe the federal government has grown into an almost uncontrollable monster, choking the freedom and liberties of United States citizens. I believe that through a well-intentioned "war on poverty" our government is systematically squelching our free-enterprise economy and getting more and more citizens addicted to government support, creating a narcissistic, lazy electorate.

I see the federal government as an increasingly strong enemy of religious freedom. Through an overload of extremely progressive judges, the government has brought us tragedies like abortion. It was incredibly initially ruled legal as an expression of a woman's right to privacy, and abortion has killed more than fifty million children under the guise of "choice". Sadly, the Church in the United States has, for the most part, chosen to sit out this battle for life.

A careful, objective study of our founding documents shows that the majority of our founding fathers were Christians. While a few of them were deists, their numbers were far smaller than progressive education and media currently spins those numbers to be. Our democratic republic is, I believe, the one form of human government that comes closest to getting it right with God. Our founding fathers recognized and eloquently stated that man's rights come from God alone—and the focus of the federal government should be to protect those individual rights. The laws of the United States were fashioned after the Law of God—the Ten Commandments. Sadly, our founding fathers would spin in their graves if they saw how the government has grown into what many believe is a monster of oppression these days.

I make this disclosure because of this fact: Jim Wallis and his organization strongly support expanded "cradle to grave" government and extreme "social justice". Both of these rub against my beliefs as a conservative. But they are not the reason I was concerned about him speaking at Lifest.

As I carefully studied the Sojourners Web site, I saw some alarming spiritual content that I did not think was appropriate to present to young Christians. For example Sojourners, which claims to be a Christian organization, referred to several "sins" on their site including:

- Immigration laws
- The Gulf oil spill
- global warming
- Poverty and disparity between the rich and poor

What sadly was missing were two crucial Christian issues they did not refer to as sin:

- Abortion
- Homosexual marriage

4

I don't care one iota if Jim Wallis wants to preach his Marxist propaganda and beliefs—that is his right as a United States citizen. What concerned me was that he would be a keynote speaker at an event where thousands of young Christians would hear his eloquent appeal for social justice and be attracted to an organization that claims to be Christian, but is anything but that. I was concerned as well that youth would connect to Sojourners and the other sham "Christian" organization Wallis founded with Tony Campolo, Red Letter Christians.[4] This would lead youth down a destructive path that would undermine the Word of God as absolute truth.

I conferred with board members, and they instructed me to meet with the organization to see if we could reach an agreement. I cannot overstate how painful the decision was for our leadership. We were risking a public disagreement with a fellow Christian organization that we partnered with for longer than a decade. But after much prayer and thought, we knew it was the right thing to do.

Our discussion with the organization led me to two direct conversations with Jim Wallis as we explored possible compromises. The first discussion was actually pretty cordial. We offered to fly Wallis up at our expense so we could introduce him to area pastors who could explore his stances and discern their compatibility with the Christian faith. I agreed that if the pastors gave him the green light, we would acquiesce. He rejected this plan out of hand during our first conversation. We hung up from our first talk agreeing to pray and to think about the dilemma we faced.

Later that week, with a self-imposed deadline to bring this to resolution less than eighteen hours away, I sat in my office on a Thursday afternoon, quite frankly getting cold feet. I started to reason that perhaps we were making too big a thing out of this and I was worried about causing division by having to take a public stance against a brother in the Lord—a man who tirelessly flew around the country sharing a message of hope with teens. I knew we had to publicly announce our reason for not supporting the event this year. We had decided to be as low-key, yet honest as possible by not mentioning anything on air, and simply announcing it on our Web site. Nancy and I were preparing a statement to be posted the following day.

My cell phone rang—it was Jim Wallis. I answered the phone expecting a reasonable conversation like our previous one. Not quite. He began ripping into us, accusing us of being right-wing fanatics, trying to silence progressive Christian view points. He stated that he was sure that if Chuck Colson were scheduled to appear we would have no objection because he leans to the right politically. I assured him politics had nothing to do with our decision. Our decision was made purely on the fact that Sojourners is very weak spiritually in their stance on sin and the absolute truth of God's Word. They are an interfaith organization, partnering with people of all religions to promote what we believe is religious syncretism and a dangerous humanist agenda. We were concerned that young, impressionable Christians would be drawn to Sojourners by the social justice call and find spiritual affinity in an organization that called themselves Christian yet refused to make right calls on obvious sin, and was also yoked spiritually with pagan religions in their quest to achieve "economic equality and justice".

I explained to Wallis that we were opposed to his call for wealth redistribution through higher taxes for two reasons: First, that charity should be voluntary with Christian donors choosing which organizations they wish to support. Secondly, their call for more and more government involvement in wealth redistribution, picking what causes and charities to support, would be dangerous to Christianity because federal monies to charitable organizations require those monies not be used to push a religious agenda. In essence Christians would be forced, through higher taxes, to support organizations at best neutral, and at worst hostile to sharing the gospel of Jesus Christ.

Now, I am a warrior, and don't mind a good fight or argument. As Wallis tried to attack me as bigoted or uncaring, strangely I felt no rise in blood pressure or tension. I felt the peace of God guiding and calming me. It was Wallis, the "enlightened and reasonable" one, who was boiling mad. I felt the Holy Spirit lead me to ask a couple questions:

First, "Mr. Wallis, do you believe homosexuality is a sin?" Three times I calmly asked and three times he refused to answer.

Second, "Jim do you believe abortion is a sin?" He yelled "I am the most pro-life person you will ever know!" I responded, "Good, then my question is an easy one—do you believe abortion is a sin?" Again, three times I asked and three times he refused to answer.

I told Wallis I was deeply concerned with his position as chief spiritual advisor to President Obama, and Wallis adamantly defended Barack Obama as a committed Christian. I pointed out that Obama's voting record in the Senate received the highest praise from both pro-abortion and pro-gay organizations. He became irritated when I suggested that he either agreed with Obama's Christian views on these issues or was an ineffective advisor based on Obama's stances.

The Holy Spirit led me to offer one more piece of bait to expose his real agenda: "Jim, I suppose you also buy in to all this global warming propaganda?" His answer told me all I needed to know about Sojourners and the social justice movement.

An Unchristian Worldview

When I asked Wallis about his thoughts on the need to aggressively fight global warming, his answer betrayed his worldview. "Absolutely, we need to have a pristine planet before Jesus can return!" There is the bottom line: Wallis is a left wing dominionist. Dominionists are people who believe mankind can control the final saga of this world's story—that the fate of this world rests upon man's ability to clean up his act, and if we did we could usher in economic equality, justice and an end to poverty and pollution. Once we purified the earth, Jesus could then return to save all mankind and rule in peace. In other words, the return of our Messiah is dependent on the work of mankind. This belief is the height of human arrogance—thinking we actually can rewrite prophetic scripture and control our own spiritual destiny. I pointed out that we must be reading two completely different bibles—mine says that when Jesus returns

7

there will be wars, rumors of war, poverty, pestilence and chaos. Wallis did not back down, reaffirming man's responsibility to clean up the earth of poverty, pollution and injustice before Jesus could return. Never mind what the bible says, we can control our own destiny.

Our conversation ended abruptly when he hung up. I informed my friend, the leader of Life Promotions, that we would post our decision to sit the event out on our Web site because of Jim Wallis being the key speaker to Christian youth.

I met with the staff the next morning and informed them of our decision. I reiterated that while we had to take this difficult stance, we hoped our relationship with our ministry partner would remain strong in the coming years, confident this was just a blip on the radar screen in our longtime relationship. We prayed as a staff that God would be glorified by whatever transpired at the event.

With that, I thought we would move on and return to normal, going back to simply being a radio ministry that played positive, uplifting music for youth. I saw this as an end to a difficult chapter in my life as a Christian. Life would return to a more normal state. But God had other plans.

Fasten Your Seatbelts!

A few days later I was enjoying my usual Wednesday morning breakfast with a board member and two other Christians when my cell phone rang. It was my lovely bride with a warning: "You better head into the station; Glenn Beck just read our statement about Jim Wallis on his national radio program."

I quickly returned to the office. I was receiving phone calls and emails from around the country. A few were critical of our stance, but most were thanking us for taking the stand we took.

As word got out locally, I was receiving hundreds of emails and phone calls. Some were supportive and some were in opposition to our stance. Most wondered why we decided to take a stand on such a relatively minor issue. How could we miss Lifest when so many youth would be there for us to interact with and minister to? Others questioned how we could bring division to the local Body by making so much out of something like this. A few listeners were furious, telling me they would never again support Q90 FM because of our stance.

Pastors were calling and wanting more information on why we made such a bold decision. Listeners wondered, considering our longstanding partnership with the event, what could we possibly have discovered to lead us to take such a strong stance? What we came to believe after a lot of research and prayer is this: The social justice movement in this country is anti-Christian. Its destructive, forced wealth redistribution policy aside, it is a movement that is dismissing the Word of God as absolute truth and promoting religious syncretism.

As I continued to research and monitor Sojourners, I found connections with many other "Christian" organizations that had been questioned by Watchmen over the years. Organizations like Red Letter Christians, founded by Wallis with Tony Campolo. We will discuss their agenda later.

I saw that a member of the Sojourners Board was one Brian McLaren. McLaren, quite frankly, is a heretic. He denies the substitutionary atonement of sins by Jesus on the cross—the central belief in Christianity.

In a lighter, but serious moment, I read on their website that Sojourners was offering a special gift if people joined their organization—a poster of Mohandas Gandhi. So why would a Christian organization offer a poster of Gandhi free to new subscribers? Because I believe they see all religions as equally truthful and valid.

As I explored the social justice movement further, I saw a disturbing pattern. The movement which claims Christian roots is more accurately a political activist organization. They actively support pro-abortion and pro-homosexuality movements, and push a radical progressive agenda of bigger government. Now, we are all sinners in need of God's grace, and all sin is an offense to God. But I believe abortion and homosexuality cut right to the heart of God. The murder of the most innocent of people and a sexual sin that seeks to destroy the biblical foundation of the family are very serious offenses. So why would a "Christian" organization promote political movements that continually vote to support abortion and homosexual marriage?

I discovered an unofficial alliance between the social justice movement and the Emergent Church movement, as leaders of one was closely knit with leaders of the other. I started seeing the list of usual suspects tied together in these and other movements that seemed to have one thing in common—discounting anything as absolute truth, including the Word of God. Experience and emotion were beginning to replace biblical knowledge and wisdom on the throne of American Christian intellect. Gradually what we feel is right was trumping what God says is right.

I Was Blind, but Now I See

A year and a half earlier, I received a tremendous blessing from God that seemed anything but a blessing at the time. Little did I know what God was preparing me to do in his perfect timing.

I was recovering from reconstructive shoulder surgery. Shoulder rehabilitation is probably one of the closest things a man will ever experience to the pain of child birth. There were times when the physical therapist would push and crank on my shoulder that I wanted to deck him. In November of 2008 my rehabilitation was complete. One day on my way back from a breakfast meeting, it began to snow—the only thing is the skies were bright and sunny. My right eye was seeing what looked like steady snow flakes falling from the sky, making vision out of that eye close to impossible.

I had undergone cataract surgery in both of my eyes years earlier, and every couple years I would have to go in when I saw a few "floaters" in an eye. It was pretty routine outpatient surgery where they use a laser to clean up the lens. I figured this new experience was just another routine visit to the eye doctor.

When I arrived, the physician sent me next door to a retinal specialist who confirmed I had a detached retina in my right eye. Surgery was scheduled a few days later and the retina was successfully repaired. At the end of the surgery they place a gas bubble in the eye to prevent infection while the eye is healing. The bubble severely impairs your vision, but gradually reduces over two-to-three weeks. So I was blind in my right eye, but no problem, that's why God gave us two eyes.

I was scheduled for a check up ten days after the surgery to make sure everything was healing properly. The night before the check up, Nancy and I went out to dinner. Usually I pray before we eat but for some reason this night I asked my bride to pray for us. This was early December and we had easily met our five-thousand dollar annual deductible on our health insurance plan with the shoulder and eye surgery. Here is a summary of Nancy's prayer:

"Father God, we thank you for the blessing of this food, our marriage and most of all the sacrifice of Jesus, by which we are your children. We thank you for all you have provided for us. Father if there are any further medical needs, please allow them before the end of the year since our deductible is met. We thank you in the name of Jesus, amen."

The next day I found out that indeed the prayer of a righteous woman is heard. I sat in the doctor's office and he pronounced my right eye was healing very nicely, and in about four to five days I should have a complete recovery of sight in that eye. I reported that I was seeing a couple small floaters in my left eye. "Well it looked fine two weeks ago when I checked it, but I'll take another look".

Then I heard two words you never want your doctor to say: "Oh, crap!" He told me that somehow I now had a central detachment of the retina in my left eye and that he needed to perform surgery immediately, because a blow to the head might lead to permanent sight loss in that eye. I had surgery that night and Nancy drove me home, same as ten days earlier. But things were much different this time. The new gas bubble in my left eye, combined with the one in the right eye, left me virtually blind for three days. I sat there unable to read the Bible or watch television. It was just God and me.

As I sought his voice, I was beginning to "hear" some very strange things. Messages like "I will bring this nation to its knees economically so it chooses if it will worship money or me". That is certainly coming about, but one other message I kept hearing was a chilling one that I just could not understand at that time: "I have taken your sight; I will restore it so you can connect the dots."

My memory raced to try and remember anywhere in God's Word where "connecting the dots" was mentioned as a spiritual gift or even mentioned at all, and of course I came up empty. I tried to dismiss the message but I could not over the following months. I had no idea what God meant by "connect the dots".

As usual, God prepares us in advance for the work he ordains within us. As I look back now, I see what he meant by "connect the dots". We tend to look at movements like social justice, the Emergent Church, Universalism or New Age Christianity as separate entities, but they are not. They are all different parts of Satan's master plan to deceive many in these final days. In fairness, most of the leaders of these movements do not realize they are pawns in Satan's chess match with God, and every one of us is used by Satan at times. But leaders of these and other movements are unknowingly advancing Satan's agenda to deceive millions in America. They have been led astray from the absolute truth of God's Word and His true character and nature. They may mean well, but they lack or reject the knowledge of the Word and seek to repackage God to fit the times, or their personal vision of who God should be.

Standing Up For the Truth

As I shared information uncovered about Jim Wallis, Brian McLaren, Tony Campolo and others with our board, God began to speak to us as a team. He encouraged us to continue the battle, and to get out of our mindset of being a radio station that just plays music, calling us to be his vessel to open the eyes of other Christians who had also been lulled to sleep. On December 6th, 2010, after a lot of prayer and preparation, Stand

Up For the Truth[5] debuted on Q90 FM.[6] Amy Spreeman and I have hosted the show ever since. The show is loved by many and hated by some, but it is not dismissed or ignored. We are asking the tough questions too long ignored by Christians and our leaders. We share the news and our opinions, along with those of our guests, and always tell people to take everything they hear back to the Word of God to see if it is true. The only measure man has for real truth is the written Word of God. It must be the absolute truth upon which every opinion and issue is measured.

There are no sacred cows on this show, and no issue is ignored. From Islam to the Emergent Church; from New Age Christianity to biblical illiteracy; and from abortion to homosexuality, the issues are discussed and the Word of God is the sole star of the show.

I am often asked just what we are trying to accomplish with Stand Up For the Truth. Some accuse us of dividing the Body of Christ at times and stirring up dissension within the ranks. Some pastors report that every week a listener is coming to them and sharing something they heard on the show, wondering where their church stood on the issue. And quite frankly, some pastors do not like the added questions and scrutiny. They would prefer to remain "Ostrich Christians", sticking their heads in the sand, believing evil and deception will just pass them by if they can't see it.

So why do we air Stand Up For the Truth? George Barna[7] reports that less than half of all self-professed "born-again believers" actually believe that the bible is absolute truth. More and more Christians believe truth is relative, not absolute. We seem to have returned to the pre-reformation days, where biblical illiteracy is the norm. Far too many Christians are going to church on Sunday to hear what the pastor or priest says is in the bible (if he reads from it at all), rather than being like the Bereans in Acts 17:11—searching the scriptures daily to determine real truth. That is the reason we air Stand Up For the Truth—and why in eighteen short months it has reached an international audience. Dedicated Christians are hungry for truth in a world of lies. They have been lied to by the government, public schools, the secular media, and even by some of our church leaders. Slow death is creeping into American Christianity—and a growing number of Christians refuse to be a part of it.

We *Are* in a War

Three years ago I was as blind as anyone to the great deception infecting American Christianity. But God used what I first saw as suffering to reveal the truth to me; the truth that American Christianity is slowly committing suicide, just like my mother. My mother's suicide could have been prevented if she had listened to her doctors and to those of us who loved her, but she chose to remain on a slow suicidal path. Will the church listen to those who have diagnosed her with cancer? Will American Christianity stop the cancer of secular culture from infecting the Body? Or will she continue a slow death and eventually pull the life support plug—the Word and truth of God?

We are in a war. Make no mistake about that. We face a tough, experienced, and powerful enemy in Satan. He has a strong, committed army at his disposal and they are pounding at the walls of American Christianity. But this army would have no power over us if we stood on the truth of God's Word by the power of the Holy Spirit. But unfortunately the enemy has sympathizers within our camp and they are weakening us from within. Weak Christian leaders and followers are allowing poison to weaken us. This poison will kill all but a remnant if we do not stop drinking it. I am at heart an optimist, and I know God can do anything. But when I see how American Christianity is evolving, my optimism is challenged.

I hope what you read will challenge you and awaken you if you find you have been lulled to sleep. I would rather be able to write a happy book about how we are defeating the enemy at every turn, but that book would be a fiction novel. I am a watchman on the wall. I did not ask for this assignment and some times I wish God would give it to someone else. But he is God and I am just Mike, and where He commands, I will follow. Whether you want to accept it or not, we are all called to be watchmen.

We have been entrusted with the truth of God's Word and the indwelling of the Holy Spirit. So read the command the Lord your God gives you as a watchman—and read it carefully.

> *"Son of man, I have made you a watchman on the wall for the house of Israel; so hear the word I speak and give them warning from me. When I say to the wicked 'O wicked man you will surely die' and you do not speak out to dissuade him from his ways, that wicked man will die for his sin, and I will hold you accountable for his blood. But if you do warn the wicked man to turn from his ways and he does not do so, he will die for his sin, but you will be saved yourself."*

Ezekiel 33:7-9 (NIV)

Footnotes

1) sojo.net
2) lifepromotions.com
3) votesmart.org
4) redletterchristians.org
5) standupforthetruth.com
6) q90fm.com
7) barna.org

CHAPTER TWO

THE DUTIES OF THE WATCHMAN

Life was a lot easier just two short years ago. I was leading a Christian Radio station that played music twenty-four hours every day. No teaching programs and no controversy except the rare caller who warned we were playing the devil's music or telling us every translation except the original King James Version was invalid and deceptive.

I had just turned fifty-six years of age and life was settling down after a year of seventy-hour work weeks as we planned for and moved into our brand new facility in DePere. Nancy and I were doing wonderfully as a couple, and the ministry was growing and doing very well as we embraced our core values and principles, challenging one another to draw closer to God individually and as a team. Life would start to slow down now and I welcomed normal work weeks once again.

I often hear that if you want to make God laugh tell Him your plans for tomorrow or next year. If true, I must have provided Him a real hearty laugh, because He indeed had other plans. He called us, as a ministry, and me personally, to step out of our comfort zone and go to battle for Him. Well, so much for a return to normality.

While the work weeks remain long and at times disruptive, I wouldn't trade it for all the tea in China. God has lit a passion in me to know Him intimately and challenge Christians to turn away from our biblical illiteracy that is causing confusion in the church and allowing dangerous teachings to lead many astray. I look at life now with a new sense of peace in my own mortality. Now at age fifty-eight, I realize statistically I have about another fifteen years to live since men born in 1954 live to an average of seventy-three years of age. If God allows me more years in this life, I will praise and thank Him. If He calls me home before I complete this book, I will still praise Him because as Paul said in Philippians 1:21 *"To live is Christ and to die is gain".*

This sense of my own creeping mortality has renewed my passion for God and the calling He has given me. Like an astronaut on a one way journey to a new world, with no worries about saving fuel for the return trip, I am going full speed to wherever God is leading me. I used to look at growing old as a problem; I now see it as a great blessing. Every day I am one day closer to being with my Lord and Savior. And each day I am still here, I feel renewed and strengthened by Him.

Sound the Alarm—But Sound the Right One!

Our calling as a watchman carries serious responsibilities. A gift or calling from God that is misused can turn into a burden very quickly, and it can be destructive if not wielded properly. No matter what our calling or gift, we must use it with biblical knowledge, discernment and a desire to restore rather than destroy.

We must resist the temptation to go on "witch hunts", always remembering that every one of us falls short of the glory of God and that none of us will ever figure God out completely. We will all be in error on some issue when we stand before Him. We must always err on the side of caution before screaming "heretic" about a leader or teacher we disagree with.

However, we must also resist the temptation to sit back in silence as dangerous teachings and leaders seem to be straying from written Biblical beliefs. Picture a watchman on the top of a wall. Inside are God's people who still believe that His Word is absolute truth. Outside the walls are people who either hate God, are ambivalent to Him, or who desire to dismantle the truth of His written Word. This is the great battle for Christianity these days.

But there is also another group of people outside the great city of truth. They may have been lured away by slick teaching that tickled their ears, or they may have decided a long time ago to remain neutral in this great battle, wanting to just live and let live. One day they feel called to enter the great city. As they approach from a distance, the watchman sees them approaching the wall, but he cannot identify if they are enemy combatants or innocent pilgrims. So he sounds the alarm--but what alarm does he sound? "The enemy approaches"--Or "strangers approaching"? What he announces carries huge ramifications. If he announces them as enemy combatants, the soldiers inside the city open fire—but if they were not enemies but rather innocent pilgrims, we have innocent blood on our hands.

However if that watchman just lets these strangers inside the walls without at least sounding the alarm, and they turn out to be enemy combatants, the result could be catastrophic for the citizens inside, as an enemy has been turned loose inside the walls. The blood of the innocent citizens would be on the hands of the watchman.

This is a burden a watchman must carry. We must be careful not to open fire on innocent people who are not a part of the enemy's army, but we must also be vigilant so we do not let enemy forces inside the camp where innocent people will be destroyed.

What we must not do is automatically sound an alarm to open fire. Instead, we must first sound an alarm for the leaders of the great city to listen and discern if the approaching people are enemies or innocent pilgrims. If it is clearly established that these people are enemy combatants, then we go to war. But we must always be cautious before we call to unleash an attack.

As I was writing the chapter on "The Demise of Christian Leadership" I suddenly felt anger toward those I was writing about. How could they call what they are doing biblical leadership when the gospel was being twisted or compromised, and leaders with worldly beliefs were being brought into church and exalted? The anger was welling up in me with each keystroke. On a Sunday afternoon as I was completing that chapter, the anger reached a fever pitch and I was starting to feel very frustrated. I immediately stopped typing and asked God to forgive me for my sinful attitude. I destroyed what I had written in the chapter and started over from my notes and research.

Some of you reading this book may think it is unnecessary that we name names and ask questions that need to be asked about our leadership. However we must not fall into the trap of thinking it is wrong to question leadership and hold them accountable to the Bible. We must be faithful to the Word of God at all times, holding every teacher to the standard of the written Word. We must start asking questions that have been ignored by too many for too long. Our desire should never be to tear down, but to restore.

I do not think the leaders I mention in this book are evil nor do I question their salvation in Jesus Christ. Like every Christian leader, they are targeted by a ruthless enemy every day. Their positions as leaders make them very vulnerable to the subtle attacks of the enemy, and we must pray for them and give them the benefit of the doubt if we find something questionable in what they say or do. However we must never allow them to be above reproach. When we start to see a pattern of words or actions that are not lining up with the scriptures, we must have the wisdom and courage to confront our leaders.

We mention names because we need these men of influence to see the errors of their ways and return to being strong leaders for such a time as this, when the church needs them desperately. I ask you to join me in praying for them and for all Christian leaders that we may stay true to the gospel and not compromise with the world. However we must never fall for the lie that leaders should not be questioned or challenged. Leadership must always be held accountable for their words and actions. Jesus did it and so did Paul. We must also.

Taking a Stand

It is painful to have to publicly challenge Christian brothers and sisters. Like most people, I would rather just believe the best in people and trust that God will shake things out. In fact that is a common critique we hear regarding Stand Up For the Truth—"just let God sort this out." There is only one problem with that argument: it flies in the face of scripture.

Jesus called out the Pharisees who were abusing the Law and acting like hypocrites, calling them "whitewashed tombs". The Pharisees were the leaders and teachers of their times, but they felt they were above reproach or rebuke. Paul publicly called out Peter in Galatians for being two-faced and trying to appease both Jews and Gentiles. Left without proper biblical accountability, even the best of leaders will be tempted to stray and think more highly of themselves than they should. We must respectfully challenge them for their own good and the good of the church.

Paul's second letter to the Corinthians is a chilling letter where Paul confronts misled believers and false teachers who preach a false gospel, preach a different Jesus or present false spirits as truth:

> *"But I am afraid that just as Eve was deceived by the serpent's cunning, your minds may somehow be led astray from your sincere and pure devotion to Christ. For if someone comes to you and preaches a Jesus other than the Jesus we preached, or if you receive a different spirit from the one you received, or a different gospel from the one you accepted, you put up with it easily enough."*
>
> 2 Corinthians 11:3-4

Talk about hitting the three major illnesses infecting American Christianity these days:

- a different Jesus
- a different gospel
- a different spirit

20

Jesus is being "refashioned" into a loving Jesus who accepts sin and would never judge anyone. He has now become our "buddy" instead of our Lord and King.

The gospel of salvation is being minimized into a simple "Ask Jesus into your heart" prayer, rather than a sincere confession of sin, repentance and a commitment to turn away from the sinful nature by the power of the Holy Spirit.

There are false spirits being introduced into the church through Buddhism, Hinduism and New Age Christianity everywhere we look. Too many Christians seek after signs and wonders that might be deceptions of the enemy.

If we do not stand against these false teachings and movements we are just as guilty as those who teach them.

Naming Names

A common argument we hear is "Talk about the issues, but you don't have to point fingers at specific people."

If you were a Mormon or a Jehovah's Witness member, wouldn't you want someone pointing out the error in your leadership? Wouldn't you take what Joseph Smith taught and hold it against scripture, pointing out the error? Funny, we have no problem naming names of cult leaders but we cringe at the sound of a Christian leader being called out for questionable teaching.

If you were a new Christian who had fallen under the influence of a leader who told you that there were ways to eternal life other than through Jesus, wouldn't you want a friend to sit you down and point out the error?

Some Christians believe Christian leaders should get a pass from accountability and scrutiny, when in fact leaders should receive greater accountability and scrutiny because of their influence over thousands, even millions of Christians. Should we not discuss Barack Obama's stances on abortion and gay marriage as he tells the world he is a born-again believer?

21

What about Mitt Romney claiming Mormonism is Christianity? Nancy Pelosi, who says she is a Catholic, yet pushes for greater and greater access to abortion, including sponsoring legislation that would allow physicians to kill a child who survived an abortion attempt and was born?

Should we not question George W. Bush's beliefs as a Christian when he states that Muslims and Christians worship the same God and calls for the division of Jerusalem in an attempt to bring "peace" to the Middle East?[1] If Brian McLaren or Jim Wallis calls out a conservative Christian politician over his views, the left applauds them. If conservative Christians call out progressive Christian leaders, we are called mean-spirited and divisive.

See folks, the beauty or disgust in "naming names" is in the eye of the beholder. When the opponent is called out we cheer, but when our guy is called out we call it mean-spirited.

National movement leaders like Todd Bentley or Paul Crouch and pastors with great influence like Rick Warren or Bill Hybels, are powerful public figures with great influence. They are open about their beliefs and programs and they are leaders. We must not cower from challenging them when we feel they have strayed from the truth of God's Word, whether they do it intentionally or unintentionally.

Another argument we hear is the "Matthew 18" argument. First of all, Matthew 18 talks about going to a brother who sins personally against you, not a public figure or teacher who shares questionable beliefs or teaching. And we have attempted to contact people like Rick Warren, Bill Hybels and Rob Bell before we shared our concerns on air, but numerous calls or emails go unanswered. So should we not discuss serious issues and the people who teach them until we sit down face to face and get to "know their hearts", as we have been encouraged? Well if we follow that logic, these teachers can hide behind their entourage and voice mails perpetually and avoid any public scrutiny. Besides, as Solomon prayed at the dedication of the temple, only God truly knows the human heart.

"For you alone know the hearts of men"

2 Chronicles 6:30

Naming names is important when the person discussed wields tremendous influence. No one had a problem mentioning Harold Camping when he wrongfully predicted the date of Jesus' return. He was publicly rebuked as he should have been. So who determines whose name is mentioned and who is exempt? Usually it depends on our personal view of the person and the subject discussed.

A local pastor who is a wonderful brother in the Lord and a friend for years is a Pentecostal pastor. He even classifies himself as a "Word of Faith" pastor, but his views are soundly biblical on what the role of faith is in answered prayer. He realizes God alone decides who will be healed but he believes our level of faith in God plays an important role when we approach his throne.

When I paid him a visit to tell him we were preparing shows about some of the outrageous claims of some "Word of Faith" pastors and leaders like Kenneth Copeland (there I go "naming names" again), and I was seeking his counsel and thoughts he paused for a moment. He looked up smiling and said something like "Keep on exposing the false teachers of the social justice and emergent church movements but leave the Word of Faith people alone." He knew of course I could not do that and he was not serious in his request.

But our discussion has led to a scheduled show where he and I will debate the Word of Faith movement before our audience. And I believe something wonderful will come of our discussion. Too often we throw words around without considering that they might mean different things to different people. This pastor's version of "Word of Faith" lines up well with scripture, but some others' do not. When some in the Word of Faith movement claim we can speak things into existence or that God cannot move without our faith, they are placing themselves on equal footing with God, and God shares his throne with no one.

We are all often selective in who we choose to question and who we choose to blindly follow. But friends we must learn to take everything we hear and everything we are taught and hold it up to scripture to verify its truth, or refute it as false. No matter if it is Jim Wallis or David Barton; Brian McLaren or John MacArthur; Barack Obama or George W. Bush. Leaders must be held accountable for what they say, what they teach and what they do. The Word of God must be our sole judge of what is true and what is false.

Statements vs. Questions

How we make arguments or enlighten people on issues is just as important as doing it in the first place. An adage we try to remember on Stand Up or the Truth is this: Questions lower tensions; Statements raise tensions.

We would all rather be asked than ordered to do something. If Nancy wants me to cook dinner "Honey, would you mind cooking dinner?" will go a lot farther than "You're cooking dinner tonight" will ever go.

Questions are our way of exploring what is going on; statements are our definitive beliefs that we know what is going on. Questions often set the table for respectful dialogue while statements often lead to emotional and defensive responses.

If I ask a question like "Do you think Bob Smith is a heretic?" I am eliciting opinion and discussion. If I state "Bob Smith is a heretic", I am making a strong statement and have boxed myself into a corner, leaving no room for honest discussion. We should always feel free to question, but be slow to judge.

Now there are times for strong statements and judgments. The one Christian leader I have called a heretic is Brian McLaren because he has denied the substitutionary atonement of the cross as part of Christian doctrine, calling the cross "false advertising" for Christianity.[2] I have not called Rob Bell a heretic; I think he is wrong on his views about Hell, but I don't think he has crossed that line yet.

As watchmen, or anyone who is passionate about the truth, we will be continually tempted to call anyone we disagree with on doctrine a heretic, but we must avoid that temptation. There is a time for that when a teacher crosses a very definitive line, but we must be careful about wielding the word heretic with every person who disagrees with something we believe. If that is the standard then we are all heretics to someone.

In the Word of Faith movement[3], some teachers have crossed a line and are teaching doctrines that are clearly refuted by the Bible. But some pastors and believers who call themselves "Word of Faith" mean something totally different than the leaders who teach false doctrine.

A listener to our show emailed me during a broadcast telling me she was offended by a post we put up on our Stand Up For the Truth Facebook site. She said she was offended "as a person who believes we can speak things into existence". I read her email on air and told her whoever is teaching her this is leading her down a very dangerous path. She emailed me later and asked if we could meet.

Nancy and I met with her that week for about two hours. She is a very nice lady who loves God deeply, is active in her church and in outreach to children in her community. I asked her to tell me a time when she spoke something into existence. She shared a time when they were reaching out to children with some sock puppets they had made as a gift for these poorer children. She said they had about forty puppets available but they were seeing probably eighty or more children coming to their event. So she and her friends prayed for God to provide what they needed to serve the children and she told me they ended up with enough puppets for each child.

I said "Oh, like the story in the gospel about the loaves and the fishes", and she responded with an enthusiastic "yes!" I pointed out to her that she did not speak anything into existence—she prayed for God's provision and He responded.

This example points to how we need to be careful with the words we use and improve our interpersonal communications between believers. If we hear something that sounds wrong or dangerous, we should first seek clarification to make sure we heard what we thought we heard. We must not give the enemy a foothold between us as Christians.

Where this does become problematic is when a leader will say or do something that is suspicious and then will hide behind his entourage despite people asking for clarification. Letters, phone calls and emails seeking clarification are not responded to, leaving us to question just why no clarification comes forward. This has been the case over the years with Pastor Rick Warren. He has been involved in some very suspicious activities and made statements that seem to contradict his actions. In fact he recently had to hire a PR firm to help him in explaining recent statements and actions. Should a church really need a PR firm?

One more word about standing up and defending the truth of God's Word as a watchman on the wall: You'd better have thick skin and you'd better not get too full of yourself. You will be loved one day by a person who admires your boldness, and the next day that same person will be upset because you raised questions about a movement he is involved in. There will be longtime friends who suddenly look at you with either pity or disdain because they feel you have gone over the deep end. You will be called courageous one day, and a bully the next. You will be called a divider, a Pharisee, a "Sanballat"[4], mean spirited, and a hater. It is not always easy, but it is the price you pay these days for discussing issues too long ignored by the church.

A former boss I worked under almost thirty years ago summed it up best when I told him I wanted to recommend to the Board of Directors that our Savings and Loan consider selling annuities to our customers, which was a controversial proposal at the time. He looked at me and said "Well, they say you can always tell who the pioneers are—they're the ones with the arrows in their backs."

No matter how loving, careful or considerate we are as watchmen, we will get some arrows in our backs, and they may come from sources you least expect. That just comes with the territory. But God is so worth any small price we have to pay for defending his Word and his church.

Footnotes

1. http://www.wnd.com/2007/10/43906/
2. McLaren interview available at www.crossroad.to/Quotes/Church/post-modern/emergent/mclaren-hell.htm
3. www.gotquestions.org/Word-Faith.html
4. Bible, Book of Nehemiah 6

CHAPTER THREE

THE RISE AND FALL OF A NATION UNDER GOD

The Birth of American Christianity

Something amazing happened in 1775. A group born of immigrants from Europe smelled freedom—a freedom birthed by God, anchored in responsibility to Him and His perfect law.

Men such as George Washington, John Adams and Thomas Jefferson started to talk treason. They and their ancestors had come to a new land called America to plant their roots and grow. They sought a new land where a man could start over to grow and prosper. A place where a man could escape a tyrannical monarchy that wanted to control everything from their pocketbooks to how they worshipped. They thought if they distanced themselves from England, they could prosper and grow—but what they got instead was, I believe, inspiration from the Holy Spirit.

As England tried to tighten the reins on their growing freedom, these men and others started to whisper "independence"—a word the British Empire simply never tolerated. After many long painstaking meetings filled with heated debate, the United States of America declared its intention to break away from England. And truly, history was made.

These men envisioned a nation unlike any in the history of mankind. A nation that recognized any rights of man came from God alone; a nation who believes that government was an impediment to worshiping God; that any time a man tried to act as an intermediary between God and another man, something was lost in the translation. Some were deists, but most were solid Christians who read the bible regularly.

The forthcoming Declaration of Independence and Constitution were modeled on the bible and were established on the example of servant leadership Jesus lived by. We would be a nation where government did not exist to be served, but rather to serve and represent the people it governed.

Was it a perfect form of government? No. The only perfect form of government is one where God is King and we are his subjects. But our founding fathers came closer than anyone in history to creating a government that could glorify God and keep man in his place.

Over the last fifty years, our constitution has been mocked, dismissed, even shredded by secular humanists and their allies. The often misquoted "separation of church and state" exists nowhere in our founding documents. To the contrary, many of our founding fathers recognized and wrote that separate from God, our republic could never survive; that a democratic republic could only survive with God's moral laws as the cornerstone.

Now, our founders were very sensitive to the relationship between government and religion. They addressed it in the First Amendment to the Constitution which reads: "Congress shall make no law respecting an establishment of religion, or prohibiting the free exercise thereof."

One could argue that our nation has remained reasonably faithful to the first portion—the establishment of a religion. But the second part "prohibiting the free exercise thereof"—well anyone with an IQ above forty can plainly see this portion of the amendment is being shredded daily. Christian children banned from saying prayers or invoking the name of Jesus when they are on school grounds; pastors being fined or arrested for sharing the gospel in public; churches being forced to rent facilities to any organization, regardless of religious beliefs; if this is not prohibiting the free exercise of religion, then just what is?

And it is not just any or every religion being attacked—it is a persecution that seems to be directed solely at Christianity. Up until the

1960s whenever the government or a public institution would attempt to silence Christians, the church responded in full force. But something happened in the sixties; something was birthed that would earmark this nation for a slow, suicidal walk. We began to step toward the edge of a cliff with a blindfold on, and with each passing year we move one step closer to falling off the cliff into the abyss. Historically when our nation would start to show early signs of self-destruction, the Christian church would intervene and convince or shame the culture back away from the cliff. But this time it was different. Not only did the church not stop the march toward suicide of this nation—she joined in, ceded her moral authority, and started walking to the cliff alongside the nation.

This attack on Christianity has been incremental and subtle. Humanists know that any attempt to overtly overthrow American Christianity would be met with fierce resistance, so over time they chipped away at its foundation slowly and meticulously. Rather than a full frontal assault that was sure to fail, they started to infiltrate American Christianity with spies and traitors. They borrowed a page from *"Rules For Radicals"*[1] by communist Saul Alinsky. He dedicated his book to Lucifer, whom he called the first radical, and spells out detailed plans on how to infiltrate and subvert government and society. A key step is to infiltrate and pollute the church, elevating new thinkers as leaders.

People like Jim Wallis, a disciple of Saul Alinsky, and progressive pastors and priests committed to the doctrine of social justice, slowly starting to twist the true gospel. Emergent leaders like Brian McLaren and Tony Campolo who question the absolute truth of God's Word in favor of feelings and experience. Alinsky taught that once people like this are elevated to leadership and positions of influence, others would follow in lock step.

These Christian leaders have been subtly undermining the basic tenets of Christianity and the absolute truth of the Bible. They relate to a postmodern culture that has been prepared by secular education and media to question everything and believe that no truth is absolute. To them, truth is subjective and dependent on our personal emotions and experiences.

Alinsky understood that the only way to bring down the republic was to apply pressure from several sources—and that the church held the key. Once the church was effectively neutralized, everything else would fall into place. Hitler realized and accomplished this in his rise to power in Nazi Germany. When you can successfully neutralize the church, victory will soon follow.

It is a mistake to view the attacks on America and American Christianity as separate battles. Founded on Judeo Christian beliefs and dependent on a strong Christian Church, a free republic and a strong church need each other. Secularists and extreme left wing progressives realize this and their attacks to implement "hope and change" are a coordinated assault on both the American Republic and Christianity in America.

And now apparently an Alinsky disciple occupies the White House.[2] President Obama claims to be a Christian but his stances on abortion and homosexuality raise serious questions. Obama has repeatedly received a one hundred percent positive rating from NARAL[3], the leading pro-abortion group in the nation. Many of the Obama appointees are anti-Christian, either atheists or secularists who believe in the goodness of man. Christian leaders who support him generally dismiss the Bible as absolute truth, no less a secular stand even though they are Christians. They have opened a two-front assault on our republic and traditional, fundamental Christianity--and they are winning.

The recent mandate under Obama Care that forces health insurers, employers and religious organizations to provide free contraceptives and abortion drugs is more than just an attack on the right of American citizens to decide if they will purchase health insurance; it is an attack on freedom of religion. It puts the federal government one step closer to mandating the religious beliefs of every American citizen.

The Era of Narcissism

The sixties were really a wonderful time to be a child in this nation. The nation was prospering economically, the boundary between socially acceptable and unacceptable behavior was well defined, and life as a whole was pleasant. Admittedly this perspective comes from a middle class white boy, and there certainly were difficult times in this nation if you were black. Racial discrimination was still a stark reality for many minorities, but the nation took steps to correct this through civil rights legislation and a growing pressure on racism as a whole.

Social unrest started to grow as the nation escalated its war in Viet Nam. College campuses began to witness violent riots and even some deaths. Illegal drugs were flowing into the country from greedy parasites looking to turn a profit off the minds and lives of young Americans.

An entire generation was calling for personal freedom. Freedom of expression; freedom to consume any mind-altering drug they chose; sexual freedom outside the established morals; freedom from laws or moral restraint; individual freedom became the rallying cry of an entire generation.

A slogan that was born in this era said it all and would have a profound effect on the future of this nation: "If it feels good, do it!"

Freedom! Freedom! Everywhere freedom! But this generation seemed to forget something our nation's founders knew all too well—that freedom without responsibility is a mirage; that freedom without responsibility would be the death of a nation and a people.

Freedom without responsibility became the cry of an entire generation— and the Christian Church in America seemed to start embracing it. Suddenly the Christian Church in America was not there to bring proper moral balance to the cry of a wicked and perverse people. The church was to be the guardian of this nation, providing righteous moral boundaries to keep this nation "under God", but it began to falter. The Church chose to remain silent at a time when our nation needed it the most. But it would get worse—much worse—just a few short years later.

Sadly, freedom without responsibility has become a hallmark for many Christian churches and teachers. We tout our new freedom in Christ Jesus as we should, but we have been deceived about just what this freedom in Jesus represents. To many Christians we are free from the law and obedience to God and we are free to continue sinning with no consequence, believing we are free to behave the way we want as Christians. This is reflected in many studies that show Christians divorce at a rate equal to non-Christians; Christians access pornography at a rate as high as unbelievers; and that Christians are just as apt to cheat on their taxes or expense reports as unbelievers.

Jesus died to free us from sin, not from obedience. In fact he raised the bar on obedience by telling us a lustful thought for another woman is tantamount to adultery. He died to free us from the punishment of sin for eternity, the power of sin in this lifetime and the presence of sin when we live with Him in heaven. He did not die to free us from obedience and the consequence of sin in this lifetime.

We expect the world to be full of narcissists. However we should not expect or accept that same attitude among Christians.

The Day American Christianity Began To Die

Sometimes the onset of insanity is a process. Sometimes it comes on suddenly, without warning, causing unbelievable actions and consequences. On January 22, 1973, insanity struck suddenly in this nation. In a shocking case of improper judicial restraint and moral bankruptcy, Roe v. Wade, seven U. S. Supreme Court Justices ruled that a woman's "right to privacy" trumped the life of the child she was carrying in her womb.

There are times when you just look at something and say "Huh?" Can someone please tell me what the "right to privacy" has to do with ending another person's life? What could possess seven intelligent men—Supreme Court Justices—to rule a woman had a right to murder her child because of privacy? I'm sure the evil depravity of man has nothing to do with it!

I love to argue the ridiculous from an equally ridiculous point of view sometimes, so here goes. Say I catch a man outside peeking at my wife in the bedroom and I go out and kill him. Do you think there is a court in the land that wouldn't convict me of murder, or at least manslaughter? I can consume alcohol to any extent I want in the privacy of my own home, but if I get in my car and run over a pedestrian and kill him, is there a court anywhere that will exonerate me if I claim a right to drink privately as a defense?

In Exodus Chapter one, we see the first recorded account of infanticide. As the Israelites in Egypt grew in numbers, the Egyptian king was fearful of their increasing numbers and ordered every male child of the Israelites to be killed at birth to control their population growth. But midwives who remained faithful to God refused to obey this hideous order and were blessed by God for their obedience to him. Their obedience also led to the survival of a man crucial to the history of the world—Moses.

These Israelite women honored and obeyed God, bringing life when there existed a culture of death, and they were blessed by God. Today, with the church sitting back idly, our nation allows the murder of more than one million children every year in the name of "choice".

> "And you took your sons and daughters who you bore to me and sacrificed them as food to the idols. Was your prostitution not enough? You slaughtered my children and sacrificed them to idols."
>
> Ezekiel 16:20-21

Our children—God's children-- are being slaughtered once again, sacrificed to our own personal idol—ourselves. We kill innocent children after conceiving them in prostitution with the world and our flesh every time we have sex outside of marriage. We give in to our carnality and then compound the sin of adultery with the sin of murder. And where is the church in all this? We are sitting on the sidelines for fear of being seen as hateful or judgmental. Our silence has cost the lives of millions.

January 22, 1973 will go down as the day that American leaders officially thumbed our nose at God and his commandments. And if we think we will escape God's wrath and judgment as a nation, we are more arrogant than we could ever imagine. God is slow to anger, but don't think for one second he doesn't get angry. Many times in the Old Testament he brought judgment and punishment down on the nation of Israel for abandoning his ways. Is his anger beginning to swell when he looks at America, a land he has blessed abundantly? Look at 9/11 and the social and economic problems we face. Is God lifting his hand of protection from this great nation? It sure looks like it and it will get worse if we continue in our wicked ways.

As tragic as the Roe v. Wade decision was, there was another tragedy that was ushered in at that time: Christianity in America sold its soul. The reaction, apart from some Catholic leaders, was pretty mute. The original decision was that a woman could only abort her child in the first trimester—and the church took the bait. I could imagine some Christian leaders actually breathing a sigh of relief over the initial decision. Their rationale would go something like this:

"Well, not a great day, but it could have been a lot worse. After all, the plaintiffs stated that the outcome would make abortions "rare, but safe". And besides abortions can only be performed in the first trimester. Now if they had allowed unfettered abortion at anytime of pregnancy, well we wouldn't stand for that!"

Well guess what? The initial ruling that abortions could only be performed in the first trimester was later expanded by the very court that initially imposed that restriction. The Christian Church in America abandoned what would become fifty million children and counting. Talk about being light and salt to the world.

1973 marked the time when American Christianity basically surrendered our moral standing within this nation. We crossed a line that should never have been crossed. We started to become that which we previously detested—an immoral, ungodly culture, and we have not recovered from this surrender. In fact we continue to surrender to the very humanist culture we are called to affect. As Pogo once said, "We have met the enemy—and he is us."

Going Down—Quickly!

Once you step off a cliff, the fall to the ground is very quick—as fast as gravity carries you. American Christianity, once a beacon of light to this nation and the world, is falling into an abyss of darkness. And short of a miracle of God, we will never return to our once prominent position of moral authority.

Once you sit by idly and allow fifty million children to be murdered, everything else becomes relatively easy. Once you have allowed evil to be seen as acceptable, you only have one way to go—down. And Christianity in America is going down at an accelerated pace.

I simply cannot understand why the outcry from Christians over the murder of fifty million babies is not deafening. Have we become so arrogant, selfish and callous as Christians that we just sit back and watch a genocide that makes Hitler look tame in comparison go on, without holding our politicians responsible? Sadly we do because we are no better than the pagan culture we bemoan. We continue to sit by idly as mass murder by the millions happen in our nation every year. In fact we do worse than just sit by idly, we participate in the genocide when we continue to vote for pro-death candidates because they appeal to us economically. We are, in essence, financially paying for the murder of innocent children.

We cheer in church when a couple has a child and marvel at the miracle of life, yet do nothing to stop the murder of other innocent children who should have the same right to be born. Is something wrong with this picture?

For Christians who vote for pro-abortion candidates, I ask you to answer this question: How many children are you willing to let die for your tax cut or an increase in your government subsidies? One? One hundred? One thousand? One million? How many murders are you willing to participate in for your personal gain? What will you say to God when you stand before him and he asks you to explain your vote? Why you cared more about your tax cut or government benefits than the life of children he knitted into their mother's wombs? If you will not at least think about these questions, please don't tell me how much you love God. It rings hollow.

I Guess It Is OK To Be Gay

I confess it—I am a Seinfeld fan. While some of the episodes cross a line with sexuality, I find the story of four narcissistic, self-centered New Yorkers to be humorous, well written—and sadly indicative of where we are headed as a nation and a Church.

In one episode, a reporter overhears Elaine pretending George and Jerry are gay and she proceeds to write an article talking about them as a couple. The episode goes on with the two of them trying to squelch the lie, saying "I'm not gay—not that there's anything wrong with that."

But there is something wrong with it—it is sin. No worse than adultery, but sin none the less. On the issue of standing up for the truth of God's Word on homosexuality, the church boxed itself in on this issue over the years, and is now paying a heavy price. For years homosexuals were demonized as the worst of sinners, and they were treated as less than human, instead of men and women struggling with sexual sin. We bashed homosexuals as evil, all the while turning our back on heterosexual adultery within Christian leadership. A Christian leader could fall because of heterosexual adultery and usually be restored at a later date. But if that leader, or even a rank and file Christian, fell due to homosexual behavior, forget about it—they were finished.

The Christian Church in America was accused of being homophobic haters—and sadly there is some truth in that accusation. We must confess of any hatred we have toward homosexuals, particularly Christians who struggle with that sin. As the Church in America singled out homosexuals as the worst of deviants, the homosexual movement was making inroads into a culture that today accepts their behavior as normal. The media, supportive of secular culture, accused the church of being homophobic and hateful.

Most church leaders have recanted of their hatred and now view homosexuality as a sexual sin no different than heterosexual sin. But, in a case of overcompensating to relieve our guilt on this issue, we have gone too far. Out of fear of ever being called homophobic or hateful again, we have chosen to not even call homosexuality a sin in many Christian churches. So we first hated the homosexual—and now we are piling on more hate by not pointing out their sin against God and offering the forgiveness and restoration of the gospel.

Homosexual marriage is now legal in eight states and within a few years it might be federally protected as a right if the Obama Administration follows through on its intention to not defend the Defense of Marriage Act in court.[4] I would like to believe the church in America will rise up to insist our government defend God's laws on marriage. But when we allow fifty million babies to be murdered because we are lazy or fear being called close minded, you will excuse me if I remain pessimistic about the church doing the right thing.

Where Is the Church?

As a whole, the Church seems content to sit the battle out. Our pastors have been intimidated into believing the church can play no role in selecting our government leaders. They are fearful that anything they say about how a Christian should vote will land them in hot water with the IRS.

The Alliance Defense Fund[5] (ADF), an organization dedicated to defending the rights of Christian individuals and organizations, spends millions of dollars every year defending Christians and attempting to educate Christian leaders and pastors about their rights to affect the political culture of this nation. In fact, they are picking a fight with the IRS, hoping they will just try to sue a pastor or church over talking about politics from the pulpit. In 2011, more than seven-hundred pastors took a Sunday service and talked about the need for Christians to vote for pro-life, pro-marriage candidates. The pastors recorded their sermons and sent them to the IRS, waiting for some kind of challenge.

According to the ADF, the IRS knows they would lose in court if they sued a church for preaching on politics the way ADF teaches churches on what they are legally allowed to say. A pastor can point out where particular candidates stand on issues like abortion and gay marriage, and he can say almost anything except who his church members should vote for. Many pastors take advantage of this freedom. The only problem is ninety-nine percent of them are progressive pastors who approve of issues like gay marriage and abortion. So while these wolves in sheep's clothing take advantage of the law to promote ungodly candidates, pro-life, pro-family pastors and churches sit back idly, allowing our nation to become a modern day Sodom and Gomorrah.

This may sound harsh, but the truth sometimes hurts. Any pastor who claims he is unaware of his freedom to discuss politics and candidates from the pulpit is either lazy or lying. Chances are he is afraid, not of the IRS, but of offending someone in his own church; afraid of criticism that might lead to a member being offended and leaving his church. I might suggest that if a church member threatens to leave your church because he supports abortion or homosexual marriage, your church should throw a party as he exits the church body. You will be a stronger, more righteous body without him. If a Christian cannot understand that abortion and homosexuality are sins, they are probably in a state of spiritual denial.

The church must engage in the political process and the culture war, but must also never forget that this is primarily a spiritual war, fought in the heavens. But simply "hiding behind prayer" is not enough. Please do not think that I underestimate God's power or the power of prayer, but too often Christians vow they will pray but are distracted and never get there. And if we as Christians do not care enough to be engaged in the battle, just how seriously will God take our prayers?

According to some exit polling in 2008, fifty-four percent of Roman Catholics and forty percent of people calling themselves bible-believing Christians voted for Barack Obama, sweeping him into office as President. Barack Obama, without question is the most pro-abortion, pro-homosexual president in our nation's history. Any Christian who took ten minutes to research his voting record, or by some fluke would have actually heard a pastor explain Obama's record, would know what values he represented. But I guess that is just asking a little too much of people these days.

I am sure many Christians now are complaining as this administration dismantles the nation economically, morally and spiritually, but many of those complaining probably voted for him. Not that John McCain was any "kiss for Christmas," but it couldn't have been this bad. But we are only getting what we asked for folks. How is that "hope and change" working out for you Christians?

The church either affects the secular culture or the culture infects the church. Millions of murdered babies and a growing acceptance of homosexual marriage clearly show us which is happening in American Christianity these days.

Which Savior Are You Voting For?

Voting is very important, but no politician, Republican or Democrat, conservative or progressive, can save our nation. Only God is capable of pulling us out of the sewer we are swimming in. But our vote does matter and we'd better start taking the time to research candidates and know their voting record and where they stand.

We must also check our own motives about how we vote and who we vote for. Are you willing to vote for a candidate who will lower your taxes or protect your union "rights", but who supports abortion or gay marriage rights? Are you voting for self-serving values of the world or in a way consistent with God's values?

Some Christians behave and speak as if the savior of this nation will be the next guy they vote for. The culture war and political involvement is important, but too often we look for human answers to spiritual problems. We must research candidates and vote for those that will restore our Christian values, but to become obsessed with one man's ability to save the nation is foolish and futile. We must fight this battle in the spiritual and cultural arenas. An either/or approach will simply not do.

> *"If my people, who are called by my name, will humble themselves and pray and seek my face and turn from their wicked ways, then will I hear from heaven and will forgive their sin and will heal their land."*
>
> 2 Chronicles 7:14

There is the savior of America—**God**! Our only real power as a nation comes not from our military, economy or ingenuity. The only source of real power that has propelled this nation to greatness is our faith in God. Over the past fifty years we have turned our back on God and his ways, and our nation, along with American Christianity, has become a shell of its former self. Nothing will change until we repent and ask for God's forgiveness and restoration.

Losing Perspective in Economic Chaos

2008 was the first presidential election in my memory where abortion was practically ignored as an issue. When Rick Warren hosted Obama and McCain for his candidate forum, why did he roll over and not pin down Obama on his one-hundred percent pro-abortion voting record? He let Obama tap dance around the issue, admitting he was pro-abortion but refusing to ask Obama how he squared that belief up with his self-profession as a Christian. Obama said he wanted to find "common ground" on the issue with pro life leaders. No wonder Warren let him slide since Warren has committed to finding common ground with Islam.[6] Rick Warren failed to take a stand for life and Christian principles.

As I write this book, 2012 is shaping up the same. Only one current candidate, Rick Santorum, is even talking about the horror of abortion. The remaining candidates are avoiding the issue like the plague. Before you blame the candidates, look in the mirror fellow Christians.

The reason this crucial issue is being ignored is this: Running on a pro-life platform is probably a sure-fire way to lose an election at this time of American history. In 2011, Gallup[7] reported that forty-five percent of Americans identified themselves as "pro-life", with forty-nine percent calling themselves "pro-choice". And many Christians who claim to be pro-life do not seem to treat the issue of life as a core voting issue. We call ourselves pro-life, but fall for the candidates who appeal more to our love of money or security over a candidate who stands for biblical righteousness. This is an extremely selfish attitude to take as Christians.

This nation was founded upon God's righteous law. We are squandering it away as the nation resembles Babylon more than a shining city on a hill. Blame the atheists, Hollywood, the media or public education if it makes you feel better. But the truth is American Christianity was entrusted by our founding fathers to be the moral guardians of this nation. If we are honest with ourselves as Christians, we need travel no further than the closest mirror to find the real culprits. We, the Body of Christ in America, have failed this nation and its citizens.

Instead of affecting the secular culture, we have embraced it. This secular culture is a cancer and that cancer is being invited into the Christian Church. The church has surrendered to this cancer and it is permeating and conquering every cell in the body. The result is a slow demise at our own hands.

Footnotes

1) Rules For Radicals, Saul Alinsky, Knopf Doubleday Publishing
2) Foxnews.com
3) www.prochoiceamerica.org/assets/files/obama-fact-sheet.pdf Barna research
4) www.huffingtonpost.com/2011/07/19/obama-defense-of-marriage-gay-rights_n_903680.html
5) Alliancedefensefund.org
6) acommonword.com
7) www.gallup.com/poll/147734/Americans-Split-Along-Pro-Choice-Pro-Life-Lines.aspx

Chapter Four

Fighting Or Surrendering To The Cultural Cancer?

God created man to live in communion with him for eternity. Adam and Eve were to populate the earth with millions of children to live in perfect harmony with God, living in a world of perfect God-directed peace and harmony. Our world would be one without sickness, disease, poverty, injustice or death; a world without sin.

Man chose an alternative world. He chose to know evil. He followed the lead of a rebellious, fallen angel who chose a similar path years or ages earlier. He chose to believe a lie over the truth. Sin entered the world and death became a part of life. Not just physical death, but also spiritual death.

Man made a choice that fateful day and choices have consequences. The eternal consequence we face out of that choice is the real possibility of eternal damnation, separated from God in a place without hope of future redemption.

Physical death comes upon us in many forms, as does spiritual death. Both can be sudden or a slow march.

Physical death can come about instantly at the hands of an armed criminal or a drunk driver, but most take a slow journey where our minds and bodies slowly break down and eventually fail us. This is the fate of man in a fallen world. Every man faces physical death--it is simply unavoidable.

Spiritual death, however, can be avoided, and we can live in eternity with God. However, this is not a right, it is a choice. Jesus said the path to eternal life is narrow and very few find it. Conversely he taught that the road to destruction and eternal spiritual death is wide and many find it.

So physical death is guaranteed, but spiritual death can be avoided, and American secular culture is leading millions to eternal spiritual death. America, built on the laws and values of God, is disintegrating rapidly as we turn our backs on the goodness of God to pursue lives of wealth, depravity and greed.

The Christian Church in America has traditionally stood strong, correcting any shift in American culture that drifted from God. But over the past fifty years the church has started to look more like the very culture it opposed for hundreds of years.

Secular culture promotes sexual promiscuity; the Church is doing little or nothing to address sexual sin among its people. Secular culture promotes abortion as a matter of "choice"; the Church stands by idly as millions of unborn children are killed every year. The divorce rate in this nation now hovers near fifty percent; divorce within people claiming to be Christians is hovering around fifty percent. Secular culture accepts, even promotes homosexuality as an acceptable lifestyle; the Church out of fear refuses to call homosexuality what it is—a sin that is dismantling God's definition of marriage.

One is hard pressed to see any real distinction between the secular culture and millions who claim to be Christians these days. In fact our self-identity as Christians has become confused, with the word "Christian" having no clear meaning anymore. I can sit in my garage and think I am a car, but I am not. I can also sit in church and say I'm a Christian and not truly be one.

> *"Many will say to me on that day 'Lord, Lord, did we not prophesy in your name, and in your name drive out demons and perform many miracles?' Then I will tell them plainly, 'I never knew you. Away from me, you evildoers!"*
>
> Matthew 7:22-23

The Great Sumo Wrestling Match

If you have ever witnessed Japanese Sumo wrestlers fight, it is an amazing thing to watch. Two huge, powerful men square off in a battle of tremendous strength and leverage. They slam together with incredible force pitting the irresistible force against the immovable object. They push on each other hoping to overpower and defeat the opponent.

Using this great strength and leverage, each attempts to get the other off balance. Once this is accomplished, the opponent is overpowered and falls back in defeat, knocked out of the battle circle.

Secular culture and American Christianity are like Sumo wrestlers-- two powerful foes attempting to vanquish and defeat the opponent. The cultural warrior is bigger, but the Christian warrior--the church--has far greater inner strength and heart, the Holy Spirit. The only problem is it seems the Christian warrior left his heart and inner strength in the training room. American Christianity is being slowly pushed right out of the battle circle, ceding ground with each passing year, and defeat seems inevitable at this point of the match. The secular Sumo warrior might soon stand alone in the battle circle, while its opponent, American Christianity, is on the outside looking in, wondering what happened.

Over the past two-hundred years, this has been a recurring battle and the church has prevailed. We fought with our heart and inner strength, the Holy Spirit, and we were for the most part continually victorious. Every time the Secular Sumo wanted to do battle, we defeated him. Not this time--we are on the brink of defeat and we either don't know or don't care. See, this cultural opponent has been training vigorously. He has learned from previous defeats and each time comes at his opponent with renewed vigor and commitment.

The church has become Rocky Balboa in the third movie edition of the series. Clubber Lang, Rocky's latest challenger, was hungry and driven. Rocky, flush with victory and all its trappings, grew soft. He didn't train as hard, thinking he was invincible. Defeat was unthinkable. All he had to do was show up and Lang would be defeated. Lang knocked him down and out. Rocky was decimated and defeated.

Rocky, recommitted to train and fight for victory, came back later and defeated Clubber Lang, regaining the title. He trained and fought harder than he ever had and the result was victory. But that is Hollywood, not always reality.

American Christianity has been knocked to the canvass by a powerful enemy, and the count has reached nine. One more wave of the referee's hand and the match is over. We will have lost, and the price for this defeat will be felt for an eternity. Satan will have claimed many more eternal disciples from the ranks of lukewarm Christians and American youth.

Christianity either affects culture, or culture infects Christianity. Which seems like the most likely scenario happening today? If you think the church is winning this battle, you are either incredibly naive or tremendously deceived.

Who is Leading This Dance Anyway?

I admit it. My wife got me to take ballroom dance lessons. Admission number two: I enjoy dancing with my wife; maybe not quite as much as I enjoy a Packer football game, but I do enjoy dancing with Nancy.

Being born with two left feet, and having no real dance experience, it was torture learning to dance. I would be constantly trying to take us in one direction while Nancy thought we were headed in another, making it look more like a wrestling match than a dance. Then one time Nancy collaborated with our dance instructor to try to straighten out my disastrous foray into ballroom dancing.

The instructor explained that in every dance there is a leader and a follower; well that much I had figured out. He pointed out that if a leader is strong and knows where he wants to go, the follower would have no choice but to go there. In other words I, as the man and leader, needed to lead from a position of strength and confidence, and then Nancy would have no option but to follow my lead. The rest is pretty easy, as long as the leader knows where he wants to go and is committed to going there.

In every dance there is a leader and a follower. In the battle between secular culture and Christianity, one will lead and one will follow. So who seems to be leading and who is following in this all-important dance? No doubt about it—culture leads and American Christianity is following, seemingly powerless to do anything about it.

Culture is redefining marriage away from God's Law and the church follows along with hardly a whimper of protest. Several states have now legalized homosexual marriage and odds are the U.S. Supreme Court will hear an argument in 2013 that could make it protected permanently under U.S. law. The church is just following along, complaining about the direction on this issue, but essentially doing nothing about it.

Abortion has brought about the murder of more than fifty million babies since 1973. The church doesn't notice or doesn't care because standing up against the murder of innocent children might be seen as harsh. Well American Christianity has been an accessory to the murder of these fifty million babies by refusing to get seriously involved—a number more than eight times the number of Jews the Nazis butchered in World War Two. We make Hitler seem tame by comparison.

We scream about the growing sexuality, anti-Christian rhetoric and violence on television and keep right on watching television instead of making our voices heard. We complain about all the sex on television and go right on watching Desperate Housewives. When sex and violence permeate new shows, we cry "outrageous!" for a month or so, and then go right on watching.

We scream about the growth of our federal government and the decreasing morality in legislation and behavior from our elected leaders. We complain that they don't listen to our wishes and how they seem to be bent on kicking God out of our society, yet we continue to help elect pro-abortion, pro-homosexual representatives because they appeal to our self-interests. We abandon our Christian principles because we think they will get us a little more money in our wallets or because we like their charm and charisma.

We continue to outsource our children's morals and values to a public education system that is a humanist organization, trying to override all the "antiquated" beliefs on morality that religion and parents have instilled. We may complain about it a little, but how many have ever attended a school board meeting or even a parent-teacher conference to find out just what our children are being taught—and by whom?

The secular culture leads, and American Christianity follows blindly. They are setting the agenda and we are just going along because we are too lazy, ignorant or fearful to question their agenda and motives. We follow blindly wherever they wish to lead.

I am not a "dominionist". I do not believe we can stop the world from going to the brink of self-annihilation before Jesus returns. I read the Bible and know that things will get a lot worse in the coming years. The Titanic is sinking and we cannot stop it, but we can fight for every person on that sinking cruise liner, running up with lifeboats to rescue them. We can work to help bail water, hoping we can buy a little more time to help a few more get off the sinking ship. We can care enough about people to stand up and make noise when we see the evil and depravity closing in on us as Americans.

We cannot do these things if we continue to let secular culture lead us around by the nose, intimidating us and marginalizing us as Christians. But the sad truth is we have twisted and abused the scripture that tells us to "be in the world but not of the world". We have used this as an excuse to believe we have no responsibility for the state of American culture decaying into evil.

Progressive Christian churches bring their favorite candidates in before elections but conservatives crouch in fear over being seen as "political". Pro-death and pro-homosexual "Christians" get involved with social justice movements while conservative, bible-believing Christians sit back and do little or nothing.

Culture leads the dance, stepping all over our toes, and we just take it, asking for forgiveness because they step on *our* toes! American Christianity led this dance for nearly two hundred years and when the culture wanted to go in a different direction we did not allow it to go there. But we have given up our leadership, choosing out of fear, ignorance or a desire to become followers, not leaders.

When the epitaph on this once great nation is read it will remember a time when America stood for God's principles and truth; a time when a Christian-led nation stood up to evil and said "no way"; a time when a strong, vibrant, moral Church was the leader of this nation.

On America's death certificate it should read "Compliments of American Christianity". God forgive us.

American Christianity: Introducing the 1976 Tampa Bay Buccaneers!

The Green Bay Packers had a remarkable ride as a team in 2011. Coming off their fourth Super Bowl Championship, many thought the team was set up to become the next dynasty of professional football.

The team had a franchise quarterback, a strong corps of wide receivers and a championship quality defense, led by a General Manager and Head Coach who were quality men on and off the field. All Wisconsin was buzzing in anticipation of a miraculous year.

There was no disappointment as the Packers steamrolled virtually every opponent en route to a 15-1 regular season. Life was good in Green Bay, but there were underlying signs of problems from day one. That championship quality defense from the previous year never looked anything like its old self. It gave up yardage at a record pace, but the offense was so prolific that the Packers managed to outscore every opponent but one.

Then the New York Giants, the eventual Super Bowl Champions, came to town on a cold Sunday for a playoff game. Fans were certain the Packers would prevail and move on to the Super Bowl a few weeks later. The Packers were heavy favorites and the darlings of the media. Fans were certain that in this game the defense would show up, and even if they didn't, the offense would continue to make up for the poor defense.

Well a funny thing happened on the way to a second consecutive Super Bowl; the defense was its usual inept self, but the offense was not there to bail it out this time. The Packers were eliminated and an entire state went into a three-week state of depression.

Championship teams need a great offense and a great defense. They need strong, committed, principled leadership and ownership that is willing to give leadership the tools they need for success. Teams with huge deficiencies on both sides of the ball, combined with poor coaching and leadership, end up more like the 1976 Tampa Bay Buccaneers, the first team in NFL history to go winless during a fourteen game season. During the season Coach John McKay was continually grilled about his offense's inability to score points. After an excruciating loss a reporter asked McKay "What do you think of the execution of your offense today?" McKay never missed a beat: "I'm all in favor of it."

The 1976 Buccaneers were a hapless bunch, further demoralized with each passing loss. Other teams would often comment that they felt the Bucs were defeated the moment they walked on the field—the malaise and ineptitude were so evident even in warm ups before the game. Well, ladies and gentlemen, may I introduce to you the latest version of the 1976 Tampa Bay Buccaneers—American Christianity. This team has become built to lose.

American Christianity was once a juggernaut, seemingly invincible. With a high powered offense and stingy defense, and strong, principled leadership, the opponent never had a chance. Run with precision to detail and a passion never seen before, this team was built for victory from the beginning.

The owner is a perfect owner, giving leadership and the team everything it needed for success. He inspires the team and disciplines them when needed. He was with them every day, reminding them how much He cares for them, even when practices and games got difficult. No team ever had a greater owner and one so committed to the success of His team.

The leadership of the team was very solid, committed to the vision of ownership, and making sure each player knows their role and the goal of the team as a whole.

But something happened. Ownership remained the same and is every bit as powerful and committed, but somewhere along the line this team developed a selfish, losing attitude. Leadership became soft and started implementing a strategic plan that was in conflict with ownership. But the owner, being patient, hoped leadership would turn from its destructive patterns and once again carry out the vision of ownership.

The players became flush with wealth and earthly success and just don't practice or play as hard as they used to. They also don't memorize the play book like they once did. They have developed an attitude of surrender instead of a passion for victory. They started doing things their way instead of following the proven method of success ownership had installed many years ago. It became all about them.

A team built for ongoing success became apathetic and lazy. It was not as committed to success as in previous years. It didn't have the confidence in the owner and leadership it once had. American Christianity had lost its passion and purpose and today is struggling to find its own identity. American Christianity these days has an ineffective, lazy offensive game plan and we are getting nowhere against the growing secular culture. This must change.

American Christianity also needs a strong defense that refuses to allow the enemy to gain one inch of our territory. We need to have spiritual eyes, ears and discernment to see how the enemy plans on attacking us. We need watchmen on the wall, warning the church of the enemy's overt and covert attacks on the foundation of the church.

American Christianity needs to return to its once powerful roots and purpose. It needs an offense that will take the battle to the enemy; an offense that is aggressive and puts the pressure on the opponent. We need to take the battle to the secular culture instead of playing passively and on the defensive constantly. We do this by being involved in the culture wars. We do this by actively supporting political candidates committed publicly and privately to God's standards of morality. We do this by flexing our muscle as a Church.

Every year in our community some of our churches engage in forty days of prayer for our community and this is a very good thing to do. But our prayers must be coupled with a willingness to be God's vessels to take the battle to the enemy. God is capable of doing anything within His divine nature, but for some reason He chooses to work through His children. We need to become willing vessels of God to reclaim the culture from the enemy. Prayer alone will just not cut it because if we pray for our community and culture but are unwilling to get off the bench and fight for it, just how seriously will God take our prayers? God commands His people to be active in the world without succumbing to it. We are called to be "in the world, but not of it". This is not a call to isolation or retreat from the world—it is a call to action and involvement with the world, being careful not to lose our spiritual perspective.

Sadly these days, watchmen are viewed more as irritants by church leadership than they are strong participants in the battle between good and evil. When watchmen stand up and warn of coming attacks, they are often marginalized as "divisive" or "unloving". When watchmen have the courage to confront leadership on unbiblical teachings or programs infiltrating the church, they are either dismissed or ridiculed. Every church would be well-served to have a team of watchmen as part of their leadership team: Men and women who are aware of dangerous doctrine or movements creeping into American Christianity; Watchmen who are willing to take the time to vet programs and speakers before they are endorsed by church leadership.

A large majority of pastors complain that they are overworked and overwhelmed by the scope of their duties, and they are probably correct in that assessment. Yet some have what seems to be a martyr syndrome, preferring to remain overworked and stressed so they can show just how valuable they are to the church. They could help themselves and the church by asking for help, and starting to invest in future leaders. Sit down with church members and find out what their passions and gifts are, and start to utilize these skills and passions to build a strong community of believers.

Leaders in the church must reclaim their roles as spiritual leaders. They must build a strong team within the local church, a team equipped with offensive warriors and defensive stalwarts. Stop complaining about the overwhelming scope of your duties and get your church members involved. If they don't want to be active participants in the church, ask them to move on—you are probably better off without them if they are that self-focused.

A strong team is comprised of an aggressive offense and a staunch defense, plus strong, principled, committed leadership that is setting the tone. It also develops depth with a strong bench willing and able to get in the game if injuries occur or if a starting player leaves the team. That is where training and educating our youth becomes so important. Today's reserves are tomorrow's starters and we need to begin training and equipping them to step in to a starting role when the time is right.

A great team also knows its identity. It knows what it believes and is committed to the goals of the team. But because of our slide into mediocrity as a church over the past fifty years, we have what looks more like a team of misfits than a powerful, effective team.

We are suffering from a lack of individual and corporate identity as a church.

Inept Leadership or Self-Centered Followers?

Does inept leadership create self-centered followers, or do self-centered followers create inept leadership?

This is a classic "chicken or the egg" question. Are our leaders the primary reason Christians have become shallow and self-centered? Or are our self-centered attitudes causing us to elevate and promote shallow, ineffective leaders? This is a fundamental question we must wrestle with as we consider the future of our nation and American Christianity.

Our government was formed in 1776 on the belief that the federal government would play a very limited role in the lives of citizens. Its primary economic purpose was to do what it could to foster equal opportunity for all citizens. That's just not good enough anymore for many Americans. We will no longer settle for equal opportunity--we want equal outcomes.

In 2008 we elected officials who promised us a quick fix to our economic recession, instead of candidates who warned us of fundamental problems that would involve some painful sacrifices. Four years later, our problems are greater than ever as we face trillions more in debt and see our individual rights threatened by increasingly intrusive government.

So as Christian animosity grows toward government policies on expanded abortion through health insurance, refusing to defend God's desire for marriage in the courts, and big government intrusion into our lives, we dare not blame anyone but ourselves. We are only getting what we asked for.

As a nation, we seem to have lost our adventurous spirit. We prefer a bird in the hand to the opportunity of two in the bush. The economic system built on free-enterprise capitalism propelled our nation to the status of the wealthiest nation in history, and provided every citizen with the opportunity to prosper if he was willing to work hard. But equal opportunity is riskier than equal outcomes, and we don't have the stomach to be at risk anymore. Besides we have become far too lazy to put in the hard work and long hours necessary to succeed.

Life is full of risk. Every time you get in your car, you put your life into the hands of another driver who is rushing carelessly or who just doesn't see anything wrong with drinking and driving. When we work for a company, our job is only as secure as the company's ability to turn a profit for the owner. As we grow older our bodies begin to break down and knees, hips and vital organs begin to fail. Life is a daily crap shoot and the future of this life always contains the unknown, lurking around every corner.

Life is also not fair. Some people enjoy good fortune or blessings; others seemingly cannot catch a break. Real control is an illusion. No matter how healthy or wealthy we are, it could all unravel tomorrow. We cannot control circumstances, only how we react to them.

These days we elect leaders out of our desire to avoid risk and pain in the short term, but the long-term devastation we will harvest is immeasurable.

We continue to accumulate massive debt that will threaten the future of our children, because we do not want to face tough decisions today.

In this case weak, ineffective leadership is the consequence of those being led---followers who want what they desire more than what is right. Whether it is our choice of political candidates or leaders within the church, we seem to vacillate to those who tell us what we want to hear, rather than leaders who tell us what we need to hear. Just as the presidential or congressional candidate who tickles our ears will likely get our vote over the candidate delivering a message of self-discipline and personal responsibility, we also want church leaders who help us feel good about ourselves rather than the leader who calls us to a life of sacrifice, turning from our wicked ways, and seeking holiness.

It is far easier to blame others than ourselves for our circumstances. The church these days has too many unprincipled leaders who cave in to the culture rather than fight it with the truth of God's Word. Leaders who embrace a corporate mentality to church growth instead of preaching the Word of God, allowing the Holy Spirit to add to our numbers as in the Book of Acts. Leaders who are compromising with the world to become popular--who think their "seeker-friendly" approach is anything but what it is--compromise with sin and admitting that deep down we are ashamed of the gospel. And an arrogance that leads us to believe a "culturally relevant" sermon carries more power than the gospel itself to transform lives.

We can blame our leaders, but we seem to desire this type of leadership. We are more comfortable coming to a church that is more like a social club instead of a place where we challenge and build one another up spiritually. Many churches seem to be places where we suppress our week-long defeats and lukewarm faith and just put on a happy face. They seem more like a class reunion, where people one-up each other with tales of phony success, instead of a place where we are honest with one another. Deep down we seem to desire leaders who will let us stay in a comfortable place rather than challenging us to be honest about our spiritual shortcomings. So if we as followers want a place where we can feel good about ourselves, even at the expense of honesty, then that is the type of leader we will seek.

As a nation and a church, we suffer from weak, unprincipled leadership, but we have no one but ourselves to blame. We have come to desire leaders who tickle our ears or help us feel good about ourselves. We do not want to be challenged to get out of our comfort zone and allow God to stretch and strengthen us. This is killing our nation and American Christianity.

Summary

Is the church fighting the poison of American culture or surrendering to it? Perhaps the best way to answer that question is with another question: Does American Christianity today look more or less like the culture than it did fifty years ago? If you believe it looks less like it, I have a bridge I'd like to sell you. There is no doubt we are surrendering to the culture instead of fighting it, and with each passing year the secular culture becomes more engrained within the church, and one day it will totally consume us if we do not wake up. American Christianity must stand firmly against a decaying secular culture, instead of compromising with it and embracing it. If we fail to do so, there will soon be little to distinguish American Christianity from the culture that seeks to destroy it.

CHAPTER FIVE

SATAN'S PAWNS

There is no shortage of enemies purposefully trying to destroy American Christianity. A simple glance at the newspaper or watching a random sitcom on television indicates what we are up against. As I write this book, the ABC Network is touting its newest program called "GCB", short for "Good Christian Belles" which was a concession from the original title, "Good Christian Bitches"[1], based on the book by Kim Gatlin. The promos show self-righteous, backstabbing, immoral and hypocritical women. These women are self-professing Christians on the outside, but adulterous, hateful, gossiping women on the inside. Christianity is again being criticized, slandered and mocked everywhere we look.

There was a time when the church would stand up and fight any effort to introduce immorality into media, government, Hollywood or public education. Sadly those days are long past us as American Christianity has become a lapdog for immorality. We have the power of the Holy Spirit within us, yet we act like obedient dogs begging for scraps the culture throws our way.

Just where and when did the Church begin to take in the cancer of secular beliefs and culture? There was no single event we can point to as the beginning of the end, and it has been more of a death by a thousand cuts. No single cut by itself was fatal, but as the cuts mounted and we failed to dress and heal the wounds, an infection began to grow within the Body of Christ in our nation. We have now reached the point where a few more cuts might lead to death.

Let's examine some of these recent cuts that are mounting to slowly bring us to the brink of spiritual suicide. With each mounting wound, American Christianity becomes weaker and more prone to serious infection leading to death.

Scientific Fact or Science Fiction?

Genesis teaches us God created the universe in six days, and God created man in his image out of the dust of the earth, breathing life into him. Adam and Eve were created to live forever in the presence of God in a world free from sin, death and pain.

These biblical facts are now being presented as an antiquated myth by many in the public realm. When Darwin wrote "Origin of the Species"[2], most people thought he was a crazed heretic. He was dismissed by the vast majority of people as a bitter lunatic who was angry at God for some unknown reason. But a select few people embraced his writings as truth and genius. These people were called Scientists.

Science is defined as *"the study and theoretical explanation of natural phenomena; knowledge acquired through experience"* according to Webster.

So science can be defined as both theory and knowledge and there is a huge difference between those. Sadly in these days where humanistic thought rules, science is often purposefully combining the theoretical with "knowledge" into humanist propaganda; a propaganda driven by arrogance to do all it can to "prove" God does not exist. Those scientists and scholars, who dare to challenge the "fact" of evolution, noting there is actually far more irrefutable proof of some kind of "intelligent design", are shamed, shunned and fired, as happened to David Coppedge, a computer specialist at NASA's Jet Propulsion Laboratory.[3] Ben Stein's documentary, "EXPELLED: No Intelligence Allowed"[4], points out several instances where doctors, journalists and academics are either fired or censored by institutions favorable to evolution, including Baylor University, a Christian institution.

You will be hard pressed to find a public school that teaches intelligent design, let alone creationism, on an equal footing with evolution. Public schools, held up as standards of learning and truth, teach evolution as fact and intelligent design as "another theory", if they teach it at all. The effects of this are far more reaching and devastating to youth than most people imagine.

When a child is led to believe that mankind is some sort of accident or chance happening, rather than humans uniquely created in the image of God, they tend to feel very insignificant. This can have a devastating effect on how the child looks at himself or views life. Life without purpose, the result of random chance, leaves one feeling empty and lost. Conversely, when a person sees themselves as the product of a loving God who values them and has a purpose for their lives, that person looks at life from a whole different perspective.

Science partnered with the medical community in the abortion debate, trying to determine when a fetus became life. Initially science determined that "viability" was attained much later in the pregnancy than we now know, jumping to premature conclusions about when "life" began. Bible-believing Christians, a shrinking minority in this nation, know that God determines when life begins. He told the prophet Jeremiah in Jeremiah 1:5 *"Before I knit you in your mother's womb, I knew you . . ."*

Science has played a key role in religion. In the middle ages, scientists including Galileo suggested that the earth was not the center of the universe. Their findings pointed to the fact that the sun did not revolve around the earth as the early church taught, but rather that the earth revolved around the sun. These scientists were threatened with excommunication, even death, if they did not recant their findings.

It turned out the church was wrong and the scientists were correct in this instance. This error by the church caused many to wonder what else the church might be wrong about, planting seeds of doubt as to the church's teachings on the origin of the universe and man himself.

We need to approach science and its findings with caution these days. Remember that the definition of science talks about being both knowledge and theory. These days scientists are much quicker to jump to conclusions as they experiment, racing for the next big grant or public recognition. A new finding that might seem to support the story of evolution sells much better than findings that prove the truth of the Bible. We should not dismiss science as totally evil, nor should we approach it as "gospel". As with all things, it must be held up to scripture to discern its reported findings.

In an era where science is making huge strides, expect to see a great deal of new discoveries. It is important to understand that scientists are human and some will seek to skew their findings or conclusions to support their preconceived beliefs about the universe or God.

Science presents itself as a pursuit of truth. But as we know, "truth" is often in the eye of the beholder. Without an anchor of absolute truth to compare everything against, the pursuit of truth often becomes a process of selecting findings that seem to support one's personal version of truth. Some scientists are atheists bent on proving that God does not exist, so be careful of what you accept as "scientific fact". In a world that hates God more with each passing day it is important that we never allow a seed of doubt as to the absolute truth of the Bible to enter our minds. Once there, it is easy to slip into doubt. Hold every "fact" that science presents against the Word of God.

Public Education or Indoctrination?

No institution has done more to discredit Christian teachings and doctrine than the public education system. For centuries, parents had educated their children at home. But public education has grown in this nation to where it has almost become a mandatory requirement for American children. With the advent of two income families, fewer parents see home-schooling or Christian education as an option.

In today's busy culture, time has become one of our most precious commodities. As parents spend less quality time with our children, public education becomes their de facto "nanny".

The average parent spends about five minutes per day in meaningful conversation with their children. The school system has their attention for seven hours every school day. Given these facts, who do you think has the greater potential influence on our children?

But who are the men and women who influence our children as teachers? I think we can safely say the majority of them are very nice people with the best of intentions. Some are bible-believing Christians who are trying to help our children navigate very difficult times in their lives. But even the best of teachers belong to a system that is definitely anti-Christian in its values and beliefs. They belong to quite possibly the most unscrupulous public organization in our nation--the National Education Association[5] (NEA).

With each successive school year we see the progression of an agenda that seeks to override the values of religion and even parents themselves; an agenda increasingly hostile to Christianity. This is not by happenstance. Quite to the contrary, this is the culmination of nearly one hundred years of scheming and gradual implementation of secular humanism.

The NEA is in lock step with the globalization plans of the United Nations through UNESCO[6]. The ultimate plan is a united world of secular humanism.

> *"The United Nations is the chosen instrument of God; to be a chosen instrument means to be a divine messenger carrying the banner of God's inner vision and outer manifestation. One day the world will treasure and cherish the soul of the United Nations as its very own with pride, for this soul is all-loving, all-nourishing, and all-fulfilling"*
> Master Sri Chinmoy[7], Head of the U.N. Meditation Room

Maybe that quote is not particularly alarming to you, but let me ask you this? Which "god" comes to rule this world before the return of Jesus Christ? Who is worshipped by the masses in the final days of this earth? Satan! The "god" that Chinmoy and other U.N. leaders deify is not YHWH, it is the ruler of this fallen world, Satan.

The custodian of the U.N. Meditation Room is Lucis Trust[8], formerly called Lucifer publishing, started by occultist Alice Bailey[9]. Many believe Bailey and her occult teachings established the foundation of U.N. spiritual beliefs, continuing to this day.

Recently, the U.N. revealed its "Declaration of a Global Ethic"[10,] commissioned by UNESCO, the U.N. entity that exercises control over the NEA and International Teachers' Union. UNESCO commissioned left-wing ideologue Hans Kung to coordinate the project. He was the perfect choice to present their agenda.

In his 1991 book *"Global Responsibility: In Search of a New World Ethic"*[11], Kung wrote: *Any form of. . . church conservatism is to be rejected . . . To put it bluntly, no regressive or repressive religion—whether Christian, Islamic, Jewish or of whatever provenance—has a long-term future."*

The United Nations, the future vehicle by which antichrist will rule all non-believers, has a tremendous influence on the education of your children. It is committed to turning them into "global citizens", wrestling them away from the "antiquated" teachings of their parents and religion. The NEA is their agent to do this in the American Public Education System.

Quite simply, our children are being brainwashed and indoctrinated. This is not an indictment of many fine teachers in our schools; it is an indictment of a corrupt teachers' union and the U.N. that believe they are charged with overriding the archaic beliefs that parents and religion have forced on our children--their words, not mine.

The United Nations has a "god complex". It envisions itself as the only organization that can save man from self-destruction. Several of its documents state that any fundamentalist religious belief is destructive to the good of man and must be eliminated.

Time and space will not permit a thorough analysis and exposure of these two anti-Christian organizations. That would be a separate book all on to its own, and there are several excellent books that go into great detail on the subject of public education. We will touch base on some larger points and encourage you to research this subject on your own.

Look at the very words and actions of NEA leaders and compare them to the Word of God.

The End of Education and the Beginning of Indoctrination

John Dewey is considered the father of American public education. His work and writings heavily influenced public education in its slide to indoctrination of our youth. Dewey equated individualized thinking with insanity. He believed only a type of "collective thought" could save humanity. He rejected the notion of God or any supreme creator.

In 1933, he co-authored "Humanist Manifesto"[12], which called for a "new world religion"--secular humanism, where man is taught that *he* is God. Dewey called for radical social transformation of the world and mankind, believing it was the only hope for mankind. He and his comrades knew American adults would reject his ideas out of hand, so they developed a system to begin public indoctrination of their humanist agenda through the public education system.

Psychology would provide the "scientific tools" for this indoctrination. These tools were refined a few decades later by B.F. Skinner, a psychologist quoted to this very day in public classrooms. In 1953 Skinner wrote that *"Operant conditioning shapes behavior as a sculptor shapes a lump of clay."* [13]This is a devious and clever twist on scripture which teaches us we are the clay, and God the sculptor. Skinner effectively inserted their humanist manifesto as an acceptable replacement for God in the public school system.

A few years earlier Skinner exposed his hand on how lumps of clay--students--were to be molded. In Walden Two[14], he wrote *"What was needed was a new conception of man, compatible with our scientific knowledge"*. In the previous discussion on science we noted how science has been transformed from seeking truth to pushing theoretical knowledge upon people as "facts". Science, in partnership with humanists shaping public education, was ready to strike, bringing slow death to pure education. The fight began to turn education into indoctrination.

Dewey continued to teach that *"all of man's experiences, in an attempt to understand and alter his environment, are continuing and variable, and therefore not subject to interpretation by any fixed or basic principles"*. Read that again, slowly and carefully, because this is the belief upon which not only public education, but progressive Christianity is based--that there is no absolute truth and that we depend on our feelings and circumstances over established truth. Dewey had started the Emergent church without realizing it.

In 1932, John Dewey became the honorary president of the NEA. His legacy as the father of American public education was cemented in history. The NEA began a systematic march to indoctrinate every American child into a humanist agenda.

The Goals of the NEA

In 1948 the NEA released the following statement: *"The idea has become established that the presentation of international peace and order may require that force be used to compel a nation to conduct its affairs within the framework of an established world system. The most modern expression of this doctrine of collective security is in the United Nations Charter."*[15]

The alliance between the NEA and the U.N. began in earnest. These two humanist organizations now dominate the landscape of American education, shaping every curriculum and transforming our children into "global citizens".

In 1956 former public school teacher and communist Dr. Bella Dodd admitted that *"the Communist Party, whenever possible, wanted to use the teacher's union for political purposes"*.[15] Bella went on to admit that virtually every suggestion communists proposed was adopted by the NEA within the next year or so.

So at a time when communists were seeking to infiltrate every level of the federal government, they also successfully infiltrated the NEA. Communists realized adults would never capitulate to their desire for total transformation from a free capital system to a state controlled system, so they began planting seeds for future generations to slowly be indoctrinated into their socialist beliefs. They knew over time the nation would be slowly transformed from the bottom up.

When you see the transformation that is taking place today as our government becomes more intrusive and more powerful, we must tip our hat to the NEA. Their plan is working to perfection.

In 1970 the Association for Supervision and Curriculum Development[16] (ASCD), the official curriculum arm of the NEA published "To Nurture Humaneness". In it they wrote the following:

> *"The old order is passing . . . the controls of the past were sacred . . . social controls cannot be left to blind chance and unplanned change, usually attributed to God. Man must be the builder of new forms of social organizations and education must play a stellar role".*

Right under the noses of American Christianity, a new Tower of Babel was being constructed. Belief in God was classified by the NEA as "blind chance"--and the church remained silent.

Communists and their NEA allies realized that to change a nation fundamentally from a capitalist to a communist nation, they would need to neutralize religion. Stalin had done it; so did Hitler. Now it was beginning to happen in America. Unlike Russia and Germany, the United States would take more time to transform. Our strong economy, love of individual freedom and strong Christian roots would require patience to undermine this nation when compared to nations facing economic collapse.

In 1972 NEA President Catherine Barrett boasted that *"We are the biggest potential political striking force in this country, and we are determined to control the direction of education".* Think about that the next time your school district's newsletter talks about partnering with you as a parent.

The NEA and its big brother, the International Teachers Union[17], are in lock step with the United Nations. These two organizations, both definitely anti-Christian, control the entire public education system of the United

States. The U.N. organization the NEA takes its marching orders from is UNESCO. The first Director General of UNESCO, Julian Huxley wrote this back in 1948: *"The general philosophy of UNESCO should be a scientific world humanism, global in extent and evolutionary in background"*[18]. The public education system was charged as the catalyst to make it so.

"Scientific world humanism, global in extent." And you thought your school system reflected the values of your community. No, the true value system the NEA is interested in is global secular humanism.

It is important to understand that many U.N. agencies and programs reflect the exact same goals. Several U.N. agencies and officials are on record calling fundamentalist religious beliefs and systems the single greatest threat to the survival of the world. When you view the above information, we see the NEA shares those beliefs.

But it is not just social studies, math and science that the NEA wants to brainwash your children about. It goes well beyond that. The NEA wants to totally take over the education of your children and actually raise them for you. Parents just cannot be trusted with the future of our "global citizens"; and we certainly cannot allow religious teachings to warp the minds of our future leaders either.

In 2011, an NEA spokeswoman spoke to the United Nations, encouraging mandatory world wide sex education for girls as young as six years old. Speaking to a panel combating "homophobia and transphobia" Diane Schneider stated the following:

> *"Oral sex, masturbation and orgasms need to be taught in education. The only way to combat heterosexism and gender conformity is comprehensive sex education. Gender identity expression and sexual orientation are a spectrum and those opposed to homosexuality are stuck in a binary box that religion and family create."*[19]

And you thought the NEA was "partnering" with you as a parent to educate your child. There is no partnership here parents. You and your antiquated religious beliefs are the problem and public education by the

NEA is the solution to how you are corrupting your child's values and beliefs. Think about that the next time you go to vote and see a candidate is endorsed by the local teachers' union or the NEA.

This is but a brief summary of the roots, history and agenda of the NEA. The damage this organization has done to American Christianity through its indoctrination of students is staggering and possibly irreversible. It has been more than instrumental in raising successive narcissistic generations that embrace humanism over the truth of God.

In these challenging economic times I wish every parent could send their children to Christian schools. I ask you as parents to take a step back, assess your financial situation, and prioritize where you are spending your money. Our children are our legacy and our future. They are the single greatest investment you will make in the future of this nation. If you can afford to invest in their education by sending them to a solid bible-teaching Christian school, it will be the best investment you ever make.

"Someone Take Care of Me, Please?" The Nanny State

On January 8, 1964 President Lyndon Johnson delivered his State of the Union speech to congress and the nation. He declared a War on Poverty[20], asking congress to fund programs that would reduce poverty in the nation and provide a basic economic safety net for Americans. It was a noble cause. But as usual the best of intentions go awry when the federal government gets involved beyond its constitutional mandate.

Johnson called for expansion in the federal government's role in healthcare and education, much to the delight of the NEA. Sugar daddy had arrived!

What started off as a necessary safety net for the poorest of Americans has grown into an uncontrollable beast that threatens the liberties and very fabric of our great nation. The NEA's goal of dominance in the education arena would soon be funded with billions of taxpayer dollars. This "War on Poverty" would also plant the early seeds of an entitlement mentality that would destroy the work ethic of millions of Americans, leading to social unrest and the eventual chaos we see today in the Occupy Wall Street Movement.

Many "Occupy Wall Street" protestors believe the government owes them a job, a home and a retirement income. They also believe the government should be required to eliminate their Student Loan debts. This is far beyond a safety net—this is economic slavery that is destroying the free enterprise capitalist system that made this nation the wealthiest in the history of the world.

Americans have historically thrived in a competitive economic environment requiring ingenuity and hard work. Today we are rapidly becoming a second-class economy as fewer Americans are productive workers, and more and more are milking a welfare system that is destroying our work ethic and moral fiber as a nation.

What does this have to do with the suicide of American Christianity? Everything, as this entitlement mentality has seeped into the very teachings of many churches today. Many Christians also have come to believe that they are owed something by God and that we have a right to dictate our needs and desires to Him. But the Word of God warns us against this mentality:

> *"Who has known the mind of the Lord? Or who has been his counselor? Who has ever given to God, that God should repay him?"*
>
> Romans 11:34-35

The Bible teaches us that man deserves only one thing—eternal separation from God because of our sinful nature. We have no rights, only privileges granted by an all-powerful holy God. Each of us deserves to spend an eternity in hell after we die, and to suffer in this life while we are alive on this earth. In reality, any good thing God grants us in this life should be treated as an unexpected bonus. We have no right to have an attitude of entitlement as Christians.

Not so fast. Welcome to American Christianity in the 21st century. Life got you down and you feel lost? Just recite this "Sinner's prayer" and everything will get better. No need for godly sorrow or true repentance, just invite Jesus into your heart. Don't know this "Jesus"? No problem, you just need to "believe" in Him, not know Him.

Having problems making ends meet financially? Would you like the blessings of a big beautiful home or that new boat like your neighbor has? No problem, just ask God for it. Hey, if you have enough faith, the world is at your fingertips. God wants only the best for you and if you think His best means a life of luxury to you, believe and you will receive.

Many Christians bemoan the fact that Americans have gained this new attitude of entitlement, but at the same time we embrace it spiritually. When the Apostle Paul was persecuted and beaten for his faith, he counted it as joy to suffer for the sake of his Lord. When we face any sort of challenge, we curl up in the fetal position and suck our thumbs wondering how God could let this happen to us. American culture has once again infected American Christianity.

As Christians it should be enough for us that God sent His Son who died as a sacrifice for our sins; that we can one day live for eternity with Him in heaven. Any other blessing we receive in this lifetime is gravy. But the entitlement mentality of American culture is infecting American Christianity. We want everything and we want it now.

Islam—The Darling Religion of Satan and American Culture

The Constitution of the United States was charged in Article One with protecting the right of every individual to worship and express their religious beliefs openly. Our nation, while established under Judeo Christian Law, was not created as a "Christians-only nation". While Christianity would be the template for the nation's laws and moral issues, individual religious freedoms were cherished by our founding fathers and they set about to make sure the rights of the individuals regarding religious preference, worship and expression would be protected.

We all know that liberal courts and legislators have succeeded in gutting many of the religious freedoms that Christians have historically enjoyed. Recently in California a homeowner was threatened with fines and imprisonment for holding a weekly Bible study in his home because so many people were attending that the street was lined with legally parked cars. A neighbor complained and the police responded by threatening the homeowner, insinuating that he was creating a public nuisance. The city backed down after threats of countersuits by organizations like The Alliance Defense Fund.

Think about that—a city threatening to shut down a Bible study under the guise of it being a "public nuisance". This is the tip of an iceberg that soon will surface and threaten the religious freedoms of Christians not only in California, but around the nation. If the Christian Church in America does not stand up and fight for its rights instead of continuing to roll over, how long will it be until Christianity itself is seen as a public nuisance or even a threat to America?

But take consolation that religious persecution is not hitting every religion in America. There is one religion that is seemingly embraced, protected and even promoted in our nation today—Islam.

Islam is more than a religion—it is a social, economic, political and religious system that is intolerant, even belligerent toward all other religions. It is the fastest growing religion in the United States and in the world—and it is a real threat to the religious beliefs and lives of people around the world.

In her riveting book "Because They Hate"[21], Brigitte Gabriel shares her personal testimony as a Christian girl growing up in Lebanon. She talks about how, when Muslims were in the extreme minority in Lebanon, some were her neighbors and were helpful to her family when needs arose. However, when the Muslim population grew to significance, the call for "jihad" went out and the nation became a breeding ground for the murder of Christians and Jews. These same friendly neighbors of the past turned into rapists and murderers.

I have read the Koran and the Hadith, Muslim "holy books", four times. I have interviewed guests who are experts on Islam, some of them former Muslims, now Christians. The truth must be told about Islam so Christians will not approach it out of fear or ignorance.

Not every Muslim is a terrorist in training. Many are very nice people who make good neighbors and citizens. But some are waiting in the wings, blending into society, and patiently waiting for the call to "jihad". When that happens, America will not know what hit her.

Islam is not a religion of peace. It is a religion of intolerance with the sole goal of world domination as the only religion acceptable for man. The Koran is a hodgepodge of stories and teachings, some of which resemble stories from the bible with others just plain bizarre and nonsensical. The Koran's Allah is not the God we worship as Christians. In the Koran, Jesus is a minor prophet, subject to the prophet Muhammed who wrote the Koran.

Reading and understanding the Koran can be challenging. The teachings are often contradictory. At times Allah commands love of Jews and Christians and at other times calls for their death if they do not convert to Islam. Some verses teach peace; others order Muslims to kill all unbelievers.

You will often hear Muslims and naive Christians refer to Islam as a "religion of peace". They will recite a "sura" (chapter) that seems to confirm their statement. But here is a key to understanding Islam--the Muslim rule of abrogation. It states in the Koran that if two verses conflict, as is often the case in the Koran, the later verse overrides the earlier verse. Early in the writings of the Koran, Muslims are commanded to love Jews and Christians, but the later verses teach Muslims to hate and prepare to kill Jews and Christians when commanded to do so. So when a Muslim cites a verse in the Koran teaching Islam as a religion of peace, they are being coy and deceptive, or at the least ignorant of their own religion.

Islam will settle for nothing short of universal conversion and eventual death to all infidels. Islam teaches that good Muslims should lie to their enemies to win their confidence. This explains how Muslims have broken every peace treaty they have ever signed with Israel or any other nation.

We will discuss Chrislam, a movement to combine Islam and Christianity later, but one more thing about the teachings of the Muslim holy books. Jesus is not the Son of God, nor did He die on the cross. He was assumed to heaven as a prophet by Allah. In the Muslim teachings of the end times, Jesus appears before Allah. Allah asks Jesus if he ever claimed to be his son and Jesus says no. Jesus then gets angry and helps the Muslim Messiah kill every Jew and Christian remaining.

Recently I watched the Republican Presidential debates where Ron Paul stated a nuclear Iran was no threat to Israel or the world. His logic was that with just one or two nuclear bombs, Iran would never dare attack Israel or the United States because the retaliation would destroy Iran. Now this is arguably sound logic when you view things from the world perspective, but obviously Ron Paul and every one of his opponents had never acquainted themselves with Muslim teachings. This sect of Muslims leading Iran believe their messiah, the Mahdi, is alive today and that he will come forward when Israel has been destroyed.

So if Iran obtains a nuclear weapon and its current regime stays in power, a nuclear attack on Israel will eventually happen. It is just a matter of time. The Iranian regime is committed to starting a war they believe will usher in the return of their "messiah". This regime is not composed of lukewarm Muslims; rather they are radical fanatics who believe they are charged with bringing about the end of the era where Allah will return to rule the entire world with an iron fist, killing all who do not convert to Islam.

With all the facts, testimonies and history available to our government leaders about this religion of hatred and violence, these warnings are not only being ignored by the vast majority of our leaders and citizens, Islam seems to be protected and elevated in this nation. Christians are fair game for the courts; Islam is the sacred cow.

As I write this book the trial of Major Nidal Malik Hasan, an Army Major and psychiatrist, is about to start. According to several witnesses, on

November 5, 2009, Hasan stormed in to the "Soldier Readiness Area" at Fort Hood, Texas and killed 13 people, wounding 29 others while yelling "Allahu Akbar" (god is greater)[22]. He was wounded, arrested and is now awaiting trial. The reaction since that day has shown just how far our government will go to pander to and protect Islam.

Government officials were quick to discount this as the terrorist attack it was. They downplayed, even dismissed the fact that Hasan had been in regular contact with known Muslim terrorists for years. Expect the coming trial to be a tragedy and a joke as every attempt will be made to convince people that Hasan was emotionally disturbed, perhaps even the "victim" of this situation—a "victim" because he is a Muslim.

Two recent events highlight the government's complicity in downplaying this event as a terror attack by a dedicated Muslim:

Two months ago, government spokesmen started spinning this brutal attack as an incident of "workplace violence"[23] instead of the terrorist attack it was. This is a blatant cover up for Islam that would never be presented that way if a Christian were the shooter.

And just a few months ago it was announced that the victims of this terrorist would not be given Purple Heart medals. The Purple Heart is given to soldiers wounded in battle. It is a symbol of gratitude given to military personnel wounded in war or wartime activities. The reason these victims will not be awarded Purple Heart commendations is this: To do so would be the government admitting that we are in a war with radical Muslims. This war has already been declared on the United States by Muslim leaders around the world and living in the United States. We are seen as the "big Satan" by Muslim leaders, with Israel cited as 'little Satan". War was declared on us when Muslim terrorists flew two planes into the World Trade center in 2001, and a third plane into the Pentagon, killing almost three-thousand innocent citizens.

One brave leader, Representative Peter King of New York, has tried to take a stand and expose the agenda of radical Muslims living in the United States. He chaired House Intelligence meetings, exposing verified information of Muslim terror cell groups and public statements made by

Muslim clerics calling for the death of America. King has exposed solid information showing many Muslim Mosques in this nation as terrorist breeding grounds. King has been labeled as a bigot for his public stance, but continues undaunted in his efforts to warn Americans of the danger of the Muslim agenda.

Islam is completely incompatible with a society that cherishes religious freedom and democracy. Islam accepts only a theocracy, with Islam the only religion acceptable. It will accept no other religions, no competing economic or political views and no legal system except Sharia Law, which would outlaw Christianity and any other religion.

What is incredibly baffling, but consistent with the spiritual blindness of many progressives in our nation, is how Islam is considered an acceptable "religion of peace" by progressives, yet Christianity is so hated. Islamic Law calls for potential death sentences for adulterers and homosexuals, while Christianity teaches we are to love all men and lead them to the truth of the gospel. We confront them with their sin, but we do not kill or even hate them. Islam treats women like property, while Christianity teaches they are equal to men in God's eye. Yet Islam is the darling religion of many progressives. They are blind fools.

Saudi Arabia, a nation committed to world wide implementation of Sharia Law, is funding American education, literally buying the hearts and minds of American children.[24] Its billions of dollars in "grants" is funding terrorism, brainwashing students into believing Islam is a religion of peace, and winning the acceptance and hearts of an entire generation. Saudi Arabia, where having a Bible warrants imprisonment or possibly a death sentence is funding American higher education. American colleges are producing the next generation of American-born terrorists that will one day bring death and chaos to our nation.

Islam is a religion of antichrist. 1 John Chapter 4 clearly identifies it as it denies the deity of Jesus Christ. Yet Christian leaders like Rick Warren, Bill Hybels, Jim Wallis and Brian McLaren call for dialogue and reconciliation between Christians and Muslims, hoping we can find a common ground of spirituality and beliefs. If this is not heresy, it walks right up to the line.

We will discuss this poisonous movement called "Chrislam" as we look at the internal agents of death slowly killing American Christianity.

Our responsibility as Americans is to welcome Muslims into our nation if they are here legally, and as American citizens they should have every right we enjoy as Christians. They have a right to worship as they please and build Mosques, but we have a responsibility as Americans to know the dangers of Islam and to keep a close eye on what is being bred within our nation.

Our responsibility as Christians is to love all men, including Muslims who belong to an antichrist religion and need Jesus as much as anyone, but they need the truth about who Jesus really is. He is not a prophet who returns with the Muslim messiah, denying he ever claimed to be the Son of God, and proceeding in anger to help kill every Christian and Jew. He is the only begotten Son of God who came to be the perfect sacrifice so that anyone who truly believes in Him could be free from the punishment and power of sin, having everlasting life with God.

It's Music to Our Ears—and Our Hearts

Music has always captured the hearts and imagination of man. Many of the Psalms are songs giving praise and glory to God with breath-taking beauty. Music has a powerful influence, speaking to us on a subconscious level. Every once in a while, I will turn on a local radio station and listen to "oldies" music from the sixties and seventies, when I was a teenager. I find that some songs I have not heard in more than thirty years are still etched in my subconscious memory and I remember every word. Music has this power—it reaches our hearts and minds and the lyrics etch themselves in our memories.

In June of 1967 the Beatles, reaching the apex of their popularity, released a song titled "Sergeant Pepper's Lonely Hearts Club Band". One of the lines in this wildly popular song says *"I get by with a little help from my friends; I get high with a little help from my friends."* This endorsement of recreational drug use encouraged millions of youth to use drugs like marijuana and LSD to "get high". Illegal drug abuse skyrocketed.

Two years later, Vice President Spiro Agnew held a press conference criticizing the negative influence that modern music was having on youth, citing the lyrics in the song. Many people dismissed Agnew's comments as paranoid behavior.

Shortly after that, Beatles members John Lennon and George Harrison began touring the nation with Maharishi Mahesh Yogi, a famous Hindu mystic, encouraging youth to combine illegal drug use with Hindu mysticism to attain "higher consciousness". Again, millions of youth blindly followed the example of their musical heroes, starting a journey down a dangerous spiritual road. Today, Hindu mysticism has a strong foothold in Christianity through many teachers of the Emergent Church movement, leading our youth away from the one true God.

Even today, when youth are asked who they admire, popular musicians are often the "heroes" they identify the most. Music has a huge influence on youth, laying a foundation for their beliefs, attitudes and behaviors. I encourage parents to take the time to know and study the musicians your children listen and look up to. Today's popular secular music is laced with music that encourages violence, drug abuse and extreme sexuality. Many popular rap musicians sing about young girls as nothing more than sexual objects available for the pleasure of young men. Our young men grow up thinking of women as nothing more than objects of pleasure, and our young girls are being taught that unless they are sexually promiscuous no man will ever love them.

Music speaks to us in a deep way, and the music we listen to can have a lasting effect on our beliefs and behaviors. Today our youth listen to music an average of thirty hours a week and the music they listen to is leading them down a very dark path—a path away from God and in to the arms of an enemy bent on their eternal destruction.

News and Entertainment: "The Opiate of the Masses"?

Life in America used to be much simpler and much healthier physically, emotionally and spiritually. Families used to spend time together and do things together. We used to spend time with our neighbors, getting to know them. When a neighbor had a project that needed to be done, families would chip in and get it done. There was a real sense of family and community. Life was good.

In the forties, television was invented. Only rich families could afford one at first but by the sixties virtually every household owned one. Today most households have three or four televisions along with the internet to occupy our free time.

Our one local television station in Green Bay used to broadcast only about ten hours a day when we were young. Now we have hundreds of channels to choose from, twenty-four hours a day. The internet, Face book and You Tube have become a crucial part of our lives.

When I was thirteen, my best friend found a Playboy magazine his father tried to hide. By today's standards it was very tame but it filled our inquisitive minds with a lot of garbage at a very early age. Today pornography is at our fingertips 24/7 in the privacy of our home, compliments of the internet. What was once a high risk venture has become easy and a low risk opportunity as thousands of websites are at the disposal of people anywhere and at anytime.

A life of family, close friendship, hard work and a sense of real community have been replaced with a life of instant gratification and communication that no longer requires face-to-face communication or even a spoken word.

We have become obsessed with and absorbed into media. The average youth now spends nearly forty hours a week immersed in media—music, the internet, television and social media. And it is not only youth who are being absorbed into media. Millions of adults are becoming addicted to social media, YouTube and Face book. We have become obsessed with social media, telling everyone about every minutia of our lives—where we eat, what we like and when we are going to the bathroom.

As with everything, the internet and media as a whole is neither a blessing nor a curse on its own, depending on how we utilize it. The internet is a useful tool for information and opinions, and social media can connect us, albeit in a very superficial manner.

Try to go anywhere and not see someone texting, talking on their phone or tweeting—it is virtually impossible. At a youth event a couple years ago I watched for twenty minutes as a circle of four young girls worked their i-phones furiously without saying a word to each other. Out of morbid curiosity I approached them and said: "Excuse me but I couldn't help but notice that for at least the past twenty minutes you ladies have not said one word to each other, just working your smart phones. Why don't you have a conversation with one another?"

One girl said "We are; we're talking by texting one another."

I asked why they wouldn't actually have a conversation with their voices and her response was alarming. "I might be saying something to one of my friends that I don't want the others to hear". Welcome to the whacky world of the American teen in the 21st century.

We utilize media, but there is a danger that media can control us. Social media is isolating people and is the easiest way to be phony, as we can present an image of what we would like to be seen as instead of the reality of who we are. Without face to face conversation, eye contact and voice inflection, it is easy to be misunderstood or to get away with lies that personal interaction can see through. While the internet can be an invaluable means of gathering information and opinion, it can also be a way for cowards to spread lies and rumors, with little or no accountability. Much damage has been done to good men and women by anonymous cowards out to slander or destroy them for a variety of reasons. The internet has become a god we worship, isolating us and creating superficial relationships that replace meaningful, personal relationships.

No News is Good News

With the explosion of cable and satellite television, news is available to us instantly, 24/7. There is a positive side to this, assuming what we are watching is news, not propaganda.

News media has always been considered the "fourth estate" of government. The news media has been a watchdog, reporting news and sharing inside information that helps us keep our government in check. It has been an invaluable tool in keeping Americans informed as to the inner workings of our government. During the Watergate scandal, newspapers and television brought us the real story of a paranoid president covering up criminal activity. The media coverage and subsequent outrage of the American people led to Richard Nixon's disgraceful resignation.

But somewhere in the past forty years, media began to cross and blur lines. There had always been a definitive line between what the media would report as news and what it would state as commentary, but not any more.

In a scene from his movie "Annie Hall"[25], Woody Allen is upstairs in the host's bedroom watching the New York Knicks basketball game while his date is downstairs having discussions with her friends who are professors and media moguls. His date comes upstairs, upset to find him immersing himself in a basketball game instead of engaging in conversations with the guests downstairs. (Hey, what man can't relate to that?)

Allen goes into a defense of his action, saying he had no desire to get into a discussion with people who specialized in "dysentery". His date corrects him: "You mean commentary".

Allen responds that he heard commentary had combined with news to create dysentery. Truer words were never spoken, except in the bible.

To remain a free people, we must have access to facts—facts necessary to make proper judgments. We need truth, not just opinions. Well, secular media abandoned their commitment to truth a long time ago. Network news has become a joke, no longer about reporting facts, rather dedicated to pushing an agenda—a progressive, anti-Christian agenda.

In recent polls, ninety-one percent of people working in the media call themselves liberal or progressive, while only nine percent identify themselves as conservative. This is reflected in the reporting of news, which has become more commentary and propaganda than real news. It seems very few stories are simply reported by secular media anymore—they always have to inject a little propaganda.

When a Muslim terrorist, Major Hasan, opens fire killing thirteen soldiers yelling "Allahu Akbar" (god is greater), the media has little to say about his ties to Muslim fanatics. This is not reported as terrorism, it's just another indiscriminate killing in America.

However when a nut case in Norway kills dozens in a premeditated shooting spree, he is presented as a "Christian" because in one of his blogs he made a vague reference to church and Christianity.

The media in this nation is unbelievably powerful, and it has destroyed many a life by reporting half truths and incomplete stories, wrapped in their destructive progressive agenda. It is an active, if unknowing, contributor to the death of this nation and to American Christianity.

The "God" of Oprah Winfrey

Oprah Winfrey is the most powerful person in media today. Millions regularly watched her television shows every day and she has started her own television network[26]. When Oprah endorses a book it is almost certain to become a best seller, and when she says someone is a great person, America listens.

Oprah was raised as a Christian, but became disillusioned at a young age. She could not accept the notion of God being a god of judgment, so she started to search for God on her own terms—something that happens every day with disillusioned Christians. But Oprah was different. This nice young lady would grow into a powerful media presence who would have the ears and hearts of millions of disciples, hanging on every word she speaks, believing it as truth.

By all indications, Oprah is a kind and very generous person. She is also one of the most dangerous enemies of Christianity in America. She has introduced Christians to many dangerous false prophets and teachers including Eckhart Tolle, Rhonda Byrne, author of the best selling New

Age book *"The Secret"*[27], Dr. Mehmet Oz who we will discuss later, and a lady you probably never heard of—Marianne Williamson.

Marianne Williamson is energetic, charismatic, eloquent—and very dangerous. In 2008 Oprah and Williamson covered a daily one year study over satellite radio on "A Course in Miracles". Millions listened, including many Christians.

"A Course in Miracles"[28] was written in 1975 by Columbia professor Helen Schucman. She claimed God spoke to her to give her new revelation and to "correct" misinterpretations in the Bible, properly defining "Jesus" away from the misunderstanding of the apostles and authors of the New Testament. Among the revelations Schucman reported were:

- There is no sin.
- The slain Christ has no meaning.
- The journey to the cross should be the last useless journey.
- Do not make the pathetic error of clinging to the old rugged cross.
- The name of Jesus is but a symbol as a replacement for the many names of God to which men pray.
- The recognition of God is the recognition of your self.
- The oneness of the creator and the creation is your wholeness, your sanity and your limitless power.
- The atonement is the final lesson man need learn, for it teaches him that, never having sinned, he has no need for salvation.

Welcome to the church of Oprah, a church that millions, including Christians, are embracing as "the new Christianity". The teachings of *"A Course in Miracles"* are exactly the opposite of what the Bible teaches, yet millions are embracing it as truth. Oprah is admired by Christians, swayed by her gentle compassion.

We have covered Oprah extensively on Stand Up For the Truth[29], sharing her theological beliefs that are leading many to destruction. In one, she adamantly insists that there is no way Jesus could be the only path to God. The book by Rhonda Byrne, "The Secret" became a best seller when Oprah endorsed it and many Christians, including some close friends of mine, read it and loved it. Byrne's message that if you send good thoughts into the universe that the universe would bring back good things to you spoke directly to some Christians seeking happiness in all the wrong places.

I could write an entire book on the deception of the Church of Oprah, but if you want more information, I suggest two great resources: The first is my friend and author Warren Smith of Mountain Stream Press.[30] As a former New Ager, Warren has written several excellent books on the new age movement, Oprah Winfrey and *"A Course in Miracles."* I also recommend a book by Josh McDowell and Dave Sterrett titled *"'O' God: A Dialogue on Truth and Oprah's Spirituality".*[31]

Summary

American Christianity is under constant attack by some powerful external enemies. Poor science, public education and indoctrination, an expanding socialist government and the anti-Christian propaganda of the media combine as a powerful force, attempting to destroy Christianity in this nation. Islam has replaced Christianity as the darling of American media. This is a powerful army pounding at the walls, seeking to destroy American Christianity. But as powerful as these enemies are, they should be powerless against the church. We have the truth and the Holy Spirit on our side.

But something is happening here that is giving the enemy a huge advantage in this battle, tilting the balance of power. There are traitors in our own camp. Some of these traitors are intentional in their mission while others are naively supporting the work of the enemy. These naïve people are being seduced, thinking they are helping the church to embrace and defeat the enemy, but they are only contributing to the destruction of the church they claim to defend and love.

Whether they are conscious traitors or unknowing pawns is an important distinction. All of us as Christians get things wrong sometimes. When we do, we need to be shown the errors of our ways so we might repent and be restored. I currently choose to believe the people and movements we are about to discuss are unknowing pawns in the enemy's chess game. They are ignorant and have been seduced by the lies of the enemy. I do not condemn these people--I grieve for them and pray that the light of truth will be revealed to their hearts and minds. The future of American Christianity depends on it.

Footnotes

1) "Good Christian Bitches", Kim Gatlin, 2011, Brown Books Publishing
2) "Origin of the Species", Charles Darwin. Random House Publishing
3) www.evolutionnews.org/2012/03/suspicious_circ057381.html
4) "Expelled: No Intelligence Allowed", Rocky Mountain Pictures
5) Nea.org
6) Unesco.org
7) Srichinmoylibrary.com
8) Lucistrust.org
9) Alicebailey.tel
10) Parliamentofworldreligions.org
11) "Global Response: In Search of a New World Ethic", Hans Kung, 2004, Wipf and Stock Publishing
12) "Humanist Manifesto", May, 1933, The New Humanist Magazine
13) http://psychology.about.com/od/profilesofmajorthinkers/p/bio_skinner.htm
14) "Walden Two", B.F. Skinner, 1948, Hackett Publishing
15) Dennis Cuddy, PhD, "The Grab for Power: A Chronology of the NEA"
16) Ascd.org
17) www.ei-ie.org
18) Dennis Cuddy, PhD, "Chronology of Education With Quotable Quotes", 1993.
19) http://www.onenewsnow.com/Education/Default.aspx?id=1310484

20) President Lyndon Johnson, State of the Union Address, January 8, 1964
21) "Because They Hate", Brigitte Gabriel, 2008, St. Martin's Press
22) Wikipedia.com
23) visiontoamerica.org/6128/obama-admin-says-fort-hood-massacre-is-merely-workplace-violence/
24) www.nationalreview.com/articles/221607/saudi-classroom/stanley-kurtz
25) "Annie Hall", 1977
26) OWN Network
27) "The Secret", Rhonda Byrne, 2006, Beyond Words Publishing
28) "A Course in Miracles", Helen Schuchman, Viking Press
29) standupforthetruth.com/2011/10/why-we-need-to-know-about-oprah/
30) Mountainstreampress.org
31) "O God: A Dialogue on Truth and Oprah's Spiritual", 2009, WND Books, Inc.

CHAPTER SIX

THE INTERNAL PAWNS OF THE ENEMY

In the movie "Braveheart", William Wallace, the warrior who led Scotland to its freedom from the repressive rule of England and its notorious king Long Shanks, surveyed the field where the battle for freedom would be fought. A mile away stood thousands of skillfully trained English infantry, cavalry and archers—the greatest fighting force of that time.

Behind him stood a rag tag group of Scots, farmers and shepherds who had taken all they could take. Their wives had been raped, their ancestors murdered, and their dignity stripped. Enough was enough! Freedom would be won this day, and their children would be free, even at the sacrifice of their own lives.

Out of view of the English were the Scottish nobles. They were greedy thieves themselves, accepting bribes of land from Long Shanks to be his proxy of oppression to the Scottish commoners. But Wallace had stirred something up in them—a desire for freedom. This day Wallace believed the nobles would stand strong for the sake of their countrymen and help Scotland free itself from English tyranny.

Wallace would first set a trap for the English cavalry, destroying it in a brilliant move. Infantry forces had never defeated superior cavalry forces before that day but Wallace had a plan. As the English cavalry charged at the waiting Scots, a fire engulfed them as the Scots fired flaming arrows into the ground they had soaked with oil the night before. The powerful

English cavalry was destroyed, setting the table for a Scottish victory that day. They attacked the English infantry, who probably figured they would never even see battle that day, as they assumed the mighty English cavalry would scatter and destroy the ragtag Scots. The battle slowly turned in favor of the Scottish rebels and Wallace's plan was working perfectly.

Wallace was ready to lead Scotland to a decisive victory. Behind a hill, invisible to the English were the Scottish nobles with hundreds of cavalry troops. When Wallace gave the signal, they would swoop in, scattering the English infantry. Long Shanks would be captured, the English army destroyed and Scotland would earn its freedom.

The time was right. With hundreds of dead soldiers around him, William Wallace picked up and waved the banner as the sign for the Scottish nobles to attack. Victory was at hand. As Wallace frantically waved the banner, his heart was about to be broken. The Scottish nobles acknowledged the signal---and slowly turned, leaving the battle area.

The valiant Scots were left to be slaughtered, scattered or captured. Defeat had been snatched from the jaws of victory. Traitors in his own camp had betrayed Wallace and the Scots.

Eventually Wallace was executed and the dream of freedom seemed a distant memory. A few months later, Robert the Bruce, one of the nobles who had betrayed Wallace, had assumed leadership of the Scots. He stood in a field, opposite English royalty, preparing to pledge loyalty to the English crown on behalf of all Scotland. But something welled up in Robert the Bruce that day. Before the previous battle his father, an evil hypocrite who only cared about power, had already arranged the betrayal by the nobles even though Robert had pledged his support to Wallace. Robert the Bruce went along, betraying his friend, out of loyalty to his earthly father.

The pain and shame from his betrayal welled up that day. Robert the Bruce had his eyes opened to what was right. He pleaded to the remaining Scots to follow him as they once followed Wallace. They responded, charging the English. Scotland would win her freedom.

We all have choices to make every day. They are often presented as an option between what is right and what is convenient. We make choices to do the right thing or the selfish thing. Robert the Bruce historically caved in to his earthly desires, choosing the selfish thing. One day he stood up ` and decided to do the right thing—and he changed history.

We need more leaders like Robert the Bruce in the church these days; men and women who recognize the errors of their decisions and make things right. Men who look deep into their own hearts and ask God to share what He sees in their hearts; men who confess they have made bad choices, and ask God for forgiveness and the strength to make things right. Men more interested in doing what is right instead of what is convenient. Men who are willing to admit they are consciously or unconsciously compromising with the world for personal benefit or because they have been seduced by the lies of the enemy.

American Christianity is having an identity crisis. It is struggling with how to be in the world but not of the world. It is struggling to understand the ever changing secular culture, trying to remain a force in confronting it, but slowly we are giving up the battle. Deep down we doubt the power of the gospel and its power to transform lives, so we have embarked on a new marketing campaign. Rather than confront the culture and call it out for what it is, we have decided to "relate" to it. The results have been nothing short of disastrous.

Too many Christian leaders have assumed the role of the Scottish nobles—compromising with evil so we can maintain some semblance of existence, and turning our backs on the people we are charged to lead in favor of embracing the culture.

As Hitler came to power before World War II, he consolidated that power through deception and intimidation. He approached church leaders of his days and convinced them that they had a common enemy--the Jew. He appealed to growing anti-Semitic passions and beliefs that the Jews were bleeding Germany of wealth, prosperity and identity.

He also let them know that he could not and would not tolerate disloyalty of German churches to the "noble" quest he was on to establish

Germany as a world economic and military power. He intimidated them by threatening to shut them down if they spoke against the Nazi movement, and the church leaders folded like cheap suits to maintain their livelihood and status.

Among the new rules Hitler imposed on the churches were the banning of all bibles and the rule that only Third Reich employees could preach. He also took down every cross.

Leaders were faced with a decision to trust God or give in to pressure and fear. They chose fear and Hitler vanquished the one internal opponent that could stand in his way. The results of this cowardly surrender speak for itself. Are some Christian leaders in America, supported by us who follow them, giving in to fear these days? Are we slowly surrendering to an evil secular culture that will one day control American Christianity and gut it of its ability to lead our nation back to God?

One internal pawn of the enemy is gaining greater acceptance among young Christians. Young people who have been trained to question anything that claims to be absolute truth are finding a home within Christianity. They are finding a place where they can accept or reject parts of the Bible so they can customize it to their perceptions of truth and reality. Truth becomes subjective, not objective, and God becomes who you want Him to be instead of who He tells us He is. This is a powerful ally in Satan's master plan to diminish or destroy Christianity. It is subtle, yet very dangerous—and it is working.

The Emergent Church—Emerging Toward What?

Brian McLaren is an intelligent, articulate writer and is well spoken and persuasive. He is referred to as the "guru of the emergent church movement", and he is leading hordes of young Christians over a cliff like lemmings.

In his book, "A New Kind of Christianity"[1], McLaren argues that our traditional beliefs about Christianity are archaic and must change. What fundamental changes does McLaren propose to this "archaic Christianity"?

On page 66 of the book McLaren states *"The question is 'Who is Jesus and why is he important?' The versions of Jesus presented by contemporary Christian institutions could hardly be more different from one another—or from the four gospels."*

I will concede the first part of McLaren's argument—that the different versions of Jesus presented in some Christian institutions these days are all over the map. Jesus is portrayed as judgmental by some, non-judgmental by others; Strong by some and weak by others; a destroyer of the Law by some, and a completer of the Law by others. To some He is a harsh taskmaster requiring sacrifice and turning our back on any good thing this world offers; to others He is our own personal genie just waiting to grant any wish if we just have enough faith. So Mr. McLaren, I concede the point—much of American Christianity is distorting the character and nature of the Son of God. But this does not warrant a call for a "new kind of Christianity". This calls for greater reading of the Word and discernment by the Holy Spirit.

McLaren goes on in later writings to talk about confusion within the gospels themselves suggesting that perhaps the Apostles might have been confused about who Jesus really was and what He taught. This casts doubt on the authority of scripture.

McLaren later goes into a lengthy diatribe about how the church has sold out the gospel by putting a "Greco Roman" spin on it. Again this is an attempt to undermine the scriptures as absolute truth. When you read the Bible in its entirety and study it in the original written languages you find a beautiful consistency from beginning to end. Are there certain teachings we may not completely understand? Certainly, because none of us will have a complete understanding of God until we stand before Him in all his revealed glory. But McLaren and many other "emergers" seek to undermine the absolute truth of the written Word, convincing naive Christians to trust in their own feelings rather than the Word of God. This is going where no man should dare go and will lead many to eternal destruction.

What McLaren is doing is subtly but effectively stating that Christians must doubt the written Word of God; that we cannot rely on the written scriptures as our source of absolute truth. Instead we must rely on our personal feelings, beliefs and experiences. Welcome to a core teaching of the emergent church: Feelings trump facts and emotions trump truth. Your personal beliefs about God are more important than what was written down by men in the Bible.

But McLaren is only warming up folks. He poses the following "dilemma":

> *"How should followers of Jesus relate to people of other religions? We wake up each day in a world whose very future is threatened by interreligious fear, hatred and violence. Many of us wonder if there is a way to have both a deep identity in Christ and an irenic, charitable, neighborly attitude toward people of other faiths. So we ask: Is Jesus the only way? The only way to what? How can a belief in the uniqueness and universality of Christ be held without implying the religious supremacy and exclusivity of the Christian religion?"*

It can't Brian. Christianity is superior to any other religion because it is truth! It is an exclusive club, not because we are special, but because of the sacrifice of Jesus on the cross. Christianity is superior because of Jesus, God in the flesh, who took our sins upon Himself. He died for our sins and rose from the dead. Did Buddha or Muhammed do this? No other religion is remotely similar in its beliefs and none can be held up as equal. True Christians will spend eternity with God, and those who are not will spend eternity separated from Him. This fact, and any fact for that matter, drives emergers crazy. They cannot stand anything that presents itself as absolute truth.

McLaren is planting early seeds of his universalism beliefs here, and planting seeds of doubts in naïve Christians who admire his open minded attitude. They are music to the ears of a generation raised early on to doubt anything that claims to be absolute.

Ready for more intellectual babble? On page 156 of *"A New Kind of Christianity"*, McLaren shares his method of learning:

> *My background was in the liberal arts . . . My training taught me to read for scenes and plots, not doctrines; for protagonists and antagonists, not absolute and objective truths; for character development and conflict resolution, not raw material to be processed into a system of beliefs . . ."*

Looking for scenes, not doctrines; not looking for or accepting the concept of absolute truth; not seeking raw material to be processed into a system of beliefs. Welcome to the cancer that is Emergent Church theology. But in the infamous words of every infomercial, but wait there's more!

> *"There will be no new kind of Christian faith without a new approach to the Bible, because we've gotten ourselves into a mess with the Bible. First we are in a scientific mess. Fundamentalism again and again paints itself into a corner by requiring that the Bible be treated as a divinely dictated science textbook providing us true information in all areas of life, including when and how the earth was created . . ."*

Boiling all this down, McLaren believes that we cannot trust the Written Word of God. McLaren also shows his incredibly weak theological understanding of God, or his deceptive nature when he writes this about God on page 269:

> *"I find a character named God who sends a flood that destroys all humanity except for Noah's family, but that's almost trivial compared to a deity who tortures the greater part of humanity forever in infinite eternal torment."*

God is now a cruel torturer instead of a righteous God who cannot tolerate unrepentant sin. It's God's fault that many will face eternal damnation, not our own. McLaren of course believes a loving God would never judge anyone, so he is setting up his shallow followers for this argument later.

Heard enough on Brian McLaren? Bear with me a little longer. McLaren goes on to argue that we have to stop looking at Christianity as good and every other religion as evil. McLaren later calls the cross *"false advertising for God"*.[2] He argues that substitutionary atonement on the cross is a false teaching—that God would never punish one person for another's sins. Hey Brian, think about something for a moment . . . Jesus, being God, took the punishment for our sins on Himself—the ultimate in sacrificial love. God didn't punish a "third party"; He took our sins upon Himself, in human form, to bring us into a righteous relationship with Him.

Who Listens to McLaren Anyway?

This is not some obscure writer out of the mainstream of Christian thought. Brian McLaren teaches at "Christian" institutions, is admired by thousands of youth pastors and has a cult-like following of hundreds of thousands of youth, youth pastors and well-respected Christian leaders and pastors.

A close friend of mine and a bible-believing Christian approached his church leadership a few years back asking permission to bring Christian teachers in who are well versed on the Judeo-Christian roots upon which our nation was formed. His idea was rejected out of hand, but a different speaker was presented as an alternative—Brian McLaren. This local church saw Brian McLaren as a godly leader and teacher who could "relate" to young adults and youth. I am willing to bet the pastoral team never took the time to study McLaren's theology before suggesting the invitation.

In Revelation 2, God writes letters to the churches, the last one penned to the church in Laodicea. Many biblical scholars believe the Church of Laodicea is representative of the last church before the end of the age because it is the final church letter, symbolizing what "Christianity" would look like just before the return of Jesus. Laodicea comes from two Greek words meaning "people" and "opinions or judgments". So the Church of

Laodicea is the church of "the opinions of the people". Today much of what we call Christianity fits nicely into this description of the Laodicean Church. Our opinions about God seem to matter more than what God says about Himself in the Bible, and we replace the clear judgments and teaching of God with our own subjective interpretations.

It is important to understand that the Emergent Church movement is not a stand alone entity. It is closely affiliated with movements like social justice, New Ageism and Christian Universalism. McLaren is one of many public spokesmen for the heresies and false teachings infecting Christianity these days.

McLaren is an eloquent, persuasive speaker and writer, and this is a real danger to a generation of Christians who place emotion above facts. He has infected American Christianity in a profound way, leading her to potential destruction. But he is hardly alone.

Red Letter Christians

Doctrine is what defines a movement or its religious beliefs. It is the groundwork for the purpose and teachings of their movement or religion—what they believe and what they profess as truth. What a doctrinal statement says, or fails to say, gives us critical information on their beliefs and goals.

Doctrine for churches and ministries is usually expressed in what is called a "Statement of Faith". We hopefully read and explore them before we enter a church or search the internet for teaching and commentaries. They define the beliefs of the organization so we can ascertain their goals and motives. Red Letter Christians[3] has no statement of faith on their site, a testament to their "God is who you think He is" belief system.

This lack of doctrinal beliefs nicely summarizes Emergent Theology— it stands for nothing and is pretty much open to anything the follower feels or thinks might be truth. In my opinion, Emergent theology is worse than atheism—at least atheists believe in something and are not ashamed to admit it. But try pinning down an emergent leader on any sort of hard doctrine, and you usually hear a fluffy response that sounds more like a romance novel than real truth.

Jim Wallis and Tony Campolo are the brainchildren behind Red Letter Christians. Their claim that Christians cannot possibly understand the entire Bible unless we read and study it through the lens of Jesus' words, thus the name Red Letter Christians. Now on the surface this does not seem to be an objectionable statement, but when you dig into their teachings and opinions you see a more nefarious purpose.

A basic cry of those in the movement is if Jesus didn't talk about it, it probably isn't all that important. In other words, don't fret about all the confusing stuff in the Old Testament or the epistles, just focus on what Jesus did or did not say. That's all that really matters. This exposes their weak theological wisdom about the Word of God.

It's as if they are saying Jesus overrode all the teachings of the Old Testament. This of course is refuted by Jesus himself in Matthew 5:17-18:

> *"Do not think that I have come to abolish the Law or the Prophets; I have not come to abolish them but to fulfill them. I tell you the truth, until heaven and earth disappear, not the smallest letter, nor the least stroke of a pen, will by any means disappear from the law until everything is accomplished."*

In the opinion of many, the real agenda of Red Letter Christians, just like Wallis' other brainchild, Sojourners, is not a spiritual agenda, but a political one. It has far less to do with the truth of God then it does in promoting a socialist utopia of "justice". It promotes a sort of "Christian communism" where having equal outcomes is more important than equal opportunities because the free enterprise system of capitalism is just too harsh, with winners and losers.

The list of contributors and recommended authors is a real "who's who" list of progressive activists including Jim Wallis, Tony Campolo, Shane Claiborne, Dorothy Day, Gabe Lyons, Lynne Hybels, Brian McLaren, Jay

Bakker and Rob Bell. There seems to be a common bond in all of them—a distaste for absolute truth and fundamental Christianity.

Apparently, anything goes with Red Letter Christians, as long as you feel good about it. No mention of sin, just a call for justice and peace. A common argument put forth by many Red Letter Christians is that homosexuality is not a sin because Jesus never overtly called it a sin. When one counters with the fact that Paul did, a common question you get in rebuttal is "Well, who do you follow, Jesus or Paul?" This speaks to their shallow understanding of the bible and culture when Jesus walked the earth.

Homosexuality was a sin under the Law, the law Jesus did not abolish by the way, and it was punishable by death. Every Jew knew this so it was probably a very limited occurrence given the severe sentence. Jesus did not have to preach on it as a sin, just like he did not have to call out rape or pedophilia as a sin—every Jew knew it.

Paul on the other hand, was the apostle to the Gentiles, mainly Greeks and Romans. Greek culture not only allowed, but often celebrated homosexuality. Historically kings and conquerors were given young boys as sexual slaves to reward them and to teach the young boys the art of servitude—disgusting certainly, but acceptable and even commendable in Greek culture. Roman culture celebrated homosexuality, recognizing it as a form of virility and superiority for the aggressor. Roman leaders used it as a way to enforce their superiority over slaves.[4] Paul had to admonish new Greek and Roman Christians, reminding them that homosexuality is a sin and that the habitually sexually immoral person would not inherit the Kingdom of Heaven.

Red Letter Christian founders, Jim Wallis and Tony Campolo, are highly respected among many Christian leaders, churches and colleges. Their books are often used by naïve youth leaders to "instruct" youth on this new form of Christianity. Tony Campolo has made some controversial statements throughout the years that cause one to question just what this new form of Christianity looks like.

"We cannot allow our theologies to separate us" (speaking on the relations between Muslims and Christians).

"Evangelicals and Interfaith Cooperation", an interview with Shane Claiborne[5]

> *"It seems to me that when we listen to the Muslim mystics as they talk about their love for Jesus, I must say, it's a lot closer to New Testament Christianity than a lot of Christians that I hear. In other words if we are looking for common ground, can we find it in mystical spirituality, even if we cannot theologically agree? Can we pray together in such a way that we connect with a God that transcends our theological differences?"*

"Evangelicals and Interfaith Cooperation", an interview with Shane Claiborne[5]

> *"Beyond these models of reconciliation, a theology of mysticism provides some hope for common ground between Christians and Islam. Both religions have within their histories examples of ecstatic union with God.*[6]

OK stop the presses for a moment. These quotes show Tony Campolo trying to find common ground between Islam and Christianity. This is called "Chrislam" and we will explore that in this chapter. I have read the Koran and the Hadith four times and consulted with former Muslims. A couple facts must interrupt Tony's love fest:

First, Allah is not YHWH. This is abundantly clear if you read the first few "suras" (chapters) of the Koran. Allah denies any sort of trinity and is a liar. God cannot lie as it is against his nature. Lying is Allah's nature and he encourages Muslims to do the same, and let's remember who Jesus said in John 8:44 is *"a liar, and the father of all lies"*.

Second, this "love of Jesus" Campolo says Muslims have; well Muslims do love Jesus—but as a minor prophet named Isa, and the teachings of Muhammed accuse Jesus of being a liar. The commonality Campolo and others seek is biblically impossible. The Koran denies that Jesus is a deity, the Son of God. In 1 John Chapter 4:1-3, Islam is biblically identified as a religion of antichrist:

> *"Dear friends, do not believe every spirit, but test the spirits to see whether they are from God, because many false prophets have gone out into the world. This is how you can recognize the Spirit of God: Every spirit that acknowledges that Jesus Christ has come in the flesh is from God, but every spirit that does not acknowledge Jesus is not from God. This is the spirit of antichrist, which you have heard is coming and even now is already in the world"*

So Tony Campolo and other Christian leaders are promoting common dialogue and beliefs between Christianity and a religion of antichrist. That's what passes for Christian leadership and influence these days. If this is not heresy, it is darned close.

Campolo has many other quotes about reaching for "christ-consciousness"—a fancy word for saying God is in everyone, a New Age philosophy. Campolo also appears to be a universalist, thinking all people go to heaven:

> *"going to heaven is like going to Philadelphia . . . there are many ways . . . it doesn't make any difference how we go there. We all end up in the same place."*[7]

Campolo tips his hand in embracing New Age teachings when he says this:

> *"That a new humanity will be brought forth from this Chris-consciousness in each person."*[8]

"Christ-consciousness" is terminology used by occultists and New Age philosophers like Alice Bailey, Helen Schuchman and Marianne Williamson. Anyone who has spent any time in the New Age movement knows these "code words" mean "Christ is in all things".

Campolo also admits he struggles with the thought of homosexuality being a sin, but at least up to now, does not endorse homosexual marriage, although his wife does. Give him time and he will be further "enlightened" I'm sure.

Earlier this year I received a call right after we covered the Emergent Church on an episode of Stand Up For the Truth. A woman asked if I was familiar with a book titled *"Irresistible Revolution".*[9] I told her I was familiar with this book, written by Shane Claiborne and endorsed by Jim Wallis. She told me her son came home from youth group the day before with the book, given to him by his Youth Leader. The leader gave every member of his group the book telling them this book would be their "Bible study" for the coming months.

This is happening regularly in our churches. The Word of God is being replaced by writings of Emergent leaders and social justice proponents. Our youth are learning a false gospel supported by many of our Christian leaders. I cannot urge you strongly enough to meet with your church leadership and find out what your children are being taught in their youth group. If your youth leader is teaching them directly from the bible, thank him and help him any way you can. If the youth leader is peddling garbage like *"Irresistible Revolution"*, demand that this ceases and if it does not, leave the church for one that teaches the Word of God.

Red Letter Christianity is not serious Christianity at all. It is an incomplete, twisted gospel that is leading many gullible Christian youth astray with its message on "love" and acceptance. There is no call for repentance and no real acknowledgment of the existence of sin in our lives. It's like a bad chick flick—full of fluff and feelings with no real content or story.

Social Justice

Wallis and Campolo are also leaders in the social justice movement that is making inroads into every denomination of Christianity. The Social Justice movement, while claiming to be a Christian movement, is nothing of the kind. Appealing more to the human perception of justice rather than God's definition of justice, this movement is damaging Christianity from within, weakening it to the external assault of Satan's army.

Jim Wallis, as noted earlier, is nothing but a progressive political activist. He has continually supported Communist regimes around the world, dating back to when he was a chapter leader for Students for a Democratic Society[10] in the late sixties. He is a disciple of Saul Alinsky and has successfully hoodwinked Christians into supporting pro-abortion, pro-homosexual candidates, including Barack Obama. In fact I believe Wallis was the key person responsible for Obama's election. A majority of Catholics and a high percentage of Evangelical Christians voted for Obama, and Jim Wallis was the catalyst.

The Social Justice Movement is a loose organization that includes some dangerous teachings that the leaders have convinced people are biblically based. Liberation Theology[11] and Black Liberation Theology teach that Jesus hated rich people and that the rich must be overthrown before Jesus can return. In fact Jim Wallis is close friends with Pastor Jeremiah Wright, Obama's former Chief Spiritual Advisor prior to Wallis. The same Jeremiah Wright who prayed God would damn America rather than bless and restore her.

The Social Justice movement that is infiltrating mainstream Christianity might sound noble on the surface. It calls for helping the poor through better housing and transportation, rehabilitation instead of incarceration for non-violent criminals, and calls for Christians to be more generous financially. It is *how* they call for this financial sharing that is a concern. They are proponents of forced wealth redistribution through higher taxes. This takes the voluntary giving of Christians, where we can choose which organizations to help, and gives that power to a federal government that has proven to be hateful of Christianity.

Jim Wallis is a staunch supporter of the Occupy Wall Street Movement, recently calling on it to expand to "Occupy Churches". This fits perfectly into Saul Alinsky's game plan in "Rules For Radicals"[12], the handbook of the social justice movement. Alinsky was a proud Communist and atheist who dedicated his book to Lucifer. Now why would a "Christian" like Jim Wallis be an avid disciple of a man who was an atheist and who dedicated a book to Lucifer?

The Social Justice movement's "crown jewel" is Sojourners' Magazine[13]. Claiming again to be Christians, Sojourners is nothing but an interfaith movement that disgraces the gospel, replacing it with a man-made gospel of communism and humanism. A frequent offer for new subscribers is a poster of Gandhi. The website refers to global warming, economic inequality and national borders as "sins", but does not call abortion or homosexuality sin.

As its Chief Editor, Wallis has a team of progressives as editors and regular contributors, including Tony Campolo, Brian McLaren and Lynne Hybels, wife of Pastor Bill Hybels. They are anti-Israel and are promoters of the Palestinian cause—these same Palestinians who partner with Syria and Iran to launch thousands of rockets into Israel every year, killing innocent children.

Wallis and Sojourners also has a "sugar daddy" in George Soros.[14] Soros is a billionaire atheist who hates Christianity and America. He invests millions of dollars every year into organizations bent on destroying Christianity and America as a nation. He sees America as the last obstacle to a one-world government that Soros believes is necessary for the survival of mankind. In 2010 when it was reported that Soros was funding Wallis and Sojourners, Wallis publicly and adamantly denied it. When documents confirmed that indeed Soros had sent Wallis and Sojourners hundreds of thousands of dollars, Wallis deflected stating he could not be expected to keep track of "every little contribution".[15]

The Social Justice Movement twists the gospel to claim that Jesus cared more about the condition of this world than He did the eternal souls of men. They promote blatant humanism and communism, along with a pattern of speaking highly of candidates who support homosexual marriage and abortion.

Wallis applauded the Arab Spring as a great day for democracy, but has remained silent as Christians in Egypt are murdered, churches are burned, and the Muslim Brotherhood controlling Egypt has announced they will disregard Egypt's peace treaty with Israel. Wallis also signed on to the "Common Word Between Us" heresy we will discuss later.

I have spoken with Jim Wallis. He is not stupid. He is smart and eloquent and knows exactly what he is doing. Combined with their close sister, the Emergent Church Movement, they are out to destroy traditional Christianity and replace it with a religion of Universalism based on humanism.

Jim Wallis is the perfect leader for the Social Justice Movement; he is as disingenuous as the movement is. Any person with a modicum of common sense can see through the flowery rhetoric of this anti-Christian movement, yet they continue to make inroads into Christian churches of all denominations.

Rob Bell

Rob Bell, now former Pastor of Mars Hill Church in Michigan, has been touted as the next wave of Christian leadership by many in the emergent movement. He is charismatic and articulate—but biblically shallow. He has produced countless "Nooma" videos that are entertaining Christian youth in youth groups around the world. Youth leaders seem to worship the ground he walks on, claiming he reaches the heart and soul of the younger generation. Teachers like John MacArthur ask if he fits the mold of the false prophets we are warned about by Jesus, Paul and Peter. Let's take a peak at the man who has a hold on our youth with his glitter and rock and roll personality.

Bell was raised an Evangelical and graduated from Wheaton University, for whatever that is worth these days. He claims to be "evangelical and orthodox to the bone" but his teachings seem to refute that claim. Historic Evangelicalism has affirmed the authority, inerrancy and sufficiency of scripture as "God-breathed". How do Bell's beliefs line up?

Rob Bell authored a best-selling book "Love Wins".[16] In it, per the emergent handbook, he asks a lot of questions but provides few if any answers. He questions if hell really exists. Would a loving God really send someone to hell? Conceding that even if the existence of hell might be possible, Bell goes on to question hell as an eternal place of suffering and separation from God.

Questions can be important. They can help you grow deeper in your knowledge of the truth, and they can help us wrestle with difficult questions of doctrine. But how Bell asks the question is just as important as the question itself.

> *"Has God created billions of people over thousands of years only to select a few to go to heaven and everyone else to suffer forever in hell? Is this acceptable to God? How is this 'good news?'"*

This frames the question in a very misleading way, claiming it has to be good news for **everyone**, not just those who choose Jesus.

Bell goes on to write: *"A staggering number of people have been taught that a select few Christians will spend forever in a peaceful, joyous place called heaven, while the rest of humanity spends forever in torment and punishment in hell with no chance for anything better . . . . This is misguided and toxic and ultimately subverts the contagious spread of Jesus' message of love, peace, forgiveness, and joy that our world desperately needs to hear."*

Sorry Rob, but that is what Jesus says. The path to eternal life is narrow but the road to destruction is wide and many find it.

But is hell a future reality or a just a present state? Is it an earthly reality or one that exists elsewhere and for eternity?

According to Rob Bell, hell appears to be more about what we do to each other in this lifetime than how we have turned away from God. Bell reads Jesus' warnings of divine punishment as addressing only the temporal, rather than both the temporal and the eternal. These warnings were for the religious leaders of the day, and had very little to do with some other reality or some other time, he argues (pp. 82-83). Instead, hell is *a word that refers to the big, wide, terrible evil that comes from the secrets hidden deep within our hearts all the way to the massive, society-wide collapse and chaos that comes when we fail to live in God's world God's way"* (p. 95). In other words, hell is here and now in this life, not a place of eternal punishment.

You also find very broad statements offered as fact. *"At the center of the Christian tradition since the first church has been the insistence that history is not tragic, hell is not forever, and love, in the end, wins."*

Scripture clearly points to hell as a place of eternal damnation, so I am not sure what Bell means when he talks about Christian tradition. The New Testament is the beginning of Christianity, and Jesus clearly taught in a literal, eternal hell.

Bell cites the Greek word "aion", a small word that is central to his arguments.

While this word is commonly translated as "eternal" or "everlasting," Bell argues that it can also mean "age" or "period of time". Using this approach, he briefly argues from the parable of the sheep and the goats (Matt. 25:31-46) that eternal punishment isn't eternal, but rather an intense period of pruning.

But if we are going to accept that definition of the word we must be consistent in its interpretation. That same word is used in John 3:16. So if we assume that these words primarily mean "age" or "period of time," what happens when we apply that definition to John 3:16 where it is used?

For God so loved the world that He sent His only Son so that whosoever believes in Him will not perish but have life for a limited period of time? You can't have it both ways Rob.

Citing 1 Timothy 2 (where Paul states that God desires all people to be saved and to come to the knowledge of the truth) Bell reflects and asks:

> *"How great is God? Great enough to achieve what God sets out to do, or kind of great, medium great, great most of the time, but in this, the fate of billions of people, not totally great; sort of great; a little great."*

A God who would allow people to go to hell is not a great God, according to Bell, and the traditional belief that He would is *"devastating . . .*

psychologically crushing . . . *terrifying and traumatizing and unbearable*"
(pp. 136-7).

Rob Bell almost seems to be attributing evil intentions and actions
to God.

If *"Love Wins"* accurately represents Bell's views on heaven and hell, it
reveals him as a proponent of a kind of Christian Universalism.

*"As soon as the door is opened to Muslims, Hindus, Buddhists, and Baptists
from Cleveland, many Christians become very uneasy, saying that then Jesus
doesn't matter anymore, the cross is irrelevant, it doesn't matter what you
believe, and so forth."*

This is just not true of the Christians I know. They desire for all people
from all religions to have their eyes and hearts opened to the saving gospel.
But God will not come to us on our terms—we must come to Him on
His terms—acceptance of Jesus as the Son of God—no other scenario
will do.

So there are the beliefs about salvation, heaven and hell from the man
your children adore—the man your youth pastor might be holding up as
"cool and relevant". And do not think for one minute that Rob Bell could
never be influencing your children or the youth pastor who is teaching
them. Bell's "Nooma" videos are extremely popular and widely used in
many churches.

In an attempt to publicize his book, Rob Bell appeared on MSNBC
in an interview with Martin Bashir[17]. Unfortunately for Bell, this occurred
in the midst of a tragedy--the massive Japanese earthquake and tsunami
that killed hundreds and devastated the nation.

Bashir started the interview by giving Bell an opportunity to share the
gospel by explaining why bad things happen. Bashir asked Bell to explain
why God allowed the devastating earthquake to occur--was God powerless
to prevent it, or did He not care for the people killed?

How I wish one day I am given an opportunity to answer a question
like that in front of millions of lost people. I would explain how God
created man to live on a perfect earth; an earth without pain, sickness or
death. How God created man to live forever, worshipping Him. But how

man chose sin, telling God we knew best how the world should function. I would tell people that since we chose life apart from God, sin and death entered the world. But how God loved us so much He sent His Son to be the perfect sacrifice for sin, so we might one day live in perfect harmony with God in heaven. I would tell the audience that in the meantime the world must still feel the consequence for our sin until Jesus returns in final, eternal victory. How those of us who place our complete faith in Jesus will one day live forever with God. I would invite the audience to repent, acknowledge Jesus Christ, and submit to Him as Lord and Savior.

But Rob Bell stumbled around the question, offering nothing of substance, failing to share the gospel of hope to millions watching him promote his book.

Bashir went onto dissect Bell's theology and Rob Bell was exposed for the fool he is. His shallow biblical theology was witnessed by millions. Watch the interview and ask yourself why millions of Christian youth and thousands of Christian Youth Pastors admire him as a leader. Is this what we want to embrace as leadership in American Christianity?

I urge you to confront your pastor and ask that he get involved with what the church's youth are being taught in youth group, and to learn more about the people his youth leader looks up to. Do not assume your children are being taught the absolute truth of the Bible in youth group. There is a good chance they are subtly learning that the Word of God is more subjective than absolute.

Christian Universalism

"Christian Universalism"[18] is the position that all of mankind will ultimately be saved through Jesus, whether we repent of sin and place our faith in him as the Son of God or not. It claims that God's qualities of love, sovereignty, and justice require that all people be saved and that eternal punishment is a false doctrine. The saving work of the cross does not save us from eternal damnation, it saves us from sin.

There are two slightly differing beliefs in Christian Universalism:

The first teaches that unrepentant sinners will be **punished proportionately in a future state**, according to the degree of sin committed in the current life. They generally hold to the belief that this punishment is moral and not physical and that there is no hell. In essence they will carry a burden with them in heaven.

The second camp teaches that **all the punishment for sin occurs in this life** and that God's discipline in our lives is for the purpose of purifying us. In eternity, there will be a loss of reward for those who did not trust in Christ in this lifetime.

So one camp generally believes they will carry a burden in heaven; the other that we will lose some blessings in heaven. But both camps maintain that everyone, regardless of their faith or religious beliefs, will be in heaven with God. It is unthinkable to them that a loving God would ever condemn anyone to eternal punishment.

Some Christian Universalists claim to hold many of the basic beliefs of traditional Christianity: The Trinity, the deity of Christ and the Holy Spirit, and salvation by grace alone. Some hold to the inerrancy of scripture but believe it has been maligned by man as history progressed.

Others deny the teaching of the Trinity, claiming the belief of Arianism, where God is a divine entity, but Jesus was created by Him. Many also claim God has taken various forms throughout history and revealed himself through other religions like Hinduism and Islam.

Many profess a belief that Jesus is the Son of the Living God, but we must examine their belief closely because of the belief of Arianism, where Jesus is the created Son of God, not a member of the Trinity. The slippery and subtle nuances of their language make this appealing to a generation that is biblically illiterate and seeking acceptance over exclusion in religious beliefs.

Many Christian Universalists affirm the physical resurrection of Jesus, but some claim He did not rise from the dead physically, that rather He was assumed into heaven to dwell with God. If the physical resurrection of Jesus is denied, as it seems it is, then anyone who holds to that position is indeed a non-Christian since it denies one of the essential doctrines of Christianity.

Many deny that the Holy Spirit is God. The "Holy Spirit" is viewed as a part of human existence—the spirit within every man that desires to connect with his creator. It is a human spirit of each man, not God Himself.

Many Christian Universalists believe in a "second chance" theology at work where people who have rejected Jesus in this life can come to faith in the next life. Some believe it is a reincarnation while others believe along the lines of what Rob Bell suggests—that eventually all humans are reconciled to God after a brief separation.

Christian Universalism is very attractive to the current generation of young people. It falls much more in line with a "loving God" then a God of justice and judgment. While you will not find many Emergent Christians that admit it, when you read the entirety of their writings and beliefs, many are Christian Universalists. That is one reason their teaching is so appealing to a biblically illiterate generation of Christians.

There is a very deep danger in how this false teaching is infecting American Christianity. It seeks to eliminate the judgmental nature of God. God is a holy God who cannot tolerate sin, and heaven will be a place that is void of the very presence of sin according to scripture.

When we eliminate the righteous judgment of God, we diminish His holy, perfect character. We reduce Him to something lower than He is, and God will not be mocked or subject to our human understanding or desires. This teaching also removes the fear of the Lord. We are instructed to have a healthy fear of falling into the hands of an angry God. He does judge and will condemn many to eternal hell. This is a healthy fear that helps us in our Christian walk. When we no longer fear the wrath of an angry God, we in essence worship a false god.

True Christians should see God as our loving Father—a Father who protects and cherishes us. But we are never to lose our reverent fear of Him if we turn away from Him.

Be watchful and have your ears open when discussing the Christian faith with young people and new Christians. Ask probing questions, drilling beneath the surface. Christian Universalist beliefs are taking hold of many younger Christians and we need to be prepared to recognize and refute it with the Word of God.

Chrislam: Sleeping With the Enemy?

Sometimes an external and internal enemy can be one in the same. Chrislam, a bait thrown out by Muslim leaders and swallowed by many Christian leaders and pastors, is such an enemy.

Chrislam is an unofficial term for a movement that seeks dialogue and common beliefs between Christianity and Islam. It is a dangerous topic to approach as televangelist Jack Van Impe discovered in 2011. He ended a longtime partnership with Trinity Broadcasting when he prepared to air a show on the network explaining Chrislam and naming names of Christian leaders and pastors embracing it, including Rick Warren, "America's Pastor". Jack you should have called me first. No person we discuss on Stand Up For the Truth leads to more backlash than our exploring Rick Warren and the path he is on. More on him later, but back to Chrislam.

We are warned in the Book of Revelation of a false prophet, representing a false unified religion that will work with Antichrist to gain world domination. The Apostles and Jesus warned that in the final days there would be many false teachers.

In 2007, one-hundred-thirty-eight Muslim leaders sent an open letter to Christian leaders. They were concerned about escalating rhetoric that, quite frankly, was occurring as Muslim terrorism became more prevalent throughout the world. This open letter was titled "A Common Word Between Us"[19]. It asked for interfaith dialogue, claiming the two great monotheistic religions shared two basic principles of doctrine: Love of the one god and love of our neighbor. These Muslim leaders were appealing to Christian leaders to find common ground to bring peace to the world through dialogue.

What is the purpose of dialogue? To find a basis for common beliefs and goals. You are willing to compromise and give up some things to reach agreement and common purpose. If this attempt was to have Christian and Muslim leaders discuss ways we could reduce the tension between the religions and respect each other as human beings, I wouldn't have a problem with it. However since it is an attempt to find common dialogue and beliefs between us, it is wrong and dangerous.

2 Corinthians 6:14-17:

> *"Do not be yoked together with unbelievers. For what do righteousness and wickedness have in common? Or what fellowship can light have with darkness. What harmony is there between Christ and Belial? What does a believer have in common with an unbeliever? What agreement is there between the temple of God and idols? For we are the temple of the living God. As God has said: 'I live with them and walk among them, and I will be their God and they will be my people.' Therefore come out from them and be separate; touch no unclean thing and I will receive you."*

The scriptures are clear: We are not to mingle God with the god of unbelievers. We are to have no part in religious syncretism with those who are not Christians.

The "Common Word Between Us" letter was a call to base all future interfaith dialogue between Christians and Muslims upon what these Muslim clerics believe is the common ground between the faiths.

> *"The basis for this peace and understanding already exists. "It is part of the very foundational principles of both faiths: love of the One God, and love of the neighbor. These principles are found over and over again in the sacred texts of Islam and Christianity. The Unity of God, the necessity of love for Him, and the necessity of love of the neighbor is thus the common ground between Islam and Christianity." And our common ground should lead to this.*

> *"Thus in obedience to the Holy Qur'an, we as Muslims invite*
> *Christians to come together with us on the basis of what is common*
> *to us, which is also what is most essential to our faith and practice:*
> *the Two Commandments of love.*
> *"So let our differences not cause hatred and strife between us.*
> *Let us vie with each other only in righteousness and good works.*
> *Let us respect each other, be fair, just and kind to one another and*
> *live in sincere peace, harmony and mutual goodwill."*

How beautiful; yet how deceptive. If one takes the time to study Islam and its "holy books" you can see right through this deception. Islam allows for peaceful coexistence with other religions only when it fits the Muslim agenda of leading to the destruction of the opposing religion. In other words, when you are in the minority, you may smile upon the infidel, but never love him in your heart. This is the historic pattern of Islam around the world: speak peace until you are in position to make war.

The Koran does not teach Islam as a religion of peace. In several verses good Muslims are commanded to kill Jews and Christians.

Muslims are taught Jesus is *not* the Son of God. He did not die on the cross. He was a secondary prophet to Muhammed. The Muslim Hadith teaches Jesus was taken to heaven by Allah and returns in the last days with the Muslim Messiah--the Mahdi--to kill Christians and Jews.

Muslims believe that as Abraham's first son, Ishmael was due Abraham's inheritance and birthright. God specifically said Isaac received the birthright and inheritance.

Read God's prophecy over Ishmael in Genesis 16:12:

> *"He will be a wild donkey of a man; his hand will be against*
> *everyone and everyone's hand against him. And he will live in*
> *hostility toward all his brothers."*

Has this prophecy come true? Of course, it is in God's written Word. Muslims kill non-Muslims and they kill one another. Shiite and Sunni Muslims are constantly killing one another, as the War in Iraq clearly shows. Islam's only real goal is this: The whole world submissive to Allah, with death to all those who refuse.

The Christian Response

Four scholars at Yale Divinity School's Center for Faith and Culture chose to respond to this with a full-page advertisement in the New York Times that was published on November 18, 2007. They titled this response *"Loving God and Neighbor Together: A Christian Response to A Common Word Between Us and You."* It was endorsed by over one-hundred Christian theologians, pastors and scholars, among whom were Rick Warren, Brian McLaren, Bill Hybels, Robert Schuller, Jim Wallis, and Richard Mouw, President of Fuller Theological Seminary.[20]

The letter was one of Christian repentance and delight—repentance for wrongs committed by Christians against Muslims, and delight for the efforts of the Islamic scholars to find this common ground between the faiths. *"As members of the worldwide Christian community, we were deeply encouraged and challenged by the recent historic open letter signed by 138 leading Muslim scholars, clerics, and intellectuals from around the world."* These Christian leaders agree with the common ground between these two faiths. The response continued:

> *"What is common between us lies not in something marginal, nor in something merely important to each. It lies, rather, in something absolutely central to both: love of God and love of neighbor. Surprisingly for many Christians, your letter considers the dual command of love to be the foundational principle not just of the Christian faith, but of Islam as well. That so much common ground exists—common ground in some of the fundamentals of faith—gives hope that undeniable differences and even the very real external pressures that bear down upon us can not overshadow the common ground upon which we stand together."*

You may want to read that several times. These Christian leaders just said that the very foundational beliefs of Islam and Christianity are virtually identical. Since these people seem to value world peace over the Word of God that should not be a surprise.

The letter concludes with further agreement that this common ground ought to be the basis for further interfaith dialogue. It concludes with the promise that these leaders will continue to labor towards the goal set by these Muslim clerics.

> *"Let this common ground—the dual common ground of love of God and of neighbor—be the basis of all future interfaith dialogue between us," your courageous letter urges. Indeed, in the generosity with which the letter is written you embody what you call for. We most heartily agree. Abandoning all 'hatred and strife', we must engage in interfaith dialogue as those who seek each other's good, for the one God unceasingly seeks our good. Indeed, together with you we believe that we need to move beyond 'a polite ecumenical dialogue between selected religious leaders' and work diligently together to reshape relations between our communities and our nations so that they genuinely reflect our common love for God and for one another.*
>
> *"If we fail to make every effort to make peace and come together in harmony you correctly remind us that 'our eternal souls' are at stake as well.*
>
> *"We are persuaded that our next step should be for our leaders at every level to meet together and begin the earnest work of determining how God would have us fulfill the requirement that we love God and one another. It is with humility and hope that we receive your generous letter, and we commit ourselves to labor together in heart, soul, mind and strength for the objectives you so appropriately propose."*

These Christian leaders just equated Islam, a religion of antichrist, with Christianity. Shockingly, the documents take for granted that the God of Christianity is the god of Islam. Nowhere in this document would one come to believe that the God of the Bible is different than Allah of Islam.

Allah denies the trinity. Allah tells people to lie. Allah says that Jesus is not his Son. Muhammed writes in the Hadith that Allah told him that when the Muslim messiah appears, Jesus (Isa) comes with him, denying he ever claimed to be the Son of God. In anger, Jesus breaks every cross and helps the Mahdi kill every Jew and Christian.

Yet Rick Warren, Jim Wallis, Brian McLaren, Richard Mouw and Bill Hybels, along with many other respected Christian leaders, endorse this deception. With any modicum of biblical wisdom or discernment they would be able to see through this deception. They are either incredibly naïve or deceivers themselves—God alone knows and will make that judgment.

I will lean to the belief they are deceived. If so, how could they be so naïve? Simply, they were dealing with an enemy much smarter than them. They were hungry, starving fish that took the bait of a crafty, experienced fisherman.

The Great Deception of "A Common Word Between Us"

The Muslim clerics stated that the common foundations between the two religions are:

- Belief in the one true God.
- The command to love our neighbor.

Both religions are monotheistic, believing in one God. But if the illustrious leaders who bought in to this deception had given five minutes of thought, or bothered reading the Koran, they would have known that Muslims worship a false god.

The command to love our neighbor is a crucial teaching for Christians by Jesus. He listed it as the second greatest commandment, behind loving God with all our heart, mind and strength. However, the command is *not* a foundation of our Christian faith, it is a command. The **foundation** of the Christian faith is belief in the one true God, YHWH, and the belief that Jesus Christ is His only begotten Son and the only way to righteous standing with God and eternal salvation. This foundation is denied by Islam as heresy and used to refer to Christians as infidels.

Nowhere in the Bible does Jesus tell us to find common ground with other faiths; we are to remain separate from them in religious matters. Nowhere do the Apostles engage in dialogue or in seeking common ground in which to pursue God together with false religions.

This unbelievable surrender to Islam by these leaders shows their lack of understanding of this antichrist religion. They fail to realize that Muslims must reject the authority of the Bible, deny the Triune God, and deny the deity of Jesus Christ.

These leaders have in essence sold out Christianity for public acclaim or the appearance of being loving and caring. Quite frankly, it is a disgrace to Christianity and they need to repent of their actions. Some of the original Christians who signed on to this abomination have repented and recanted their support. Those who have not recanted owe every Christian they lead or influence an apology. But most importantly I pray that God will show them the errors of their ways, and that they will repent for their sake.

Summary

There are many more internal pawns of the enemy within the walls of American Christianity. Many Christian universities and seminaries are a shell of what they once were, abandoning doctrine and sound biblical teaching for emergent, post-modern theology. The adoption of homosexuality as acceptable behavior by a growing number of churches, a church more concerned with image rather than substance, and growing biblical illiteracy are chief among the internal subversives.

We must not fail to understand that these movements are not separate, stand alone entities. They are intricately interwoven with leaders of each movement tied in with leaders of other movements. Leaders like Brian McLaren, Rob Bell, Tony Campolo, Bill and Lynne Hybels, Rick Warren and Jim Wallis are a network of leaders supporting and interacting with one another to advance a larger movement than any one of their individual entities represent on their own. This "octopus" is getting its tentacles into every denomination of Christianity and will soon be in position to squeeze the life out of American Christianity.

Any entity—a business, an army, a ministry or a church--will only go as far as leadership is able and willing to take it. Leadership is crucial to the direction and success of any organization, and next we explore the condition of leadership in American Christianity.

Footnotes

1) "A New Kind of Christianity", Brian McLaren, Harper-Collins
2) http://www.lighthousetrailsresearch.com/brianmclaren.htm
3) Redletterchristians.org
4) http://en.wikipedia.org/wiki/Homosexuality_in_ancient_Rome
5) http://www.crosscurrents.org/CompoloSpring2005.htm
6) Tony Campolo, "Speaking My Mind", 2004, Thomas Nelson Publishing
7) "Carpe Diem: Seize the Day", Tony Campolo, 1994, Thomas Nelson Publishing
8) "A Reasonable faith", Tony Campolo, 1983
9) "Irresistible Revolution" Shane Claiborne, 2006, Zondervan Publishing
10) Newsds.org
11) Liberationtheology.org
12) "Rules For Radicals", Saul Alinsky, 1971, Random House Publishing
13) Sojo.net; www.discoverthenetworks.org/groupProfile.asp?grpid=7018
14) Georgesoros.com
15) www.discoverthenetworks.org/groupProfile.asp?grpid=7018
16) "Love Wins", Rob Bell, 2011, Harper Collins Publishing
17) www.youtube.com/watch?v=Vg-qgmJ7nzA
18) Christian-universalism.com
19) Acommonword.com
20) www.yale.edu/faith/acw/acw.htm

CHAPTER SEVEN

THE DEMISE OF CHRISTIAN LEADERSHIP

A word about our pastors as we take a look at leadership within American Christianity:

I meet with local pastors regularly and have known many of them for more than a decade. The vast majority of them are kind, hard-working, wonderful men of God and they work long hours with ridiculously low salaries. Some are forced to have their wives hold jobs to help support their families, while she also plays a crucial role within the church. This can cause tremendous stress on the pastor and his family. These pastors care deeply about the people they lead, often giving up a lot of their personal time to meet with members of the church when needs arise.

Pastors are forced to wear many hats. Preacher, teacher, friend, marriage counselor, parental advisor, financial manager and often janitor; and that's by no means the total extent of their duties. They work countless hours, preparing a weekly sermon that must sadly be a near perfect balance. Too soft and some will not feel fed; too strong and some will feel he is being awfully harsh, not understanding what they are going through in their lives.

Tragically, pastors are often held hostage by the financial condition of the church they lead. Consciously or subconsciously, this puts a lot of pressure on them. They are forced into the role of performer too often, having to be entertaining when delivering a message--the gospel-- that shouldn't need to be "entertaining".

Our pastors need our prayers, financial support and our help. Somewhere over the past few decades, churchgoers started embracing an attitude that pastors worked for us. They were "hired" to run the church, and at our beck and call. We simply show up on Sunday like we were going to lunch, expecting to be served. We the people *are* the church. We must take ownership in our part of the Body of Christ, and stop expecting the pastor to carry the load on his own.

Pastors are under tremendous pressure these days, and members and elders need to step up and help them. Many are on the verge of physical and emotional burn out and often tempted to quit, finding a secular job where they can work more manageable hours and support their families.

Pastors are not the problem. A dysfunctional church system and self-centered followers are the problem. These godly men carry too heavy a burden with pressures from those they serve and their elders. This must change.

Defining Leadership

Leadership is difficult, requiring courage, commitment, passion and wisdom. It also requires a servant's heart and humility.

Leaders are often placed on pedestals that are much higher than we deserve, and when people continually look up to you and tell you how wonderful you are, pride begins to lurk around every corner.

I have been blessed to serve and lead here at Q90 FM for more than ten years. Our Board took a chance on me when they hired me with no radio experience. They figured that the station had plenty of people who knew radio, and that I possessed a heart and skill set that would serve our listeners well. I hope I can always live up to their faith and expectations. About six years ago a listener stopped in and thanked me for the role I play in this ministry. She told me she was blessed when she watched me interact with youth at concerts and felt that I had helped bring the ministry to a new level serving the Christian community.

I thanked her, somewhat embarrassed by the praise, and when she left I returned to my office. And then it happened . . . I began to believe my own deceptive heart. I started thinking to myself "man, I am doing a pretty good job. The ministry is growing and financially we are becoming more secure. Boy I am good!"

Then I learned that God is the master of all things—even instant messaging technology. I heard an immediate soft voice whisper to me "Mike, I love you . . . but if you don't think I can take any drunk, homeless person off the street and make him a better leader than you, then you don't really know me."

I had been given a piece of dessert—humble pie—and it didn't taste very good at all.

Pride is the most dangerous enemy of any leader, not insubordinate followers or external challenges. Pride can undo a lifetime of accomplishment the moment it becomes entrenched in our ego.

Leadership is tough and we as leaders are often the greatest obstacle to becoming truly great leaders. We become puffed up, start to coast by living on past laurels and accomplishments, and believe we are infallible and should never be questioned. In a "what have you done for me lately" world, there is no time to coast, and the day we feel we should never be questioned or challenged as leaders we become gods in our own minds.

Leadership also requires an understanding of, and commitment to, the core principles and values of the organization you lead. It is not enough to simply agree with them, it is crucial that you commit to not wavering from them. Four years ago the team at Q90 FM underwent a painful assessment of what our core values as Christians in this ministry should be, and one we decided on after a lot of prayer was relational honesty. We decided that if we really loved one another and were committed to the Christian organization and God that we serve, relational honesty must be a core principle.

We have learned to be honest, and when necessary argue. We have learned to get beyond the superficial and challenge one another when our words or actions seemed to contradict biblical teachings. It has not always been easy, but it has been beneficial.

Two years ago as I sat in my office, a couple team members wanted a word with me and of course I obliged. They proceeded to tell me that I was not enforcing my own rules on operational procedures. My first reaction as a leader was to deflect and deny, but I just listened. Their message was basically I was killing them by not following procedure, making their jobs more difficult.

Those that know me know I can be stubborn and defensive at times, and that I am not good with details. As they finished confronting me they awaited my reaction. They had just told their boss to shape up! I purposefully milked the tension for a moment, and then looked at them and said "Thank you. I needed to hear that. I know I stink at basic procedures sometimes. Will you please help me?"

The entire ministry has rallied around me. While not enabling me, they recognized that detail is a weakness for me and they have put in systems to make up for that weakness. They have freed me to do what I do best as a leader and the ministry has been blessed. I am not holding myself up as a perfect leader by any stretch, and those who work with me will tell you I am far from a perfect leader. But one area where I do lead well is by giving those I lead the freedom to challenge me whenever they think I might be straying from the Word of God in any decision, word or action that comes out of me. In fact I insist that they do this. It has been a blessing to me knowing those I lead are watching the example I set and are there to hold me accountable for my words, actions and leadership. It has made me a better leader.

Leaders lead, but they must also be accountable to those they lead. If not, they foster a potentially poisonous work environment. Leaders are ultimately accountable for the performance of the organization and people they lead. Leaders establish the framework for values, principles and expectations.

American Christianity is suffering from a lack of real leaders who lead like Jesus taught us to lead. He scolded the Pharisees for not doing what they taught others—hypocritical leadership. He scolded them for adding more burdens upon the people while not carrying those burdens themselves—selfish and arrogant leadership. He rebuked them because they knew the letter of the Law, but not the heart of the Law—a lack of discerning, wise leadership.

Leaders are the ones ultimately held responsible for the performance of the organization. If you look at American Christianity as an organization, how would you rate its performance over the past fifty years? Is it a stronger or weaker church because of its leadership over the past fifty years? Is it impacting the culture for better or worse? Is it an organization that is truly transforming lives?

Surrounding Leaders With the Right People

In the mid 1990s I was charged with taking a start-up organization and leading it to viability. It was a unique organization that would provide newly available, even unheard of services to employers. One of the charges was to build a team that would serve customers twenty-four hours a day in a traditional "9 to 5" industry. Needless to say there were challenges.

We would be hiring about twenty new employees so we posted job positions in the local newspaper and were flooded with applications. I interviewed probably close to one hundred people over the course of two years. Inevitably some of the hiring decisions would come down to hiring a person with a college degree or hiring a person with practical experience and working knowledge.

In theory, the person with the impressive college degree would probably have more upside, while the person without the degree but with practical experience was probably the safer bet—the thought being that the person with a verifiable track record was more of a known quantity. So at times I hired the college graduate and other times I hired the better known quantity. What I eventually found out was *who* I hired would not matter if I hired them into a dysfunctional system.

If an organization knows its mission and is dedicated as a team to attaining that mission, that is a great starting point. If the organization has effective systems in place and proper accountability for goals, corporate performance and individual performance, the odds were much greater that the person hired would succeed. If the organization lacked in any of these areas, even the best of hires would ultimately fail or at least turn out to be mediocre in performance, and the organization would suffer.

In other words, an organization's values, principles, mission, and systems were more important factors than the individual we hire, assuming an acceptable level of competency and character was present in the employee.

In spite of the efforts of leaders we will cover in the next chapter like Peter Drucker, Bill Hybels and Rick Warren, the church is not a corporation. It has only one mission—making disciples for Jesus Christ. But the character, values and principles of its leaders are crucial to developing an effective church.

The values, principles, character and commitment of a leader matter far more than that individual's qualifications, especially in a Christian organization. Leaders who understand and fully embrace the values and principles of an organization are best suited to lead that organization. When we hire people who agree with those values and principles the odds are much higher that it will be a successful hire.

Crucial Characteristics Needed for Christian Leadership— Values, Principles, Character and Commitment

Values, principles, character and commitment are vastly more important in leaders than potential, charisma or charm. But how do we define these necessary qualities for a Christian leader? I would propose the following as a starting point for any Christian organization:

Values

- **Honesty,** no matter what the cost
- **Love,** as God defines love.
- **Wisdom** to discern truth by God's standards, not man's standards
- **Spiritual Integrity and Mutual Accountability**

Principles

- Non-compromising with sin or human culture.
- No shortcuts for immediate gain at the sacrifice of long-term success.
- Always doing the right thing—even if it is painful.
- Willing to be held accountable by those we lead and serve.

Character

- Doing the biblically correct thing when no one is watching.
- Consistent behavior at work, home or when alone.
- Looking internally first when issues or conflict occur.
- Never saying something about someone you would not say if they were present.

Commitment

- True Kingdom focus--Matthew 6:33.
- Commitment to developing strong leaders.
- Commitment to developing disciples, not just members of the organization.
- A willingness to release team members who are continuous problems.

So how does this relate specifically to the church and its leadership? Do we overlook values, principles, character and commitment in favor of the educational level of a person we elevate as a leader? A degree in Religious Studies or thirty years of experience does not make a good pastor—biblical values, principles, character and commitment do. Without these foundations, a leader will eventually fail.

Dysfunctional Leadership Systems

Staying on my pesky urge to ask hypothetical questions, I offered this scenario to twelve pastors I know well a few years ago: If you as a pastor feel God is telling the church to do "A", and the elders feel God is leading them to do "B", who wins? Remarkably I got the same initial answer—"We would meet and pray together about it". I countered—so you do that but the conflicting messages remain, who wins? Only one of the twelve could cite how the conflict would be handled.

Christian leadership needs to be thoughtful, wise, discerning and above reproach whenever possible. It must also be well organized and purposeful, with duties and accountability clearly spelled out. And leaders must be appointed not by their human credentials, but by their spiritual credentials.

Pastors and ministry leaders must have a clear understanding of where their authority begins and ends. They must clearly know what decisions they are empowered to make and when they need to consult those they are accountable to.

I sit on several Boards for Christian non-profit organizations. Recently the Executive Director of one of them offered the name of a new potential Board member for our consideration. I asked why he felt this person would be a positive addition and his response centered on the fact that he was a CPA and knowledgeable on fundraising techniques. When I asked about his spiritual qualifications, the Executive Director said he didn't know.

This is a sad situation that happens way too frequently within Christian organizations and the church. Human qualifications are often elevated above spiritual qualifications when we consider people for leadership. A local church recently hired a pastor that it had to dismiss just six months later because they discovered spiritual flaws in his character once he assumed a position of leadership. They also discovered this man would fall to pieces when conflict arose.

How should a church decide on who the elders and leaders should be? The amount of their tithes? Their position and qualifications in the corporate world? Or should we seek elder and leader qualifications as outlined in the scriptures? Of course we will all answer that the scriptures should determine the qualifications of church elders—but do we practice it?

Leadership sets the tone for the entire organization. However, even the best, most biblically solid leaders will still fail if they are surrounded and suffocated by a dysfunctional system.

Dysfunctional systems lead to dysfunctional leadership. And dysfunctional leadership is a disaster waiting to happen in a church. When church leaders do not anticipate conflict and consider how it should be handled biblically, we find ourselves one day facing a crisis—a crisis that could have been averted by prior planning and discussion.

The Status of Christian Leadership Today

Generally, it's a mess boys and girls. When people like Rob Bell, Brian McLaren and Joel Osteen are held up as leaders, we are in deep trouble. When Pastors like Jim Wallis, Bill Hybels and Rick Warren seek compromise and common ground with an antichrist religion, has leadership sold out to the world? When the size of a church means more than the spiritual depth of the church, American Christianity is on its last breath.

In fairness to these leaders, as we will discuss in the next chapter, they are primarily by-products of our own fleshly desires as Christians. We seem to want leaders who tickle our ears or make us feel good about ourselves more than we want the truth. The truth can hurt; and our tolerance for pain as Americans and Christians is at an all-time low.

When watchmen stand up and question the teachings and activities of Christian leaders, we are told we are not to question God's "anointed". In the Old Testament, the Israelites had fallen under the same spell, being led by false teachers and false prophets into compromise and apostasy. How did God respond?

> *"Among the prophets of Samaria I saw this repulsive thing: They prophesied by Baal and led my people Israel astray. And among the prophets of Jerusalem I have seen something horrible: They commit adultery and live a lie. They strengthen the hands of evildoers, so that no one turns from his wickedness. They are like Sodom to me; the people of Jerusalem are like Gomorrah.*
>
> *"Therefore this is what the Lord Almighty says concerning the prophets: I will make them eat bitter food and drink poisoned water, because from the prophets of Jerusalem ungodliness has spread throughout the land.*
>
> *"This is what the Lord Almighty says: Do not listen to what the prophets are prophesying to you; they fill you with false hopes. They speak visions from their own minds, not from the mouth of the Lord."*
>
> Jeremiah 23:13-16

A question for you: Does American Christianity look more or less like Sodom and Gomorrah under the leadership of those currently leading the church? Are we strengthening the hands of evildoers or disarming them? Is the trend more toward God and his Word, or away from it?

Christian leadership in America is in a state of crisis and we seem to be lacking in strong, principled leadership at a time when we need it most. When any organization is in crisis, strong, principled leadership is necessary to navigate difficult times and get the organization back on track. But as we will see, just the opposite is happening in American Christianity.

Instead of steering us away from rough waters, many of our leaders seem committed to taking the ship right into a hurricane.

A Hypothetical Situation (?)

As I have shared, I love to ask hypothetical questions of pastors and leaders. Today's hypothetical questions often become tomorrow's real questions, so my pastor is often subjected to my torturous hypothetical questions.

Nearly two years ago a bible-teaching church in Michigan became the center in the fight for homosexual rights. The video shot hit YouTube and was broadcast by Fox News. The church choir had just completed a song and the elderly pastor ambled up to the pulpit to deliver his sermon message. But before he could, four homosexual activists created a chaotic scene. Two of them started passing out fliers and screaming "It's OK to be gay", while at the same time two females starting kissing passionately at the front of the church.

The pastor and congregation sat back, stunned and speechless. One elderly gentleman tried to gently convince the demonstrators to leave but they continued for several minutes until they finally left peacefully.

I asked my pastor and several other pastors what they would do if that happened in their church. None of them could answer the question. I suggested they might want to consult with the elders of the church so they would be able to handle the situation in a biblical way if it happened in their church. Trust me, it will occur more and more folks.

This is a difficult situation if it arises. Do we physically remove them from the church? Or just pray for them as they rant? The important thing is that the church leaders know ahead of time how to react if these types of disturbances occur. Failure to act decisively and biblically will create a lot of confusion and lingering problems.

I asked my pastor another hypothetical a couple months ago. And yes, this is a hypothetical situation. I proposed a fictitious scenario where my wife meets with him, telling him I am having an affair. So the pastor meets with me and I admit to the affair but insist on continuing the behavior. Would he kick me out of the church? He answered "No." I said he was crazy, that I should be kicked out of the church if I did not repent after talking with church leadership—and that it should be done publicly as Paul states to warn the rest of the church. Would our church be stronger or weaker with an admitted adulterer in its midst? It would be weaker.

Defining the Mission of the Church

Leaders and organizations love to throw around vision and mission statements, looking for a silver bullet to solve the problems of the organization. But Christian churches do not need new vision and mission statements—Jesus gave them their vision and mission in Matthew 28:19-20.

> *"Therefore go and make disciples of all nations, baptizing them in the name of the Father and of the Son and of the Holy Spirit, and teaching them to obey everything I have commanded you. And surely I am with you always, to the very end of the age."*

Seems like a pretty clear vision and mission statement to me. Go make disciples; (note Jesus did not say "convert people", he said **make disciples**). Christian leaders and pastors need to stop improving on Jesus' perfect mission statement. When you tinker with perfection, nothing good can result from it.

Now, developing a strong plan to carry out that vision or mission statement is a different story. ***How*** will we make disciples? What does a true disciple even look like? How can we truly invest in the spiritual growth of our church members? These are much tougher questions to answer for leadership than just getting our heads together to develop a nice sounding, but meaningless vision or mission statement.

Many churches in America are "spiritually bipolar". They aren't sure if they want to increase numbers of members, or increase the depth of spirituality, making true disciples. Now certainly any church would want to accomplish both simultaneously, but that is a very difficult thing to accomplish without the Holy Spirit. How do most churches act? Well, ask a pastor to tell you about his church and the first thing he will probably share is how many people attend—a nod to the superior importance placed on numbers over spiritual depth.

The church in Acts gathered regularly, listened to the teaching of the apostles, prayed, ministered to one another and shared all God was doing. Great signs and wonders were experienced and **the Lord added to their numbers daily.** (Acts 2:42-47) Wow, the Lord added to their numbers; not culturally relevant messages or cool praise and worship bands—the Lord! Might the Word of God just be trying to tell us something here? When our goal is to increase numbers, any warm body will do. The early church was more intent on true discipleship and fellowship than it was on reaching into the community for new members.

There were no marketing plans, no evangelism committees, and no pastors spending days trying to make the sermon sound just right. They met, prayed, shared and praised God. A simple formula for success has been replaced by a modern marketing plan that leads to dismal failure. Oh you may counter that your church has hundreds or thousands attending every week, but what is the level of spiritual depth and maturity? You probably don't know. Granted that is a difficult thing to measure as most Christians are great salespeople, telling you they are doing great. But most struggle just to get through the week, hoping to get a little Jesus on Sunday—enough gas in the tank to make it through another week.

There is nothing wrong with having a large congregation. However bigger numbers do not necessarily mean a better church. The power of any church congregation comes from a passionate love of God. When we gather in unison to worship and praise him, learn from his Word and challenge one another to a deeper intimacy with God, the Holy Spirit will begin to add to our numbers. But when we seek to add to our numbers out of human ambition or plans, are we weakening the church?

Bigger is Better—and a Ticket to Fame.

When numbers become more important than raising real disciples and developing strong Christian leaders, we get ourselves into serious trouble. When "nickels and noses" become the benchmark for success, Satan is laughing and God is broken-hearted.

But that is what appears to be happening in American Christianity, as the mega-church has become the standard of success. Can a church have huge numbers but still be truly successful? Certainly, but it is a difficult balancing act as large numbers plant a desire for larger numbers. Large collections and tithes breed a desire to bring in even more so we can "do more work for God". God doesn't need our money folks—He wants our hearts. When He truly has our hearts, He accomplishes great things through us regardless of our financial status.

Why is it that virtually every Christian pastor viewed as a leader these days pastors a mega church? Rob Bell, Bill Hybels, Eddie Young, Rick Warren and Joel Osteen all pastor huge churches. Seems you're not a leader if you don't pastor a mega-church. There certainly are exceptions, but it seems bigger is better—and bigger automatically elevates you to national leadership and the acclaim that comes with it.

Now there is nothing wrong with leading a mega-church, but it can be a trap. Suddenly you get the feeling you are King Midas and everything you touch turns to gold. You are held up as a model pastor and leader; you hit the national speakers' tour—maybe even have your own national television show! Ask Jim Bakker, Ted Haggard and Jimmy Swaggart how that worked for them.

Leaders and teachers will be held to a higher accountability and standard by God when we stand before Him. And leadership, with all its trappings, is waiting to snare us and drag us down. Many of the leaders in American Christianity might be headed down the path of Bakker, Haggard and Swaggart, because the enemy has his eyes on Christian leaders, setting subtle but effective traps for leaders in the church. Any of us can step into those traps when we become filled with our own self-importance and "success." That trap, invisible to the all-important leader, has two characteristics—arrogance and power.

The people I am about to comment on are recognized leaders in American Christianity. I do not think they are evil men. Quite to the contrary I am pretty sure they are wonderful husbands and fathers; men who love God and believe they are doing the right things. They are men who very much want to grow Christianity in America. It is not their heart or even motives that I question—it is their methods. In my opinion, they may be blindly leading American Christianity to the brink of suicide, and we, the lemmings, are only all too happy to follow them right off the cliff.

If these men are to blame for what is happening to American Christianity, others must share in that blame. Are their elders and mentors holding them accountable to the Word of God? Or do they fear that if they do, the leader will pack up and move to the church across town, taking many members and dollars with him?

What about those of us who follow these leaders? Are we more enamored with their eloquently worded sermons that get us excited than what they are actually teaching in those sermons? Are we excited that we attend the biggest church in our community even if the Word of God is not being preached in its entirety? Has the charismatic, charming pastor replaced God on the throne of our lives?

Leaders and followers are a direct reflection of each other. They form a symbiotic relationship, feeding off and needing one another. Is this symbiotic relationship killing American Christianity?

Anointed or Appointed Leaders?

On Stand Up For the Truth we question everything—except the Word of God. I find with each show I am forced to question my own level of dedication to God, as still too often I wander into sin. We question movements like Word of Faith, Signs and Wonders and The Emergent Church Movement. We question all of us as Christians when we claim to love God more than anything, but continue to give in to our sinful nature. And we question Christian leaders like Rick Warren, Bill Hybels and Joel Osteen. No subject or person should be above question or reproach.

When we question the words or actions of popular Christian leaders we get a frequent question from those who are their followers: "Who are you to question the Anointed of God?" In 1 Chronicles 16:22, God does warn us about harming his anointed prophets so we should be very careful when we question or accuse leaders. But exactly how do we know if a leader is anointed by God or appointed by men?

In Romans 13:1 Paul writes this:

"Everyone must submit himself to the governing authorities, for there is no authority except that which God has established."

Yet several times in scripture we see examples of God's people disobeying man's authority because it conflicted with God's teachings. In Acts 5:29 the High Priest forbad the Apostles from teaching the gospel, but they responded by saying *"We must obey God rather than man"*.

So how can we be sure if a leader is anointed by God or is appointed by men? Or perhaps even self-appointed? And even if God allows or anoints a leader, do we automatically obey and never question them? God ordained Saul as King and later rejected him because of his wicked ways.

> *"But Samuel replied: Does the Lord delight in burnt offerings and sacrifices as much as in obeying the voice of the Lord? To obey is better than sacrifice, and to heed is better than the fat of rams. For rebellion is like the sin of divination, and arrogance like the evil of idolatry. Because you have rejected the word of the Lord, he has rejected you as king."*
>
> 1 Samuel 15:22-23

Saul was rejected because he disobeyed the Word of God. If "anointed" leaders these days are disobedient or teach questionable gospels or messages inconsistent with God's Word, do we just blindly follow? Or do we question them and confront them when necessary? Is our allegiance to earthly leaders or to God?

A Balanced Approach to Leadership

Every one of our leaders will make mistakes, saying something the wrong way or perhaps teaching something that might contradict God's Word. Leaders will fall for slick presentations like *"A Common Word Between Us"* because they have a heart for people and want to build bridges of peace. Every one of us will get things wrong sometimes.

When our leaders do teach something that appears to contradict the Bible, they should be confronted in love and given an opportunity to clear the air. Did they simply misspeak? Did we fail to clearly hear what they were trying to say? Did they have a temporary lapse in judgment and fall for a slick presentation? Did they get wrapped up in the excitement of bringing in a well-known speaker and not check his teachings and affiliations? If any of these happen the leader needs to be treated with love and grace, given an opportunity to explain their words or actions, and if appropriate, apologize and repent for their mistake.

But what do we do when the questionable statements or teachings become a pattern? What if the leader says one thing with his mouth but his words conflict with his actions? What if there is a pattern of bringing in speakers or leaders who conflict with the teachings of the Bible? At what point does grace no longer apply, replaced with a tough rebuke?

> *"The Lord says: These people come near to me with their mouth
> and honor me with their lips, but their hearts are far from me.
> Their worship of me is made up only of rules taught by man."*
> Isaiah 29:13

These are important questions we must wrestle with as Christians. God has abundant grace with us and we should always extend abundant grace to others. But at some point, when a pattern emerges of questionable teachings and affiliations that conflict with scripture, a strong rebuke might be in order.

If I proclaim that I have been anointed by God to do a radio talk show, does that exempt me from being held accountable for what I say on air? If a ministry leader claims to be anointed by God, should he go unquestioned if the ministry is suddenly faced with financial problems or personal scandal?

Have we become so shallow that we are looking to men as pure and righteous instead of the only truly righteous one, God? When a pastor has an affair and divorces his wife while leading a church, should we just blindly accept it because he is "anointed"? When some Word of Faith preachers teach that our words can overpower the will of God, or that men have the power to speak things into existence, do we just accept it as fact because they claim an anointing? Should we hold Barack Obama accountable to his claim as a born-again Christian while he is pushing for easier access to abortions and an agenda to legalize homosexual marriage? What about George W. Bush when he proclaimed that Muslims and Christians worship the same God?

Leaders are to be respected, but they should never be above accountability and reproach. The day we give leaders a pass from accountability and rebuke when they cross a line, we are in serious trouble. But that is what is happening more and more in our nation and within American Christianity.

Leading Christians—But To Where?

I can guarantee that many of you reading this book will bristle at some of the thoughts, opinions and facts I am about to share. None of us wants to think poorly of our leaders or to think they are deceived. I am not asking you to be judge or jury on their faith or even their motives. A day might come when we do have to judge them harshly, but if we must, we should remember that their ultimate place in eternity can only rightly be judged by God—and we should never assume His throne of judgment. God never gives up on us and we should never give up on anyone else. We seek to restore, not condemn, when we see a brother faltering.

I ask you not to approach what I am about to share as if you were a judge, determining the guilt or innocence of a defendant. Rather, picture yourself as a member of a grand jury. A grand jury is assembled when the district attorney believes there might be enough evidence to try a case. Evidence is presented to the grand jury and their verdict is not one of guilt or innocence. Their verdict is either there is enough evidence to consider bringing charges or there is not, determining if the case should go to trial or not.

I offer this research and opinion not with the goal of convicting any individual or movement mentioned. I offer it to you as the grand jury to determine if we should watch these leaders and where they are leading us, or if we should just continue to follow and trust in them.

Every major character mentioned in this book has been reached out to in an effort to allow them to refute any information we have shared on Stand Up For the Truth, but no calls or emails to them have received a response. I encourage you once again to do your own research and be a good Berean, searching the scriptures on all issues. The Word of God is the only source for absolute truth—so study it, learn it and hide it in your heart.

I caution all of us one more time that if you start to feel anger or even hatred well up in you as we share what these leaders are up to, we must first look at ourselves as the people who follow them and have elevated them into leadership positions. They lead because we allow them to, and the fact is we seem to desire mushy, soft leadership these days that tells us what we want to hear, not what we need to hear.

CHAPTER EIGHT

DRUCKER, HYBELS, WARREN AND OSTEEN—IS THIS REALLY WHERE WE WANT TO GO?

Bill Hybels, Rick Warren and Joel Osteen are among the most powerful and visible leaders in American Christianity today. All lead huge churches and have tremendous national influence. All have millions of Christians who look to them for teaching, guidance and mentorship. They have charm, charisma and an appearance of humility.

I have no doubt that each of them is a very nice man. I do not doubt their love of God and I do not question that each of them is doing what he thinks is right. What I do question is their methods and perhaps some of their motives.

I do not sit in eternal judgment of them or any other person and neither do you. But just like Jesus and Paul, we are to respectfully question our leaders and, when necessary, rebuke them. As we review some of our prominent Christian leaders, we sit not as ultimate judge, but as a grand jury to decide if enough evidence exists to warrant further investigation.

Incorporating American Christianity

To understand where Christian leaders are leading the church in these perilous times, we must first look at a man historically known as one of the most influential people in the business world. The book you are reading is built on the premise that either Christianity positively affects the culture, or the culture infects Christianity. Allow me to introduce you to the man who is probably most responsible for the infestation of secular culture into American Christianity:

Peter Drucker[1] was born on November 19, 1909 and died in 2005. He rose to a "god-like" level in the business world, consulting for organizations like General Motors, Coca-Cola, IBM, CitiCorp and Intel. Drucker believed and taught that if the church wanted to be successful, it needed to adopt a business model in how it was structured and how it treated its "customers". Drucker believed the church needed to bring the corporate model into American Christianity.

Drucker was a disciple of Christian Universalist Soren Kirkegaard[2], who believed every person, regardless of their beliefs, would go to heaven. Peter Drucker was a highly influential mentor to both Bill Hybels and Rick Warren, along with universalist Robert Schuller. He also mentored Bob Buford of Leadership Network, and in the words of one of the founders of the Emergent Church Movement, Doug Pagitt, without Drucker and his disciples listed above, there would be no Emergent Church movement.

Drucker taught that like corporations, churches needed to become "customer friendly", and he spawned the growth of seeker-friendly churches like Saddleback and Willow Creek. And while Warren and Hybels will never verbally endorse the heresies of the emergent movement, they have continually aligned themselves with many of them who also admire Drucker.

Warren helped launch the Emergent movement by writing the foreword for Dan Kimball's book *"The Emerging Church"*[3], directly associating himself with other Emergent leaders who endorsed this same book, such as Brian McLaren, Tony Jones, Chris Seay, and Spencer Burke. Warren wrote:

> *"This book is a wonderful, detailed example of what a purpose-driven church can look like in a postmodern world. My friend Dan Kimball writes passionately from his heart, with a deep desire to*

> *reach emerging generations and cultures. While my book, The Purpose Driven Church, explained what the church is called to do, Dan's book explains how to do it with the cultural-creatives who think and feel in postmodern times. You need to pay attention to him because times are changing."*

Rick Warren just stated that the Emergent church movement is the ***how*** in relation to ***what*** Warren's Purpose Driven Church wants to accomplish. The ultimate goal of Emergent leaders is religious syncretism and universalism to some extent.

In his book *"More Ready Than You Realize"*,[4] Brian McLaren says this:

> *"I first heard Rick share this material in 1985, when I was a college English professor. As I heard Rick share the story of Saddleback Valley Community Church, for the first time in my life I could envision a church that had authentic evangelism running through its veins, and for the first time I sensed that God might be inviting me to leave teaching to do this kind of church-based disciple-making. I literally would not be doing what I am doing if not for Rick's impact on my life."*

Bill Hybels and Willow Creek have repeatedly endorsed and yoked themselves with Emergent leaders. In 2005, a session of the Willow Creek small group conference was hosted by Brian McLaren. In 2008, McLaren was invited back to Willow Creek to speak to youth ministers. McLaren told these young ministers that the emphasis Christians place on the doctrines of hell and the second coming of Jesus inhibits their ministry.

When we understand the teachings and influence Peter Drucker has on Christian leaders like Bill Hybels and Rick Warren, along with emergent leaders like Dan Kimball and Brian McLaren, we are able to focus on Christian leadership with fresh eyes. Our churches are being run more like corporations instead of a house of worship.

Here is the danger of running a church like a business: Businesses are customer focused, seeking to identify and meet the desires of their customers. Their products and services constantly change at the whim of those customers. When this principle is applied to the gospel, it ceases to be the true gospel of repentance, forgiveness and a call to holiness. The gospel and Word of God is not a product we can change to suit our whims. It is the unchanging absolute truth of God, and not subject to our personal preferences and desires. But Peter Drucker convinced many of today's prominent Christian leaders that being consumer-driven is more important than being truth-driven.

Armed with this new corporate mentality, many of today's Christian pastors now lead churches that are more focused on the number of customers in their church instead of teaching the hard truth of the gospel. This philosophy fits perfectly with the vague theology of the Emergent Church movement and as we see, many emergent leaders like Brian McLaren have been embraced and promoted by prominent church leaders.

Now that we see how Peter Drucker inspired Bill Hybels and Rick Warren, along with their connections to the Emergent Church movement, let's take a closer look at three prominent Christian leaders of our day.

Bill Hybels

Pastor Bill Hybels is the leader of Willow Creek Community Church in Barrington, Illinois. Willow Creek has a total of seven "campuses" and has a network of hundreds of churches under its Willow Creek Association. While it does not seem to have any direct authority over these churches, WCA is a resource for pastors and churches and helps plant churches around the nation.

The Willow Creek web site[5] shows a doctrinal statement that is pretty solid and I have heard no major complaints about any sermon Pastor Hybels has given. So what's the issue? As we noted above, there seems to be an infusion of social justice and emergent theology influencing Willow

Creek, causing some concern. What a person or organization *says* must be consistent with their actions. If not, which are we to believe?

Homosexuality

In 2011, Willow Creek announced they had severed a long-standing relationship with Exodus International. Exodus is a leading Christian organization, helping homosexuals leave the lifestyle and find hope in Jesus Christ. This decision came after a series of meetings between Willow Creek leadership and gay activist organizations who claimed that Willow Creek was "anti-gay".

The leader of Exodus International, Alan Chambers, responded with an open letter on August 10, 2011, expressing his sadness at the decision. He disclosed at a meeting between Willow Creek and Exodus leaders that the church's leaders stated that they didn't want to help people overcome homosexuality because that wasn't possible.[6]

Is this a denial of the power of the gospel, stating that sexual sinners could not be released from the bondage of sexual sin by the power of God? Willow Creek leaders went on to say they wanted to tell people that abstinence was the only option for unmarried people and that the church would provide a comfortable place to abstain. Is this the right way to handle the temptation and sin of homosexuality?

In fairness to Hybels and Willow Creek, they continue to teach that marriage is biblically defined as between one man and one woman, and that all others are to practice sexual abstinence. But it is sad if Willow Creek leadership is now denying the power of God to release people from the bondages of sexual sin. Thousands have been released by the power of God through Exodus International and several other Christian organizations presenting the gospel and salvation of Jesus Christ.

If it is true that Willow Creek leadership now believes that sexual sin is not "curable" by the power of the gospel and the Holy Spirit, is this sending a very dangerous message to Christians and the unsaved alike? Are we giving up on the power of God, settling for human answers and understanding? If that is the message, is that what American Christianity should stand for? Is this effective leadership or compromising with the culture?

Lynne Hybels

Could this shift in policy and teaching have anything to do with Lynne Hybels, Bill's wife, becoming very active in the social justice movement?

Lynne Hybels is a contributing editor for Sojourners Magazine, the leading social justice organization in the nation. We covered their dangerous theology earlier, but it is a good time to remind you that Sojourners and Jim Wallis refuse to classify homosexuality or abortion as sins. Is it appropriate to ask if Willow Creek is embracing the social justice movement's deception and false teaching because of Lynne Hybels' deep connection with Sojourners?

Lynne Hybels is a Palestinian apologist, partnering with others to discredit the nation of Israel and label them the aggressors in the conflict, in spite of the fact that Palestinian forces continue to fire hundreds of rockets a day into Israel, killing innocent children. She has criticized the "occupation" by Israel of lands they hold since the latest attacks on their nation by her Muslim neighbors. She partners with Tony Campolo and others to spread propaganda supporting a two-state solution and the division of Jerusalem in the hopes of bringing about "peace". We know through biblical prophesy that this would be no real peace. The documentary "Christ at the Checkpoint"[7] paints Palestinians as the victims and Israelis as occupiers in this conflict.

Are there Palestinian victims in this conflict, some of them Christians? No doubt. But history and scripture are clear who the aggressors are— Muslims and those seeking to destroy Israel. The land currently "occupied" was promised to Israel by God in Genesis and the fact is Israel did not seek to conquer these lands; they were attacked several times and have now decided to no longer trade land for peace as they have in the past, all to no avail.

139

The contested area is of strategic defensive value, providing a buffer between Israel and her enemies who are sworn to destroy her and kill every Jew. These neighboring Muslim nations have attacked Israel repeatedly since 1948, yet Lynne Hybels and her friends are undermining public opinion in America toward Israel by repeating the propaganda of Muslim leaders around the world.

Is this an issue we should be concerned with as Christians? Is Lynne Hybels' role as a contributing editor with Sojourners, an organization that refuses to acknowledge homosexuality as a sin, behind Willow Creek's confusing stance on homosexuality?

Willow Creek Leadership Summit

"When God wants to begin a new work in the world, He almost always starts by speaking into the heart of one person. Drawing up the courage to listen, obey and share the vision with others, these are the people we call leaders."

This statement on the Willow Creek website explains why since its inception in 1992, Willow Creek has brought in religious, social and world leaders, holding them up as examples of effective leadership.

American Christianity does need strong leaders these days. The church is in crisis and leadership is crucial to getting us through these difficult times. But just what kind of leaders is Willow Creek bringing in to this worldwide conference that millions of Christians attend in person or via satellite?

The list of speakers that have questionable views compared to traditional Christianity is extensive, so we will concentrate on a select few. In fairness there have also been many solid Christians presented at the annual event over the years. But I question why we feel the need to hold up leaders who may be Christians, yet openly support anti-Christian beliefs, or non-Christians at an event teaching leadership to millions of Christians.

Remember the word "obey" from the Hybels' statement about leaders and ask yourself if the leaders discussed are obeying God's Word.

Bill Clinton

As President of the United States, Bill Clinton met an intern in 1995 named Monica Lewinsky. He started a sexual relationship with her, which he repeatedly denied publically. He lied under oath about the affair and was impeached by the Congress in 1998[8].

Shortly after his impeachment, where he lied under oath and was reprimanded, Bill Clinton spoke at the Willow Creek Leadership Summit in 2000. He had disgraced the office of the Presidency with his sexual affair and perjury, and Clinton's actions also spawned a significant increase in sexual activity by teens when he claimed oral sex was not really sex. Is this the type of leader we want Christians to emulate? Should he have been deemed worthy by Willow Creek leadership to be held up as a great leader for Christians?

Rob Bell

In 2000 Rob Bell was also a leader touted at the Summit. The up and coming Evangelical Pastor was hailed as an example of what God is doing. Ten years later Bell would write a book, *"Love Wins"*[9] where he questions the existence and permanence of hell, a direct contradiction of scripture and the words of Jesus himself.

Rick Warren

We will cover Rick Warren in depth later. "America's Pastor" is seeking compromise and common theology with Islam and bringing in Muslims and New Age believers to teach holistic health to Christians.

Bono

U-2 rock sensation Bono presented at the Willow Creek Summit in 2009. He has done a lot of good on humanitarian fronts, but his "Christianity" is highly suspect. On the website of Relevant Magazine[10], a progressive Christian periodical, an article was posted by Terra Cobble about what she witnessed at a Bono concert:

> *"About five songs into their set, Bono stopped the show and strapped on a headband with a message on it: COEXIST. He began to sing 'Jesus, Jew, Muhammed all true' repeatedly."*

Bono has made several statements denying traditional Christian beliefs, including:

> *"God's Spirit moves through us and the world at a pace that can never be constricted by any one religious paradigm."*
> *"Be wary of people who think theirs is the only way. Unilateralism before God is dangerous."*

Bono does talk about Jesus Christ as the Son of God in other interviews, but there is clearly a belief in universalism. Do universalist religious beliefs qualify as an example of great leadership to Christians according to Willow Creek Leadership?

Tony Blair

The former Prime Minister of England certainly knows what it means to lead. But where is he leading people these days? Blair touts the legalization of homosexual civil unions as an important accomplishment of his administration. Since leaving office he has founded the "Tony Blair Faith Foundation[11]". One of the goals of the foundation is religious syncretism, bringing all faiths together for the common good of humanity and the earth.

On his website, Blair brags of how as Prime Minister he successfully advocated for adoption of the United Nations Millennium Goals[12] because he "believes they represent the world's values". The U.N. millennium goals are, simply put, a movement toward a one world government and religion. The U.N. through its sub-organizations like UNESCO has already succeeded in promoting a global curriculum adopted in many American school systems—an education platform that seeks to mold children into "global citizens" and lead them away from what they call "antiquated beliefs set in place by parents and religion".

Should a man who brags about getting homosexual unions legalized in the country he led be held up as an example to Christians about what a successful leader should look like? What about a man who is working toward religious syncretism?

Cory Booker

Cory Booker is the current mayor of Newark, New Jersey. He recently blasted New Jersey Governor Chris Christie for his refusal to sign homosexual marriage into law[13]. Booker has been outspoken in his promotion of gay marriage, stating *"marriage equality is not a choice, it is a right."* He has also refused to conduct traditional marriages between a man and a woman in City Hall to protest what he sees as inequality in marriage.

We start to see a pattern emerging where leaders who support gay marriage are continually brought in by Willow Creek and touted as examples of great leaders. Is Willow Creek considering embracing homosexual marriage as acceptable in God's eyes? Are these examples of leaders we should ask Christians to emulate?

Howard Schultz

Howard Schultz, CEO of Starbucks, was slated as the lead speaker at Willow Creek in 2011. In his biography he talks about the need for leaders to stand on their principles. Well, apparently Mr. Schultz didn't read his own biography because he decided to cancel his appearance as keynote speaker when seven-hundred-twenty-eight people signed an on line petition suggesting they would boycott Starbucks if Schultz spoke at an "anti-gay" church.

This story is fascinating on several fronts. First that a few hundred on-line protestors could cause this man of "principle" to back out of an agreement to speak shows the power of the radical homosexual lobby in this nation.

Second, it shows the quandary many churches are in these days because Willow Creek does clearly state the biblical belief that homosexual relations are wrong, yet they continue to invite people in who endorse homosexuality—including Howard Schultz of Starbucks, holding them up as leadership examples for Christians. Starbucks recently came out in enthusiastic support of the movement to legalize homosexual marriage in the state of Washington and is pouring a lot of money and time into making sure homosexual marriage is legalized there.

The question must once again be asked: Why would Willow Creek Leadership insist on bringing in leaders with clearly anti-biblical positions, holding them up as examples of model leaders to Christians?

Summary on Bill Hybels and Willow Creek

Willow Creek is a highly respected mega-church and Bill Hybels a highly respected pastor among evangelical Christians. The Willow Creek Association influences thousands of churches around the world with their teaching resources, and has influenced millions through their Leadership Summit.

Is confusion a quality we want to see from our leaders? Hybels and Willow Creek seem to be uncertain of how to handle the homosexual issue. They don't condone it, but they certainly don't condemn it. Their leadership reportedly told Exodus International that they don't believe homosexuality can "be cured". Do they deny the power of the gospel and the Holy Spirit?

Lynne Hybels is extremely active in the social justice movement, partnering with Jim Wallis and Tony Campolo in activities damaging to Israel, and in promoting an unbiblical social justice movement. She is a contributing editor to Sojourner Magazine, clearly an organization promoting syncretism among the religions of the world.

A friend of mine recently visited Willow Creek Church and said he could not find one cross in the church. Many emergent and seeker-friendly churches employ this tactic to appear more welcoming, since the cross is seen as offensive by many. Should this be an additional concern?

Given Willow Creek's frequent invitations to have Brian McLaren teach should we be concerned over their recent direction?

If you were on a grand jury, would you see enough information that would make you want to investigate more? Or are we just "overreacting"?

Rick Warren, "America's Pastor"

Rick Warren pastors at Saddleback Church, a mega-church in California. His books, "The Purpose Driven Life" and "The Purpose Driven Church"[14], have sold millions of copies and are used by thousands of pastors and Christians as blueprints to successful church life.

Saddleback's statement of faith is solid and Rick Warren seems to teach that salvation comes through Jesus as the Son of God. Thousand of pastors subscribe to Warren's daily emails and receive teaching ideas and daily devotionals. To say he is an influential leader in American Christianity is an understatement of epic proportions.

But there is a disturbing pattern in what Rick Warren has been doing over the past several years and who he partners with. To begin to assess his motives and methods we must first learn about the man he was mentored by years ago.

Rick Warren's Mentor

To have a better understanding for what drives Rick Warren, we need to look at who influenced him as a young Christian leader. We already shared the great influence Peter Drucker had on Warren, but in addition Rick Warren and his wife spent years learning everything they could from another leader in Christianity who is no longer on the main stage—Robert Schuller of Crystal Cathedral fame. Below is a transcript from the Berean Call[15] Radio Show with T.A. McMahon and Dave Hunt. This will give you a pretty solid indication of the man Rick Warren learned his theology from:

> *I'll never forget being on a panel with Walter Martin. This was in Denver and this was at a cult conference. I think somebody asked something about Robert Schuller and I mentioned that Robert Schuller had gone to LeSaint, Missouri Unity School of Christianity, one of the worst cults out there. They deny everything in the Bible. They are into yoga and hypnosis and New Age. They deny the gospel of Jesus Christ. Robert Schuller went there not to correct them, but to commend them and to share his church growth principles with this horrible cult. And in the question and answer time one of them asked, "Well what is the function of a minister in this New Age which we are all a part?" . . . Robert Schuller didn't skip a beat, he didn't deny he was part of the New Age. He said, 'Well what we have to do is positivize religion' and he said 'now that's easy for you being Unity ministers, ministers-in-training. You are already very positive, but you understand I deal with people you would call fundamentalists. They use terms like sin and guilt, repentance, and redemption. What we have to do is positivize this.'*
>
> **Tom:** *Right.*
>
> **Dave:** *. . . Anyway, Walter Martin said 'Dave, I don't want to hear you say that again about Robert Schuller, because I've gone to him personally about this in private and he's agreed that he's not going to be involved with Unity anymore. Now he understands how bad it is."*
>
> *"Well I said to Walter, 'Okay if that's what he says.' A few months later I'm driving in my car and I turn on the Bible Answer Man and it's Walter Martin telling how Robert Schuller is back with Unity, speaking at their functions and so forth. And Walter Martin says, 'And now he won't return my phone calls and he won't answer my letters.' So this is the experience we've had. You talk to someone in private, but it doesn't benefit people out there who have been publicly taught things."*

There is a growing pattern among some Christian leaders to speak out of both sides of their mouths these days. Messages seem to be tailored to specific audiences, lacking a cohesive message of the saving gospel of Jesus Christ. Truth has taken a back seat to being culturally relevant, and the hard truth of the gospel is being replaced with a more "positive message". Robert Schuller was one of the early pioneers of this "positive" message, and Rick Warren was one of his greatest disciples. In Schuller's own words:

> *"And there's Rick Warren, a pastor who today is phenomenal. He came to our institute time after time. And in 'Christianity Today,' his wife was quoted as saying, 'When we came to that institute, we were blown away.' How God has blessed him. And today Rick Warren is blessing millions of people."* **Crystal Cathedral, April, 2004**

Robert Schuller was long ago exposed as a universalist and a New Age proponent, and Rick Warren was mentored by him. This is important to remember as we look at Rick Warren and what he is doing within the confines of Christianity these days.

Also remember that Rick Warren was mentored by Peter Drucker, the man most responsible for turning churches into corporations instead of houses of truth and worship.

Warren has been called "America's Pastor", and he conducted the prayer for President Obama's inauguration in January, 2009. When I first heard that President Obama had selected Warren for his inaugural prayer, I thought that perhaps Warren would be light and salt to the world as millions watched on television. Obama was hailed as a savior to our nation by many, and I thought this would be an opportunity for a strong witness to many who are not Christians.

The prayer started off solid and it was thoughtful, respectful and referred to God. Many had wondered building up with all the speculation about Obama's true religion, if Warren would mention the name of Jesus. Well he did—and so much more:

"I humbly ask this in the name of the one who changed my life, Yeshua, Isa (Koranic term for Jesus), *Jesus* (Hey-sous, as in the Spanish way of saying Jesus), *Jesus, who taught us to pray"*[16]

Rick Warren had just not only prayed in the name of Jesus, he prayed in the name of the counterfeit "Jesus" of Islam. I was stunned and felt betrayed as a Christian.

As we covered earlier, Isa is not Jesus. Isa is not recognized as the Son of God in Islam; Isa did not die on the cross for our salvation, and Isa returns in Muslim prophecy to renounce that he is the Son of God, and helps kill every Jew and Christian who does not convert to Islam.

Is Rick Warren ashamed of Jesus and his gospel? Is he pandering for the sake of popularity?

> *"What good is it for a man to gain the whole world, and yet lose or forfeit his very self? If anyone is ashamed of me and my words, the Son of Man will be ashamed of him when he comes in his glory and in the glory of the Father and the holy angels."*
>
> Luke 9:25-26

Rick Warren did a lot of damage that day. He wrongly placed Islam, a religion of antichrist, on an equal footing with Christianity. He promoted, or at least did not refute, a lie that millions of Americans and many Christians believe—that Allah and YHWH are the same. The same lie that President Bush pronounced just a few years earlier.

Just one year earlier, Rick Warren was signing on to an abomination we covered earlier, the infamous *"A Common Word Between Us"*[17] document. He either bought the deception of these Muslim clerics or he really believes these two religions are equal. Should this raise serious questions about Rick Warren's true beliefs or his status as "America's Pastor"?

Compromising With the Enemy?

Islam is a spiritual enemy of Christianity. I know that sounds harsh but sometimes the truth hurts. That does not give us license to hate Muslims or deny them their rights as citizens, but we must understand that Islam is in direct conflict with Christianity and that the Muslim faith mandates worldwide dominance and implementation of Sharia Law. No dedicated Muslim can wish otherwise, just like any dedicated Christian must hope that every human being one day comes to know Jesus Christ as Lord and Savior.

> *Dear friends, do not believe every spirit, but test the spirits to see whether they are from God, because many false prophets have gone out into the world. This is how you can recognize the Spirit of God: Every spirit that acknowledges Jesus Christ has come in the flesh is from God, but every spirit that does not acknowledge Jesus is not from God." This is the spirit of antichrist, which you have heard is coming and even now is already in the world."*
>
> **1 John 4:1-3**

These scriptures clearly show that Islam is a religion of antichrist by their denial of Jesus Christ as the Son of God who came in the flesh. No committed Christian could possibly think that there is common ground to be found between the two religions. But because we are becoming more and more biblically illiterate, the lie that Muslims and Christians worship the same God is spreading throughout the church.

By signing on to the "Common Word" deception were Warren and the others simply naïve or being deceptive with an ulterior agenda? Could Rick Warren actually be at the center of a movement toward a one world religion?

Look, we all make mistakes. Several Christian leaders who initially signed the "Common Word" deception have since recanted, admitting they were swept up in the emotion of seeking peace with Muslims. Anyone can make a mistake. So all Hybels, Wallis and Warren had to do was admit they were deceived in a moment of weakness and they would have been forgiven. But Rick Warren didn't apologize; he doubled down.

In 2009, Warren spoke to eight thousand Muslim leaders at the 46th annual conference of The Islamic Society of North America (ISNA)[18]. ISNA has been charged by many with having links to foreign terrorist organizations, including the Muslim Brotherhood. Below is a report with information received through the Freedom of Information Act as reported by Steven Emerson:

New Disclosures Tighten ISNA-Muslim Brotherhood Bonds[19]

Steven Emerson
IPT News
July 22, 2008

"The Islamic Society of North America's (ISNA) roots in the Muslim Brotherhood have been strengthened by newly declassified FBI memos and from a second, highly unlikely source.

The records, recently obtained by the Investigative Project on Terrorism through Freedom of Information Act requests, show that FBI agents investigated a parent organization to ISNA, the North American Islamic Trust (NAIT), during the mid 1980s.

The FBI investigation concluded that the Muslim Brotherhood members who founded U.S.-based groups had risen to "leadership roles within NAIT and its related organizations," including ISNA, "which means they are in a position to direct the activities and support of Muslims in the U.S. for the Islamic Revolution." The FBI memo also stated that within the organizational structure of NAIT, there have been numerous groups and individuals identified as being a part of a covert network of revolutionaries who have clearly indicated their support for the Islamic Revolution as advocated by the Ayatollah Khomeini and his government, as well as other fanatical Islamic Shiite fundamentalist leaders in the Middle East. This faction of Muslims has declared war on the United States, Israel and any other country they deem as an enemy of Islam. The common bond between these various organizations is both religious and political with the underlying common goal being to further the holy war (Islamic Jihad).

The FBI memos date back to 1987-88. Dozens of pages of the released files are redacted in their entirety. But others contradict ISNA claims that it "never was, and is not now, affiliated with or influenced by any international organizations including the Muslim Brotherhood." Furthermore, ISNA still considers NAIT an affiliated organization. ISNA's president is an ex-officio NAIT board member and Muzammil Siddiqi, NAIT's chairman, serves on ISNA's governing board."

NAIT holds the deeds to more than a quarter of the mosques in the United States and continues to build additional mosques around the nation.

When Warren spoke, he shared the platform with Siraj Wahhaj[20], an unindicted co-conspirator in the 1993 bombing of the World Trade Center, a precursor to the 9/11 attacks. He was the only Christian invited to speak and he was warmly received.

Among Warren's quotes from his presentation: *"I will tell you that I am not interested in interfaith dialogue; I am interested in interfaith projects. There is a big difference. Talk is cheap. You can talk and talk and talk and never get anything done. Love is something you do; it is something we do together."*

Now you may believe that it is admirable to cooperate with other religions in doing good works. But two questions for your consideration:

First, what is our mission as Christians? Is it to do good works or to share the gospel of salvation? Which is considered the "great commission"? Good works, while admirable, are a method to share the gospel. They are a means to an end, helping us be in position to share the message of eternal life and salvation. If I feed a man for thirty years, but never share the gospel and he is not saved, what have I really accomplished in light of eternity? Works are an expression of our faith and our mission to share the gospel.

Second question: When we conduct these interfaith projects, which faith gets to share their religious message with those being helped, assuming evangelism takes place? Quite frankly the answer is probably moot because

I don't believe these interfaith projects that Christians get wrapped up in intend to share our faith—I think they are just a way for us to feel good about ourselves, thinking we are accomplishing something great.

In fact, I think interfaith projects are cowardly. They alleviate the responsibility in our own minds of actually sharing the gospel of salvation. We have a responsibility as Christians to help the poor and needy, but sharing the hope of eternal life must be our ultimate goal. If we feed a man but fail to be God's instrument to lead him to eternal salvation, what has really been accomplished? One can argue the only thing we have accomplished is we have fed him and loved him right into hell.

We certainly should try to learn how to live with Muslims, not approaching Islam out of fear or ignorance. But to agree with them that Allah and YHWH are the same and promise to not share the gospel with them? This is nothing short of a betrayal of Christianity, and hatred, not love, for Muslims—people who need to know who Jesus really is and find salvation in Him. What about "go and make disciples of all nations"? What about 1 John 4 proving the fact that Islam is a religion of antichrist as Islam denies that Jesus is the Son of God?

Welcome to "leadership" in American Christianity.

So Rick Warren signs on to the "Common Word" travesty, and then doubles down by speaking to a Muslim organization accused of supporting terrorist organizations. What could be next? Plenty.

Tony Blair's Faith Foundation

Tony Blair, who also presented at the Willow Creek Leadership Summit, is at the front of a movement to embrace the United Nations Millennium Goals that many think are leading to a one-world religion and one-world government. In cooperation with the United Nations, Blair's organization encourages interfaith dialogue and cooperation in hopes of solving the problems of poverty, discrimination and global warming.

Through its subsidiary, UNESCO[21], the United Nations has successfully presented and is implementing a global school curriculum around the world, and in many communities within the United States. Our children are being educated by organizations like the National Education Association populated with secular humanists who have stated that they must undo the damage parents and religion are doing to the children.

Blair is busy building spiritual bridges between Catholics, Evangelicals, Muslims, Buddhists and Hindus and Rick Warren is on Tony Blair's Board. Warren is also a member of The Council on Foreign Relations, a somewhat secretive organization that has its fingers everywhere.

Many would never believe that Rick Warren would ever intentionally try to equate Islam and Christianity. After all he is "America's Pastor" and leads a mega-church. He is admired by Christians and non-believers alike.

More Confusion on the "Gay" Thing

In April, 2009 Rick Warren appeared on Larry King Live[22]. He apologized for his support of Proposition 8 in California, the referendum calling for state law to legally recognize marriage as between one man and one woman. Proposition 8 passed, but has been overturned by the extremely liberal 9th Circuit Court of Appeals in California. The fate of it now will probably lie in the hands of the Supreme Court of the United States.

Not only did Rick Warren apologize for his support, he went on to deny ever publically supporting Proposition 8. Well Rick, if you didn't support it, why the need to apologize to the homosexual community? Rick Warren is trying to have things both ways, because he did publicly support Proposition 8. Below is a transcript of Warren's statement to his congregation two weeks before the election:

"The election's coming just in a couple of weeks, and I hope you're praying about your vote. One of the propositions, of course, that I want to mention is Proposition 8, which is the proposition that had to be instituted because the courts threw out the will of

the people. And a court of four guys actually voted to change a definition of marriage that has been going for 5,000 years.

"Now let me say this really clearly: we support Proposition 8 -- and if you believe what the Bible says about marriage, you need to support Proposition 8. I never support a candidate, but on moral issues I come out very clear.

"This is one thing, friends that all politicians tend to agree on. Both Barack Obama and John McCain, I flat-out asked both of them: what is your definition of marriage? And they both said the same thing -- it is the traditional, historic, universal definition of marriage: one man and one woman, for life. And every culture for 5,000 years, and every religion for 5,000 years, has said the definition of marriage is between one man and a woman.

"Now here's an interesting thing. There are about two percent of Americans [who] are homosexual or gay/lesbian people. We should not let two percent of the population determine to change a definition of marriage that has been supported by every single culture and every single religion for 5,000 years.

"This is not even just a Christian issue -- it's a humanitarian and human issue that God created marriage for the purpose of family, love, and procreation.

"So I urge you to support Proposition 8, and pass that word on. I'm going to be sending out a note to pastors on what I believe about this. But everybody knows what I believe about it. They heard me at the Civil Forum when I asked both Obama and McCain on their views."[23]

So Warren initially supported Proposition 8 in California, but since then has apologized to the homosexual community for something he said he never did. Is this the type of leadership we should look for in American Christianity? Do we want leaders who might lie and pander for the sake of being popular or being seen as compassionate?

Who or what got to Warren? I don't know. Does he now privately support gay marriage? Given his P.E.A.C.E. Plan, closely tied with U.N. Millennium Goals, and his close ties to Tony Blair, I believe that day will soon come.

The Daniel Plan

Rick Warren, by his own admission, was getting fat. He decided he had to do something to get his weight under control, helping his body and mind become a better temple of the Holy Spirit. Physical and emotional health is very important and we should all strive to have strong minds and bodies. But what price are we willing to pay for this effort? Apparently Rick Warren was willing to pay a very high price.

In challenging his congregation, and now the millions of pastors and Christians following him to join in this quest for fitness, Rick Warren exposed them to some unusual, to say the least, experts he had recruited to teach the plan. When discipline to exercise more and eat less would have sufficed, Warren decided to call in some big guns—and those guns might be pointed right at the spiritual condition of Christians whom Warren leads.

Dr. Mehmet Oz

Oprah Winfrey is a leader in the New Age movement and sadly one of the most influential "Christians" in the world, and she calls Dr. Oz her "favorite doctor". He was raised as a Muslim and has been influenced by the mysticism of Sufi Muslims. He subscribes to the ideas of cultist mystic Emanuel Swedenborg:

> *"As I came into contact with Swedenborg's many writings I began to understand Swedenborg's profound insights and how they applied directly to my life."*

Swedenborg believed he could pass between the life to come and the present. He claimed he had conversations with spirits of the dead as well as angels. Swedenborg wrote that the last judgment of man occurred in 1757, though it was only visible in the spirit realm which he visited frequently. He claimed that the second coming of Christ occurred, not to all men as the bible teaches, but to Swedenborg personally in the spirit world.

In his book *"Life On Other Planets"*[24], Swedenborg claimed he spoke with spirits from Jupiter, Mercury, Mars, Saturn, Venus and the moon. He also denied the Trinity and salvation through faith.

Swedenborg's followers started a church called "New Church". In a 2008 edition of their magazine, "New Church Connections[25]", Dr. Oz wrote an article exposing that his spiritual beliefs are connected to Swedenborg's theology. In an article he wrote titled "Mehmet Oz Finds His Teacher", Oz shared his spiritual journey and awakening. I have taken excerpts due to its length, but the entire article is available for viewing at newchurch.org.

> *"I was raised a secular Muslim . . . I hungered for a scientific rationale to help me reconcile my newly found insights into our bodies and the deeper spiritual longings that we all possess. Help came in the form of an eighteenth century Swedish philosopher (Swedenborg).*
>
> *Soon after I met Lisa, (his wife) she introduced me to insights into heaven and hell that challenged my status quo. Swedenborg, I later learned, was a scientist and theologian whose great and defining quest was to find the nature of the relationship between the body and the spirit. In his mid-fifties he came into an altered state of awareness in which he experienced simultaneous dual consciousness of this life and the afterlife. I began to understand his profound insights and how they applied directly to my life.*
>
> *His emphasis on overcoming the delusion of the self and on the profound interdependence of all things in both the spiritual and natural worlds aligns so closely with Buddhist thought that the Zen Master D. T. Suzuki referred to him as "the Buddha of the North".*
>
> *According to Swedenborg, heaven and hell are not merely places but spiritual states. We do not "go there" when we die. We are already there . . . .I have always had trouble with the idea of a selective redemptive. How could a compassionate God condemn his children for nothing more than being born into the "wrong*

faith"? How could an all loving God choose to extend that love to only a select few? Swedenborg taught that God loves us all and all the various religions allow us to approach him in the way best suited to our needs. He argued that we are all born for heaven, and that it is what we love that determines our fate, not what we profess to believe . . . Further Swedenborg claimed that God never judges us.

Angels as described by Swedenborg aren't a separate species but people who are regenerate—literally reborn humans."

Is Rick Warren endorsing these beliefs by endorsing Dr. Oz to teach in his church? Does Warren also believe in this universalism view, so contrary to the Bible? When a pastor parades someone in front of the church as a teacher, can we assume that the beliefs taught are consistent with the Pastor? I think that should be a fair conclusion. The teacher should be properly vetted to be as certain as possible that what he teaches is consistent with the teachings of the church. If the teacher strays and teaches something that conflicts, a disclaimer should be made afterwards. There has been no disclaimer made by Rick Warren to Dr. Oz's beliefs.

Dr. Oz is also a proponent of transcendental meditation and Reiki meditation, and his wife is a Reiki Master. What is "Reiki"? Let's hear it from their own website, reiki.org:

"The word Reiki is made up of two Japanese words—"rei" which means "God's wisdom or the higher power" and "ki" which is "life energy force". So Reiki is actually spiritually guided life force energy . . . Reiki is a simple, natural and safe method of spiritual healing . . . While Reiki is spiritual in nature, it is not a religion. It has no dogma, and there is nothing you must believe in order to learn and use Reiki."

Note the definition of being "spiritual in nature . . . and with no dogma." This is a free-form spirituality—the kind that Satan just loves.

Dr. Daniel Amen

Another of the Daniel Plan doctors and teachers, Dr. Amen[26] has done some breakthrough research on how the brain works. Based on some of his beliefs, I wish he hadn't.

> *"I teamed with Drs. Dharma Singh Khalsa and Nisha Money to study the impact of meditation on the brain. We chose a simple 12 minute form of meditation, Kriya Kirtan that is easy for busy people to practice. It is based on five principal sounds:' Saa, Taa, Naa, Maa, aa.'*

Now call me a conspiracy nut, but do you see any sounds in this mantra that when connected give you pause for concern?

What about this "Kriya Kirtan" meditation Dr. Amen promotes? Well, let's go to the official website of Kriya Kirtan[27] meditation to find out:

> *"Kundalini yoga as taught by Yogi Bhajan is a scientific technology for happiness. It extends the brain to imagine Infinity in its totality, and then it is a gradual process to work for that experience. Every movement is scientifically originated, organized and projected. This is a discipline in which there is nothing but success.*
>
> *When practicing Kundalini Yoga, your inner power is awakened to unite with the Universal life force, empowering you with awareness beyond the ordinary. This awakened state gives you the capacity to expand your perspective and experience each day with increasing inspiration and joy."*

But wait, there's more! The site goes on to explain the benefit of identifying and connecting with your inner divinity, a New Age term for "you are god". There are also mantras and chants to bring physical healings, wealth and increased memorization.

Dr. Amen has also teamed up to create a six-part series for improved sexuality using ancient Hindu mantras and teachings.

Daniel Plan Summary

What could Rick Warren be thinking? Or was he thinking at all, bringing in these men to teach physical and spiritual health to Christians? Is this a case of being naïve or is there a real agenda?

Warren is either a careless pastor, not vetting teachers he brings in and endorses, or he is a willing participant to introduce Buddhist, Hindu and New Age teachings into Christianity. Since he has not refuted any of the views of these teachers, we must assume he endorses their beliefs. Pastors, if this does not lead you to take a closer look at this man many of you follow and emulate, I'm not sure what will.

P.E.A.C.E. Plan of Saddleback Church

Who doesn't want peace? Not me, if it compromises the gospel and sharing it with the lost. And Rick Warren's ill advised "P.E.A.C.E. Plan"[28] will compromise the gospel and our ability to share it with lost people, no matter how good his intentions are.

One cannot escape how similar Warren's PEACE Plan goals line up with the United Nations Millennium Goals. If you are a fan of the United Nations and think it is an organization that is interested in anything short of global humanism and universalism, I strongly suggest you research the historical facts and statements made by U.N. leaders and in their various charter organizations like UNESCO, the global governance organization that is implementing a global education curriculum for all students. See if you can find anything remotely Christian in their beliefs and goals.

U.N. Millennium Goals

- End Poverty and Hunger
- Universal Education
- Gender Equality
- Child Health
- Maternal Health
- Combat HIV/AIDS

- Environmental Sustainability
- Global Partnerships

PEACE Plan Goals

- Promote Reconciliation
- Equip Servant Leaders
- Assist the Poor
- Care for the Sick
- Educate the Next generation

"Promote Reconciliation" replaced the former goal of "Planting Churches". Does this say anything about the ultimate plans and purposes? What are we reconciling and toward what purpose? Is the goal to develop a watered-down religion that all people can agree on?

And while Warren's PEACE Plan goals might be admirable, is there anything missing? Nowhere is there a mention of Christianity, the gospel or making disciples.

There are strong similarities between the Millennium Goals and the PEACE Plan goals—both are strong social justice agendas. Now taken on their own, none of the PEACE Plan goals are wrong. But we must step back and analyze the partners involved and the current state of affairs when Christianity partners with the secular world to solve problems.

The mission of disciples of Jesus was given in Matthew 28:19:

> *"Therefore go make disciples of all nations, baptizing them in the name of the Father and of the Son and of the Holy Spirit, and teaching them to obey everything I have commanded you."*

This is the calling of all Christians. We are to share the gospel of salvation to the lost. Feeding the poor, caring for the sick and educating children are a means to this end. If we stop short at helping the poor, but are not God's instruments in leading them to Him, what have we really accomplished in light of eternity except loving them into hell? This is a problem for the PEACE Plan and every other multi-religious collaboration effort: as men and women of various religions interact with those in need, which religion shares their version of the truth? Christianity? Islam? Hinduism?

The United Nations, who partners with Rick Warren in the implementation of the PEACE Plan, has been proven to be an anti-Christian organization. They promote human secularism and earth worship through every program they offer. They seek world control and have made it clear in many publications that they see religious fundamentalism as an obstacle to world peace.

The PEACE Plan may be well-intentioned but it is an ill-advised program that will waste billions of dollars with no real affect on the eternal souls of men. By partnering with the United Nations, it has ceased to be a means to spread the gospel and has become the greatest effort of secular social justice in the history of the world.

There is an excellent, in depth article on the PEACE Plan at crossroad. to. It goes into great detail about the people and organizations involved in this program.

Summary on Rick Warren

Here is a summary of information to consider on Rick Warren's activities and associations:

- Mentored by Peter Drucker and Universalist Robert Schuller of the Crystal Cathedral
- Equated the Muslim "Isa" with Jesus at the Obama Inauguration prayer
- Signed on to the deception of the "Common Word Between Us" document
- A welcome guest at The Islamic Society of North America, an organization with ties to terrorist groups
- Agreeing to not evangelize to Muslims

- A Board member on Tony Blair's global spiritualization organization
- Sent contradictory messages on Christian acceptability of homosexual marriage
- Brought in New Age teachers who promote Hindu and Buddhist meditation and follow cult leaders like Emmanuel Swedenborg to teach holistic health to Christians
- The PEACE Plan which compromises with the world and will spend millions on social justice programs, consistent with U.N. Millennial Goals

As I complete this book, more controversy is swirling around Warren and his cooperation with Muslims. Muslim leaders with whom Warren partners have openly stated that they embrace Warren because of his promise to not evangelize Muslims. And Saddleback's "Interfaith Outreach Pastor", Abraham Meulenberg, teaches the concept of "Kingdom Circles"[29] around the world. "Kingdom Circles" theology teaches that all members of any religion can be saved without professing Jesus Christ as the Son of God. Does this sound like solid Christian theology or more like New Age gibberish?

Rick Warren and Saddleback Church have hired a nationally known public relations firm to handle and respond to media inquiries. Just what does a Christian Church need with a public relations firm? I guess standing on the truth of God's Word just won't cut it anymore. As Christians, should we need PR firms to spin things the right way, and to make sure we can deflect any questions or criticism? Is Saddleback a church of God or a corporation, like Peter Drucker proposed? Is this the future of American Christianity?

If you sat on a grand jury, do you see enough evidence to warrant further investigation into Rick Warren's activities, affiliations and motives? I can tell you from personal experience that no leader elicits more criticism or passionate defense than Rick Warren. He is held in almost god-like status by many pastors and Christians, however he must be examined as any other leader, regardless of how big his church or influence is.

Joel Osteen

We have all gone to a place that offers a huge buffet dinner. There is salad, fruit, meat, vegetables---and a huge table of fattening desserts.

When parents take their children to a buffet place for dinner, the children want to sprint to the dessert table and load up on cookies, cake and ice cream. But parents will first make sure they eat food with proper nutrition before filling up on fattening desserts.

We need fruit to give us healthy sugars and fiber for our body. We need vegetables for necessary vitamins and minerals. We need meat for iron and protein; and every once in a while it is perfectly fine to indulge in some dessert. But if we overindulge on the desserts and ignore the fruit, vegetables and meat, we will become obese and very unhealthy.

Christianity is a buffet. Hebrews tells us the "milk" is the death and resurrection of Jesus, the forgiveness of sins and the resurrection of the dead. It tells us that solid food (meat and vegetables) is righteousness and the pursuit of holiness. The dessert is whatever blessings God chooses to give us to bless others in this lifetime—health, wealth and prosperity, when actually we deserve none of these because of our sinful nature.

When I picture walking in to this Christian buffet setting I see Joel Osteen at the dessert table, inviting us to partake of all things sweet. He is luring many over as they bypass the nutritional teachings of scripture in favor of the dessert bar. Joel Osteen is to Christianity what cream puffs and chocolate éclairs are to the body—they taste good but you'd better not overindulge on them.

Joel Osteen is attractive, charismatic and likable. He is the embodiment of what seems to define success in several leaders of American Christianity these days—a lot of words without saying anything substantive; a leadership that is focused on numbers, not spiritual depth; and a willingness to compromise core Christian values and beliefs when convenient.

Osteen's sermons appear on national television every week on Christian and secular outlets. Granted, his message of love without obligation might be effective in reaching the lost initially, especially those who feel unworthy of God's love, but once these seeds start to sprout they will wither and die quickly because Osteen does nothing to help them develop significant roots in their faith. I watch him every week just to hear his latest teachings and I have yet to feel challenged once by anything he has taught. His message is constant—God loves you and wants the best for your life. Health, wealth, prosperity and a life free of pressure or stress. If only Paul, Peter and John had been able to listen to Osteen, maybe their lives would have been much easier.

Joel Osteen missed his calling; he should have been a politician. He's had many opportunities to stake out strong biblical beliefs, but prefers to remain as neutral as possible, so as not to offend anyone. He has an international platform to share the true gospel, but his inability to take a firm stand on core biblical teachings makes him an ineffective, even destructive leader, as he continues to push an incomplete and dangerous gospel.

In an interview with Larry King, Osteen covered a lot of topics with his usual style of half-answers and questionable theology.[30]

KING: *But you're not fire and brimstone, right? You're not a "pound the decks and hell and damnation"?*

OSTEEN: *No. That's not me. It's never been me. I've always been an encourager at heart. And when I took over from my father he came from the Southern Baptist background and back 40, 50 years ago there was a lot more of that. But, you know, I just -- I don't believe in that. I don't believe -- maybe it was for a time. But I don't have it in my heart to condemn people. I'm there to encourage them. I see myself more as a coach, as a motivator to help them experience the life God has for us.*

KING: *But don't you think if people don't believe as you believe, they're somehow condemned?*

OSTEEN: *You know, I think that happens in our society. But I try not to do that. I tell people all the time, preached a couple Sundays about it. I'm for everybody. You may not agree with me, but to me it's not my job to try to straighten everybody out. The Gospel is called the good news. My message is a message of hope, that's God's for you. You can live a good life no matter what's happened to you. And so I don't know. I know there is condemnation but I don't feel that's my place.*

He preached a "couple of Sundays" on sin and hell? Perhaps the collection was smaller those Sundays as Osteen saw that his congregation found the message too harsh. "I'm for everybody?" How about being for Jesus Christ and the true gospel of salvation?

KING: *There's a lot of books about improving yourself.*

OSTEEN: *Yeah. I don't know. I think coming from the Christian base, and I think the fact that I don't know, it's a book of encouragement and inspiration. And to me it seems like there's so much pulling us down in our society today. There's so much negative. Most of my book is about how you can live a good life today in spite of all that. So I think that had a big part of it.*

KING: *But it doesn't quote a lot of biblical passages until the back of the book, right?*

OSTEEN: *It doesn't do a whole lot of it. My message, I wanted to reach the mainstream. We've reached the church audience. So I just try to, what I do is just try to teach practical principles. I may not bring the scripture in until the end of my sermon and I might feel bad about that. Here's the thought. I talked yesterday about living to give. That's what a life should be about. I brought in at the end about some of the scriptures that talk about that. But same principal in the book.*

Read between the lines: The bible and gospel are too negative and negativity doesn't sell.

KING: *Because we've had ministers on who said, your record don't count. You either believe in Christ or you don't. If you believe in Christ, you are going to heaven. And if you don't no matter what you've done in your life, you ain't.*

OSTEEN: *Yeah, I don't know. There's probably a balance between. I believe you have to know Christ. But I think that if you know Christ, if you're a believer in God, you're going to have some good works. I think it's a cop-out to say I'm a Christian but I don't ever do anything . . .*

KING: *What if you're Jewish or Muslim, you don't accept Christ at all?*

OSTEEN: *You know, I'm very careful about saying who would and wouldn't go to heaven. I don't know . . .*

KING: *If you believe you have to believe in Christ? They're wrong, aren't they?*

OSTEEN: *Well, I don't know if I believe they're wrong. I believe here's what the Bible teaches and from the Christian faith this is what I believe. But I just think that only God will judge a person's heart. I spent a lot of time in India with my father. I don't know all about their religion. But I know they love God. And I don't know. I've seen their sincerity. So I don't know. I know for me, and what the Bible teaches, I want to have a relationship with Jesus.*

So, Osteen has an opportunity to explain the gospel, and what is the response of one of America's top pastors? *"I don't know."* Every time Osteen speaks truth—*". . . you have to know Christ", "If you're a believer in God, you're going to have some good works",* and King questions him on it, Osteen waffles. Why not quote John 14:6? John 3:16? John 15:5-6? Seemingly, the answer is because Osteen is more concerned with appearing non-judgmental and being liked than he is in standing up for the gospel. After all, quoting what the bible says about salvation and pointing out that YHWH is the only true God, and all others are false, does not help him sell books.

KING: *What is the prosperity gospel?*

OSTEEN: *I think the prosperity gospel in general is -- well I don't know. I hear it too. I don't know. I think what sometimes you see is it's just all about money. That's not what I believe. It's the attitude of your heart, and so you know, we believe -- but I do believe this, that God wants us to be blessed. He wants us to be able to send our kids to college, excel in our careers. But prosperity to me, Larry, is not just money, it's having health. What good is money if you don't have health?*

KING: *Also many in the Christian belief are wary of too much material, aren't they?*

OSTEEN: *Yeah, I think some of them are. But to me, you know, I hope people get blessed if they can handle it right. Because it takes money to do good. You know to do things for people. To spread the good news. So I think it's all a matter of your heart.*

Osteen doesn't know what the prosperity gospel is? He preaches it virtually all the time. And he goes on to preach it to King right after he says he doesn't know about it.

And on the point that it takes money to do good: how much money did Paul and Peter have? How much money did Paul spend in marketing plans and social justice programs to "relate" with people? Is the power of the gospel held captive to our financial resources?

KING: *Don't you ever doubt?*

OSTEEN: *No. I don't – I wouldn't say that I do. I guess I do and I don't think about it too much.*

Talk about living in denial! "I don't doubt . . . I wouldn't say that I do . . . I guess I do."

KING: *Do you ever involve politics in the sermons?*
OSTEEN: *Never do.*
KING: *How about issues that the church has feelings about? Abortion? Same-sex marriages?*
OSTEEN: *Yeah. You know what, Larry? I don't go there. I just . . .*
KING: *You have thoughts, though.*
OSTEEN: *I have thoughts. I just, you know, I don't think that a same-sex marriage is the way God intended it to be. I don't think abortion is the best. I think there are other, you know, a better way to live your life. But I'm not going to condemn those people. I tell them all the time our church is open for everybody.*

Of course, a strong biblical answer here would have meant taking a tough stand that might be unpopular. Gay marriage and abortion aren't "God's best"? No, they are abominations to God as his innocent children are slaughtered and marriage is demeaned to fit sinful human desires.

Is Joel Osteen selling out the Christian faith for personal gain? He has a huge platform to spread the good news of the bible but it seems he would rather sell books and be loved and admired. Is this where we want our leaders to take us?

KING: *You don't call them sinners?*
OSTEEN: *I don't.*
KING: *Is that a word you don't use?*
OSTEEN: *I don't use it. I never thought about it. But I probably don't. But most people already know what they're doing wrong. When I get them to church I want to tell them that you can change. There can be a difference in your life. So I don't go down the road of condemning.*

Hey Joel, breaking news: Sin is the disease that is leading men into spiritual death for eternity. Sinners need to repent and accept the forgiveness, grace and mercy of God, available because of the painful sacrifice by the Son of God.

Joel Osteen is like a cancer doctor refusing to properly diagnose and treat cancer in his patients. Any physician who did that would be sued for malpractice and lose his license forever. Is Joel Osteen guilty of spiritual malpractice? Osteen has great influence and we need to pray he will be convicted by the Holy Spirit to preach the entire gospel, not just the "feel good" gospel.

Osteen has also weighed in on the controversy surrounding the faith of presidential candidate Mitt Romney, who is a Mormon. Here is an excerpt from his an interview on Fox News[31] with Chris Wallace:

Wallace: *"And what about Mitt Romney? And I've got to ask you the question, because it is a question whether it should be or not in this campaign, is a Mormon a true Christian?"*

Osteen: *"Well, in my mind they are. Mitt Romney has said that he believes in Christ as his savior, and that's what I believe, so, you know, I'm not the one to judge the little details of it. So, I believe they are. And so, you know, Mitt Romney seems like a man of character and integrity to me, and I don't think he would—anything would stop me from voting for him if that's what I felt like."*

Wallace: *"So, for instance, when people start talking about Joseph Smith, the founder of the church, and the golden tablets in upstate New York, and God assumes the shape of a man, do you not get hung up on those theological issues?"*

Osteen: *"I probably don't get hung up in them because I haven't really studied them or thought about them."*

So let's analyze Osteen's response:

- Romney and Osteen both believe in Jesus as savior (note the absence of the word "Lord")
- Osteen admits he has not studied Mormonism. Some shepherd of the flock.
- Osteen says he is not the one to judge if Mormons are Christians or not. Perhaps, but is God qualified to make that judgment? I certainly hope your answer is "yes".

What do Mormons believe?

The Mormon[32] religion, whose followers are known as Mormons and Latter Day Saints (LDS), was founded less than two hundred years ago by a man named Joseph Smith. He claimed to have received a personal visit from God the Father and Jesus Christ who told him that all churches and their creeds were an abomination. Joseph Smith then set out to begin a new religion that claims to be the "only true church on earth."

Mormons believe that there are four sources of divinely inspired words.

- The Bible "as far as it is translated correctly." Which verses are considered incorrectly translated is not always made clear.
- The Book of Mormon, which was "translated" by Smith and published in 1830. Smith claimed it is the "most correct book" on earth and that a person can get closer to God by following its precepts more than any other book.
- The Doctrine and Covenants, containing a collection of modern revelations regarding the "Church of Jesus Christ as it has been restored."
- The Pearl of Great Price, which is considered by Mormons to "clarify" doctrines and teachings that were lost from the Bible, and adding its own information about the earth's creation.

Mormons believe that God was not always the supreme being of the universe, but attained that status through righteous living and persistent effort. They believe God the Father has a "body of flesh and bones as tangible as man's." Brigham Young taught that Adam actually was God and the father of Jesus Christ, though this teaching has now been abandoned by modern Mormon leaders.

But Mormon leaders have taught that Jesus' incarnation was the result of a physical relationship between God the Father and Mary. Mormons believe Jesus is *a god*, but that any human can also become a god, and that salvation can be earned by a combination of faith and good works.

Mormons do tend to be good moral people; but it is clear they are not Christians. To refer to Jesus as *a god* distorts his nature. He is the only begotten Son of God, and he is God (John 1:1). To infer that we can all become gods is not a Christian belief. And to teach that God has not always been the all-powerful, omniscient God who created all things is heresy. If that is true, then who created God?

Osteen simply does what Osteen always does—deflect tough questions and show that he is an empty suit. Unfortunately, this empty suit has millions of followers who think he represents sound Christian doctrines and teachings.

Summary on Joel Osteen

In many ways Joel Osteen embodies the state of Christian leadership these days. Soft-peddling or denying sin; suggesting all gods might be the same; more concerned with health and wealth in this life instead of our eternal spiritual destination; and afraid to call out false religions and beliefs. Is Joel Osteen ashamed of the gospel, and more worried about his public image than the truth of the gospel?

Summary

Bill Hybels, Rick Warren, and Joel Osteen. Welcome to leadership in American Christianity. These men represent the new "incorporation" of American Christianity, where the desires of "customers" are cherished, often at the expense of clear biblical doctrines. Are we witnessing the future of the Church? A future of religious syncretism, the discounting of sin, a social justice gospel, and truth sacrificed for numbers, popularity and power?

A future that redefines love as total acceptance of any behavior; a future where what we feel trumps cold hard facts; and a future where we can pick and choose which characteristics of God we want to accept, discounting the rest?

This future is right here, right now and it is increasingly disturbing. Sadly it may have unstoppable momentum, fueled by biblically illiterate and lazy Christians who find it easier to listen to a twenty-minute sermon to select our theology, instead of taking time out of our busy lives to read what God teaches us about Himself, sin and salvation.

And the next generation of leaders is appearing on stage to carry the torch forward. Mentored by these men and others like McLaren, Wallis and Campolo, this next generation of leaders is preparing to take us to new places and possibly greater depths of depravity. Men like Rob Bell and Steven Furtick[33] are ready and willing to lead us farther from the truth of scripture and deeper into the spiritual abyss.

American Christianity is on life support and continues to be infected with the cancer of secular culture, and the body is starting to shut down. Vital organs are starting to fail, the blood is poisoned and we are gasping for air. At our current direction there may be no clear distinction between secular humanism and American Christianity ten years from now.

Our leaders are leading us to where we really want to go deep down in our hearts. They have tickled ears that asked to be tickled and they have closed eyes that desired to be closed. While they are partly responsible for this slow poisoning, it is we who follow them who must share at least equal blame.

> *"So all the elders of Israel gathered and came to Samuel at Ramah. They said to him 'You are old and your sons do not walk in your ways; now appoint a king to lead us, such as all the other nations have.'*

"But when they said 'Give us a king to lead us' this displeased Samuel, so he prayed to the Lord. And the Lord told him 'Listen to all that the people are saying to you; it is not you they have rejected, but they have rejected me as their king. As they have done from the day I brought them out of Egypt until this day, forsaking me and serving other gods, so they are doing to you. Now listen to them; but warn them solemnly and let them know what the king who will reign over them will do."

1 Samuel 8:4-9

History is repeating itself. Just as the Jews rejected God as king in favor of men, we are repeating the same mistake in American Christianity. We are rejecting the knowledge of God in his Word, choosing "kings" to be our leaders instead of God himself. These kings will tell us what to believe and what to do. We mistake their apparent "prosperity" as a blessing from God. We emulate them and try to be just like them, hoping our churches can grow and become financially prosperous.

Surely these "kings" would not lead us astray, because they have been trained in Christian seminaries, so they must be a lot smarter and wiser then we are. They pastor mega-churches so they must be doing something right. They have charm and charisma and are kind, loving and accepting and they make us feel so good about ourselves. They are our leaders—shouldn't we just follow where they lead us?

How did that work for the Israelites? About as well as it will work for us. Welcome to our future American Christians. Enjoy it because we asked for it, and just like in 1 Samuel, God is allowing it. Is he hardening our hearts like he did to Pharaoh? Are we feeling his wrath spoken of by Paul in Romans 1?

"For although they knew God, they neither glorified him as God nor gave thanks to him, but their thinking became futile and their foolish hearts were darkened. Although they claimed to be wise, they became fools and exchanged the glory of the immortal God for images made to look like mortal man and birds and animals and reptiles.

"Therefore God gave them over in the sinful desires of their hearts to sexual impurity for the degrading of their bodies with one another. They exchanged the truth of God for a lie, and worshipped and served created things rather than the Creator---who is forever praised. Amen.

"Because of this God gave them over to shameful lusts. Even their women exchanged natural relations for unnatural ones. In the same way the men also abandoned natural relations with women and were inflamed with lust for one another. Men committed indecent acts with other men, and received in themselves the due penalty for their perversion.

"Furthermore, since they did not think it worthwhile to retain the knowledge of God, he gave them over to a depraved mind to do what ought not to be done. They have become filled with every kind of wickedness, evil, greed and depravity."

Romans 1:21-29

Footnotes

1. druckerinstitute.com
2. sorenkierkegaard.nl
3. The Emerging Church, Dan Kimball, 2003, Zondervan Publishing
4. More Ready than You Realize, Brian McLaren, 2002, Zondervan Publishing
5. willowcreek.org
6. http://exodusinternational.org/2011/08/the-fullness-of-the-gospel-letter-from-alan-chambers-for-august-2011/
7. christatthecheckpoint.com
8. United States Congressional Record, 1998
9. Love Wins, Rob Bell, 2011, Harper Collins Publishing
10. http://www.relevantmagazine.com/culture/music/features/3252-how-to-dismantle-an-idolized-bono
11. Tonyblairfaithfoundation.org
12. un.org

13. www.onewhiteduck.com/2012/02/08/newark-mayor-cory-booker-stands-strong-in-fight-for-marriage-equality/
14. Purpose Driven Church, Rick Warren, 1995, Zondervan Publishing
15. thebereancall.org
16. christianitytoday.com
17. acommonword.com
18. isna.net
19. www.investigativeproject.org/730/new-disclosures-tighten-isna-muslim-brotherhood-bondsunesco.org
20. www.discoverthenetworks.org/individualProfile.asp?indid=716
21. unesco.org
22. transcripts.cnn.com
23. www.abpnews.com/content/view/4007/53/
24. Life on Other Planets, Emanuel Swedenborg
25. www.newchurch.org/materials/pdf/2008issue3-science-and-religion.pdf
26. amenclinics.net
27. kundalini-yoga-info.com
28. thepeaceplan.com
29. kingdomcircles.net/#/islam-circles/4539645452
30. transcripts.cnn.com
31. foxnews.com
32. gotquestions.org
33. stevenfurtick.com

CHAPTER NINE

A MOVE OF THE SPIRIT—
BUT WHICH SPIRIT?

Signs and Wonders Movement

> *"And afterward, I will pour out my spirit on all people. Your sons and daughters will prophesy, your old men will dream dreams, your young men will have visions. Even on my servants, both men and women, I will pour out my Spirit in those days. I will show wonders in the heavens and on the earth, blood and fire and billows of smoke.*
>
> Joel 2:28-29

> *"At that time if anyone says to you 'Look here is the Christ' or 'There he is' do not believe it. For false christs and false prophets will appear and perform great signs and miracles to deceive the elect—if that were possible."*
>
> Matthew 24:23-25

> *"The coming of the lawless one will be in accordance with the work of Satan displayed in all kinds of counterfeit miracles, signs and wonders, and in every sort of evil that deceives those who are perishing. They perish because they refused to love the truth and so be saved. For this reason God sends them a powerful delusion so*

that they will believe a lie and so that all will be condemned who
have not believed the truth but have delighted in wickedness."
2 Thessalonians 2:9-12

OK, strap on your seatbelts and reconcile these three verses! God says in Joel that in the final days he will pour out His Spirit with great signs and wonders yet Jesus and Paul warn us of incredible false miracles, signs and wonders, not of God, but of the enemy.

These verses call for biblical wisdom and discernment, testing the Spirits to determine true from false. There will apparently be real signs and wonders from God, but also a lot of false, deceptive signs and wonders from Satan that will deceive many. In telling His disciples about the end of the age, Jesus warned us once about wars and pestilence, but we are warned **four times** about false signs and wonders. No movement we discuss on Stand Up For the Truth brings stronger emotions and opinions than the "Signs and Wonders" Movement.

God created the universe and all that is in it, sustaining it by His might, and He has the power to suspend natural laws in order to fulfill any purpose He desires. Miracles were a huge part of the ministries of Moses, Elijah and Elisha, and of course Jesus and the apostles. Today, many people still seek to experience miraculous signs and wonders, and some go to great lengths to experience what they believe are signs and wonders from God.

Some want confirmation of the truth of God and there is nothing inherently wrong with that. In fact, God willingly gave signs to Moses (Exodus 4:1-9) and in John 2:23, *"Many people saw the miraculous signs he was doing and believed in his name."* However, there comes a time when enough miracles have been presented and the truth should be known. God should not have to prove Himself over and over again.

Jesus visited the Samaritans, and *"because of his words many more became believers"* (John 4:41). However just a few verses later, Jesus rebukes the Galileans: *"Unless you people see miraculous signs and wonders . . . you will never believe"* (John 4:48). So to continue to seek signs, wonders and miracles in the pursuit of knowing God can be an insult to Him.

Signs and wonders appeal to us on an emotional level. While we are creatures of deep emotion and passion, our passion and emotions can have a dangerous hold on us when we allow them to govern us. When we desire something strongly enough, our emotions can fool us. That is why God gave us His Word, so we could measure every thought, word, action and feeling against His absolute truth.

Some people seem to almost develop an addiction to witnessing signs, wonders and miracles. The danger in this is that God becomes a "high" in our lives. Grounded Christians should not need continuous signs, wonders and miracles--just knowing He is God and we are His children should be sufficient. Now some argue that miraculous signs bring them continually closer to God, but there is a real danger in becoming addicted to signs and wonders. The danger is that Satan is also capable of demonstrating his power through signs and wonders.

> *"Then the devil took him (Jesus) to the holy city and had him stand on the highest point of the temple. If you are the Son of God throw yourself down, for it is written 'He will command his angels concerning you, and they will lift you up in their hands, so that you will not strike your foot against a stone.' Jesus answered him, 'It is also written: Do not put the Lord your God to the test."*
>
> *"Again the devil took him to a very high mountain and showed him all the kingdoms of the world and their splendor. 'All this I will give you if you will bow down and worship me'.*
>
> Matthew 4:5-8

The devil transported Jesus from the desert to the top of the temple to a mountain so high they could see all the world's kingdoms. That, my friends, is a sign and wonder, but not one from God. And therein lies a serious problem in the Signs and Wonders Movement—both God and Satan are capable of performing them. So when people claim to see angel feathers or gold dust, or claim they were transported to another place or time, how can we tell with one-hundred percent accuracy that it is God, not Satan, performing the "miracle"?

Nowhere in God's Word do we see examples of gold dust or angel feathers connected with God. So if people are seeing these signs, are they more likely from God or a counterfeit sign from a false spirit?

People I have spoken with who claim to experience incredible signs and wonders always report a euphoria accompanying the sighting. In such an emotional state, how can we be certain our emotions have not overwhelmed our common sense and biblical discernment? We must remember that Satan is a great counterfeiter who will make his signs and wonders seem just like God's whenever possible.

Is there selective manipulation present at many of these events? Is "signs and wonders" exclusively a "Christian thing"? Many who have come out of leadership from the "signs and wonders movement" are deeply concerned by what they were taught on orchestrating these events and what they have experienced. One such man is Mark Haville, who was a leader in a one-thousand person church deep into the movement. Here is a partial copy of the transcript from his appearance on Stand Up for the Truth on December 22, 2011:[1]

> "Even in the few services that I put on or was instigating, I would blow on people, they would fall down; I would just touch them on the head, they would fall down, semi-conscious for 10, 15 minutes and so on. These were exactly the things that we had been taught. And of course, if you're taught if you follow steps A-B-C, this is what will happen, and then you do A-B-C, in your natural mind you think, "well this must be God, then", it does seem on a pragmatic level to work. But the problem is it worked for a whole lot of other reasons, and for a whole bunch of different people as well around the world who are not Christians, not believers, not praying in the name of Jesus, or maybe even from other religions or from the occult.
>
> "So when you look around the world and see that this same phenomena is duplicated exactly, and using the very same techniques, then that's the time to go back and question, what I'm reading in scripture, is that describing what I'm seeing in

charismatic meetings today or in word/faith meetings today? And of course, the answer is 'no'. When you look in scripture, you do see one or two occasions where people fall down: Jesus when they come to arrest Him says, 'Who are you seeking?' and they say 'We're seeking Jesus of Nazareth'. He says 'I am He', and when He says the 'I AM' word they all fall backwards, but I don't think that was a blessing. These people were coming to arrest Him to be crucified.

You see another occasion with Ananias & Sapphira in the book of Acts, when they are challenged about lying to the Apostles and before God, about the money that they had given and the land that they had sold, and they both fell down backwards dead. Again, that is not a blessing, that is not a Holy Spirit slaying us and imparting some kind of blessing to us. So when you examine more carefully, you can't actually find one occasion where Jesus or the apostles did this."

And what we're actually seeing is hypnosis, but hypnosis in 'Jesus' name'. And the way to achieve this is to get people into a suggestible state. People who attend large crusades are, to an extent, in a suggestible state when they arrive, because they have a heightened expectation that they're going to experience the supernatural, they're going to see miracles. So once you add the music and the lights, and the large crowds--these are all common techniques that you see at events held by people of other religions, or people using the occult, at hypnotic shows, and it's absolutely identical."

Mike: *"Mark, is hypnosis a tool used by many in this movement?"*

"It is group hypnosis because everybody is being subject to the same experience. The only thing that varies is the level of susceptibility. And some people can't be hypnotized, as they are not susceptible to hypnosis and hypnotic technique, that's all. So because of that, the Hypnotist, in our case, the Preacher, say someone like Benny Hinn, goes through a selection process, exactly the same as a stage hypnotist. And they go through various procedures to select people in the audience that are going to be susceptible to what they

> call 'slaying in the spirit', which is the hypnosis. And that's why you
> have the various staff who are positioned around the auditorium,
> to pick out people they see are starting to manifest, to shake or
> to laugh or weep, or whatever the case may be, and then they go
> through a further selection process when they come out of their
> seats into the aisles to meet with the staff and say "well I believe
> I had this kind of sickness, and now I don't have pain anymore".
> That selection process is to eliminate mostly the organic disorders
> from the functional ones, and those are generally the ones they will
> bring up on stage."

The fact that religions other than Christianity, along with hypnotists, use the same techniques and achieve similar results should bode as caution for Christians seeking to get involved in this movement.

A recent phenomenon over the past several years is the claim of people seeing "angel orbs." Coincidentally, this has started to surface with the development of digital photography, and can easily be manufactured by dust particles seen by these high tech cameras. But "angel orbs" are really nothing new. Early Christian Gnostics and Jewish Kabala teachers talked constantly about seeing "angel orbs", and the New Age and occult realm have taught about the sighting of these orbs for centuries. Nowhere in the bible is there anything remotely suggesting that God sends his angels as orbs. Some point to Ezekiel, but a study of this passage clearly refutes the suggestion that Ezekiel saw "angel orbs".

Another claim of some in this movement is being "drunk in the spirit". They fall down and slur their words like a man who consumed a quart of brandy, yet claim this is a manifestation from God. Benny Hinn once claimed to be so drunk in the spirit that he forgot where he was or what he was teaching, falling down like a fool.[2]

> But the fruit of the Spirit is love, joy, peace, kindness, goodness,
> faithfulness, gentleness and **self-control**."
> Galatians 5:22-23 (emphasis added)

Does being "drunk in the spirit", falling down and slurring words, sound like self-control?

When we are looking for the next great thrill of a sign or wonder, could our mind be open to suggestion? Open to suggestion from an enemy looking to speak to us when we want to believe we are hearing from God? This sets us up for tremendous deception as Satan is very clever and devious, and can twist scripture ever so slightly to advance his agenda of deception.

> *"For such men are false prophets, deceitful workmen, masquerading as apostles of Christ. And no wonder, for Satan himself masquerades as an angel of light. It is not surprising then, if his servants masquerade as servants of righteousness. Their end will be what their actions deserve."*
>
> 2 Corinthians 11:13-15

Why, with such clear teachings from the bible, would people flirt with the dangers of the spiritual realm, when Satan and his servants are so crafty and deceptive? People who seek signs and wonders are like moths attracted to a flame—and sadly many are going to be burned.

Sadly, sensuality seems to be replacing genuine spirituality in much of Christianity these days. More and more Christians are seeking greater depths of sensuality in everything they feel and encounter. This sensuality can overwhelm our common sense and send us in pursuit of dangerous passion, like a dog in heat. We become obsessed with the sensuality and will pursue it at all costs, even at the expense of sound doctrine.

There is no doubt that many of the "signs and wonders" proclaimed by someone like Todd Bentley are bizarre and not found anywhere in the Word of God. But a defense put up by some is "Just because God has never done it in the past doesn't mean he cannot do it now." Very true, as God is capable of doing anything within his nature and character and that is what makes this issue so difficult to discuss rationally at times. Emotion runs high on both sides of this issue and we must approach it with great wisdom and discernment.

But what I often find in defenders of this movement is, at times, curious to say the least. They will call skeptics closed-minded and not open to the possibility of God doing "something new". However I challenge them that perhaps they are the ones who are closed-minded because they seem to automatically think every new sign and wonder is from God instead of the enemy. When Jesus talked about the final days before His return, he warned us once each of wars, rumors of war and pestilence. Yet we are warned **four times** about dangerous false prophets, false teachers and false christs. When God warns us of something four times, I think He is quite serious about the point He is trying to make. But in the pursuit of sensuality over truth, we are often led by our emotions and passions instead of using discernment and the Word of God. We dive head long into something we may not understand and just assume it is from God because we are Christians.

Now in fairness, many defenders of the signs and wonders movement recognize, as one supporter puts it, that whenever "signs and wonders" appear there are three camps at work: The Holy Spirit, the enemy, and people who get swept up in the emotion of the event and fake it. When they raise this defense I thank them for making my argument. It is so easy to get caught up in our emotions that sound judgment and discernment can be abandoned, and it may result in dangerous connections to false spirits. It places young believers in a very dangerous situation. As they see "mature" Christians swept up in the emotion of the event, they are tempted to seek the same out of fear they will be seen as immature in their faith. So they either fake an incident, or actually open a door to demonic spirits waiting to deceive.

Back in 1996, three years before I committed my life to Jesus, I was in the Dallas-Fort Worth Airport, waiting to catch a plane home after a business trip. A woman was in the chair next to me and I could tell she was really struggling with a deeply emotional issue. I asked if she was alright and she shared what was causing her so much emotional grief. At age forty, she had become unexpectedly pregnant and her husband wanted her to have an abortion. Even though I was not a true believer at that time, I was staunchly pro-life and I encouraged her to not make a hasty decision to end the life of her child. After our hour-long discussion, she gave me a book that she said I just had to read.

The book was the best selling *"Conversations With God"*[3] by Neale Donald Walsch. At this time my eyes were not open to who God was and for the need to become born again in the Holy Spirit. I thought I was good to go since I was raised in the Catholic Church and still attended church a whopping two times a year.

I read the book on the flight to Green Bay and found Walsch's "conversations" with God to be intriguing and heart warming. Walsch talked about how God is in every one and every one is in God; about how Jesus, Buddha and Mohammed were all God's sons; and that we are all gods if we just realize the divinity within us. Without the Holy Spirit of God, I actually found the book to be interesting and beautiful. I began to question what I was taught about God and Jesus. Satan was reaching out to me in my blindness and ignorance, and I must confess, I found the message interesting.

Fortunately, I forgot about the book within a few days, as I returned to my job and the pursuit of worldly happiness. But for a few short days, I was caught up in the emotion of bliss, harmony and peace. Had I received a dream or "vision" that seemed to confirm the heresy I was flirting with, I could have easily fallen for the lies of the enemy and been the worst of heathens to this day. I thank God that He loved and protected my mind and heart even when I hated Him.

Emotions and feelings are often our worst enemy. They deceive us and encourage us to believe in what we feel, instead of the truth. Satan will play on our emotions, and disguised as an angel of light, can trick us and lead us astray if we are not anchored in the Word of God.

Our IT Manager at Q90 FM loves trains. About two years ago he shared some wisdom he had received from a mentor about trains and God. The "biblical train" lines up like this: Faith, then facts, then feelings. Our feelings must always be filtered through facts, which must be identified through our faith. Faith dictates facts, and facts sort out feelings as proper or improper. If we allow our feelings to override our faith, we are headed into very dangerous territories.

"Signs and wonders" appeal to us emotionally, but if they are not held up against the facts in God's Word, these emotions can trick us, leading us astray into a very dangerous spiritual world.

There are many outrageous teachers and leaders in the "signs and wonders" movement, but one is most worthy of study and critique. There is one man who seems to embody what many in the movement believe. This man teaches we can transport our bodies and minds to and from heaven anytime we desire. He believes that God has "angels of wealth" waiting at our beck and call to provide whatever we desire. He believes that angels will appear to us anytime we call them, serving as our spiritual guides and mentors—a belief that the New Age Movement promotes regularly.

Todd Bentley

While there are many "signs and wonders" teachers like Benny Hinn and Rick Joyner, Todd Bentley[4] is among the most controversial, and for good reason. Bentley was born on January 10, 1976 and raised in Gibsons, British Columbia in Canada. According to public records, at age fifteen he was convicted of sexually assaulting a seven year old boy. He struggled with alcohol and drug addictions and at age seventeen was hospitalized after an overdose of amphetamines and hallucinogenic drugs. At age eighteen, he claims he committed his life to Jesus Christ.

In 1998 the "Fresh Fire Ministry"[5] group asked him to give his testimony at one of their weekly meetings and soon after he became the leader of the group, traveling worldwide on religious crusades. In 2008 Bentley was invited by Stephen Strader, pastor of Ignited Church in Lakeland, Florida, to lead a weeklong revival. An event of powerful light flashes with rock music and colorful light shows attracted up to ten-thousand people a night and became a media phenomenon. Bentley's ministry was unique indeed, as he often physically abused attendees by kicking and punching and knocking them over, claiming God told him to do it.

At these events Bentley would pray for miraculous healings from God and then claimed miraculous healings did occur, but to my knowledge none have been confirmed independently.

Later in 2008, Bentley announced a legal separation from his wife due to an "unhealthy relationship" with a female member of his staff, and stepped down from active ministry for a short period of time. He initially submitted to restoration at the hands of church leaders, but in November 2008, the restoration oversight team at Fresh Fire announced he was no longer submitting to the process. Three short months later Bentley married the object of the "unhealthy relationship", staff member Jessa Hasbrook. He agreed to come under the restorative hand of Rick Joyner, a key figure in the signs and wonders and New Apostolic Reform movements. After only a few short months Joyner claimed Bentley had been restored, so he resumed leading a ministry.

We all make mistakes and God can forgive and restore anyone. But many Christians feel Bentley's apologies were shallow at best, and that Joyner's decision to restore him was premature to say the least. Let's look at some of Bentley's "experiences" and teachings, holding them up against scripture to discern if this is a movement of the Holy Spirit or a different source.

Bentley's events try to call down angels from heaven—angels that he thinks carry very specific blessings to those who seek them in the supernatural realm. He often screams "angels, angels, angels", encouraging the crowd to do the same as thousands are whipped into an emotional frenzy and chaos breaks loose. He then claims to see angels, and encourages acknowledgment from those in the crowd. It is utter chaos.

> So when I need a financial breakthrough I don't just pray and ask God for my financial breakthrough. I go into intercession and become a partner with the angels by petitioning the father of the angels that are assigned to getting me money. 'Father, give me the angels in heaven right now that are assigned to get me money and wealth."
>
> 2003 Article titled "Angelic Hosts"[6]

> *"In my ministry, I teach my disciples 'Power first, then the Word of God! Go in and prophesy first, or demonstrate the power of God first in some way."*
>
> "The Reality of the Supernatural World" by Todd Bentley

> *"We can preach the Gospel all day long, but that won't win souls. They won't win the hearts of the people."*[7]

Bentley alleges that angels give him advice about all sorts of things, from finances to healing.

An angel named "Healing Revival" worked with Bentley in many past healings. *"When He comes,"* said Bentley, *"I get . . . the ability to diagnose people's sicknesses with my left hand. I get very accurate details from God. . . . And whenever this angel shows up the miracles go off the charts."*[8]

Bentley claims that six angels operated on him during one of his heavenly visits. He saw "a pillar of fire" rise up through the roof of a church and when "God" told him to "get into the pillar," he did and landed on an operating table in heaven. Six angels tied him down and began surgery. *"They pick this thing up . . . and they stuck it in me right here on my neck and it didn't hurt . . . everything inside of me popped out onto the table, my heart, my liver, like everything. . . . The angels start taking these white boxes . . . and they start stuffing these things inside of me."*[9]

More quotes from Todd Bentley:

> *"In the middle of the service . . . in walks Emma. . . . She floated a couple of inches off the floor . . . emitting brilliant light and colors. Emma carried these bags and began pulling gold out of them. Then, as she walked up and down the aisles of the church, she began putting gold dust on people. 'God, what is happening?' I asked. The Lord answered: 'She is releasing the gold, which is both the revelation and the financial breakthrough that I am bringing into this church."*[10]
>
> *"I went into a trance-like state and I saw . . . the angel of finance . . . In that trance I experienced one of heaven's realities and then that experience became a reality here on earth . . . I found*

> *myself in a treasure room in heaven. The only item in this room was gold coins, and I began stuffing those coins into my pockets until they were falling out."*[11]

Since the uproar over "Emma", Bentley downplays any knowledge or revelation of "Emma", but his previous claims are well-documented and available on YouTube videos.

Bentley held up a letter at one of his events claiming proof of a thirteenth resurrection from the dead because of his ministry, but when pressed to release names or proof he comes up empty time after time. [12]

Bentley tells stories of remarkable healings. In fact, he now claims that in his ministry twenty-one people have now been raised from the dead. Are these stories credible? Bentley claims that one man had been dead for forty-eight hours and was in a coffin. When the family gathered around at a funeral home, the man knocked from inside the coffin to be let out.

If any of these resurrections were true, every media outlet in the country would be reporting it. But to date I have not seen one first hand testimony.

At another event Bentley called his first wife and three children up on the stage with him. He said his family was "prophetic proof" that God was ready to heal families and marriages. While this event was taking place, Bentley was involved in an affair with one of his employees and shortly thereafter he and his wife got divorced. Some "prophetic proof"-- dragging your children on stage and humiliating them, at a time you are committing adultery with a staff member. And by the way, when he asked his wife to speak she couldn't because she was "drunk in the spirit"; her eyes were glazed and she had to be held up by leaders on stage.

Todd Bentley claims to have been brought to heaven by God and the angels several times, putting him in lofty company with the Apostles Paul and John. On his website he claims he can teach people how to spiritually transport themselves from one dimension to another.[13]

In Acts 8, the Bible tells a remarkable story of Philip baptizing the eunuch. Philip lowered the eunuch into the water then disappeared, appearing at Azotus. This seems to be a case of spiritual transportation, but if it was, it was an act of God, not something you can train people to do on their own.

> *"The coming of the lawless one will be in accordance with work of Satan displayed in all kinds of counterfeit miracles, signs and wonders, and in every sort of evil that deceives those who are perishing. They perished because they refused to love the truth and so be saved. For this reason God sends them a powerful delusion so that they will believe a lie and so that all will be condemned who have not believed the truth but have delighted in wickedness."*
>
> 2 Thessalonians 2:9-12

Compare the fruit and teachings of Todd Bentley with the Word of God. Look at the fruit he bears: lying about "Emma" after being confronted; parading his children on stage claiming they are prophetic proof of God, healing marriages and families, while he is having an adulterous affair, later divorcing his wife; claiming dozens of miraculous resurrections from the dead without a single testimony from any of the "risen". Claiming the Gospel will not win any souls. Is this the fruit of a disciple of Jesus Christ?

Bentley is one of the higher profile "signs and wonders" teachers out there today. Rick Joyner and Benny Hinn are two other notables. We hear miraculous story after miraculous story, but do we see one shred of proof to back up their incredible claims?

The greatest tragedy in all this is that it will bring into doubt any genuine miracle or sign or wonder one might see these days. As we approach the end of the age, I do believe God will pour out His Spirit in miraculous ways as He chooses, but He will not be at anyone's beck and call like a genie in the lamp waiting to appear when He is called. And all the false claims by people like Todd Bentley will not only lead immature Christians astray, it will also cast a shadow on any real move of the Holy Spirit that believers or non-believers may hear about.

Events like these are often marked by chaos and uncontrolled emotion. People are screaming at the top of their voices, walking around "drunk", barking like dogs and clucking like chickens. Bentley often goes into a near rage, calling down angels to come minister to those in attendance. Two points on scenes like this:

First, according to scriptural accounts, angels are God's messengers. God usually sent them when an important message must be delivered and there are no indications whatsoever that there are angels of "finance" or "healing" as Bentley and others teach. Secondly, is chaos like this biblical or is God a god of order?

> *"The acts of the sinful nature are obvious: **sexual immorality**, impurity and debauchery, **idolatry** and witchcraft; hatred, discord, jealousy, **fits of rage, selfish ambition**, dissensions, factions, and envy; **drunkenness**, orgies and the like. I warn you, as I did before, that those who live like this will not inherit the kingdom of God.*
>
> *"But the fruit of the Spirit is love, joy, **peace**, patience, kindness, goodness, faithfulness, **gentleness** and **self-control**. Against such things there is no law."*

Galatians 5:19-23 (emphasis added)

Fits of rage, drunkenness and a lack of self-control are often evident at events by Bentley and others in the movement, yet countless thousands still consider them moves of the Holy Spirit.

In 1 Corinthians 14:32-33, Paul teaches that worship should be orderly and that *"the spirits of prophets are subject to the control of prophets. For God is not a God of disorder but of peace."*

Order and peace are almost always absent from events that Bentley and other "signs and wonders" teachers conduct. They are usually marked by chaos.

The Bible warns us of many false miracles, signs and wonders in the final days, and Christians should be careful not to fall for slick words or special effects. We must not let our feelings drive facts and faith. God gave us the bible for a reason—so we could come to know His perfect nature and character and He could show us a pattern of His works so we might be able to discern the real from the counterfeit. The Bible clearly teaches us that God is a God of order, not chaos, and this must be a guiding thought when we assess movements like this. Is God capable of doing something new that He has never done before? Yes, as long as it is consistent with His nature. The gospel is an account of what Jesus did, not men. And we should be very careful not to confuse the two.

Word of Faith Movement

The life of a Christian is a battle between our flesh and the Spirit of God we receive when we are born again. When we commit our lives to Jesus Christ as Lord and Savior, our problems do not magically disappear--in fact sometimes our troubles intensify. We live in a fallen world led by Satan, and he will use every means to lead us away from our new life as Christians. Things of this world--fame and fortune--are always ready to distract us from a life of righteousness and humility.

Some Christians have been blessed by God with wealth and prosperity. However, this blessing can turn into a curse if we allow wealth to become our master. Jesus taught us several important lessons while He walked the earth. He taught that no man could serve two masters--God and money--that men would come to love one and hate the other. He taught us that we would be hated and persecuted for the sake of following Him.

He also taught us that He would provide for our needs, even in the most difficult of times. Never once, however, did He teach us that we would automatically be filled with earthly riches if we followed Him. In fact, He warned us to not pursue earthly wealth that is temporary, instead encouraging us to accumulate treasures in heaven.

As we have become a wealthy nation and people, something very wrong has happened to us. **Wants** now become seen as **needs**. These days just having a home to live in is not enough-- we desire earthly mansions far larger than we truly need. Having a dependable automobile for transportation has been replaced with the "need" for new luxury automobiles that testify to our social status. Having simple clothes has been replaced with the "need" to look fashionable and hip at all times. Simple meals of provision have been replaced with feasts fit for a king.

American Christianity is being seduced by the same fleshly desires that are sought by the secular culture. A simple life is no longer good enough for us. We want Jesus in addition to the desires of our flesh, instead of dying to our flesh daily as the Bible instructs us.

Every good thing we receive in this life is a blessing from God. But it is so easy to cross a dangerous line where we *expect* more blessings from God. The entitlement mentality gripping Americans is invading and infiltrating American Christianity, spawning an explosion of television evangelists preaching prosperity to feed this entitlement mentality. Some of these preachers are accumulating massive wealth on the backs of naive Christians who believe God is like a personal butler, at our beck and call to provide every desire of our human heart.

Faith: Hebrews 11:6 says without faith it is impossible to please God. In Matthew 13, the Bible says that when Jesus returned to his home town he did not perform many miracles because of their lack of faith. The Old and New Testament teach us not to be double-minded, but to have a strong, immovable faith in God.

So let's settle one thing first: Faith is what the Christian life is all about. Christianity is all about faith in Jesus Christ as the Son of God, faith in our eternal destination because of what Jesus did on the cross, and faith that when the whole world is crumbling around us, God has us in the palm of His hand. And I believe that our level of faith is very important when we make our petitions to God, whether they are for someone else or ourselves.

But there is a huge difference where that faith is placed. Just what is it that commands and holds our faith? Is our faith in God or is it in our "faith"? God is capable of doing anything consistent with his perfect, sinless nature. Man is capable of nothing good according to scripture.

192

God is to be worshipped, but not manipulated. And while *"without faith it is impossible to please God"* (Hebrews 11:6), faith is not a silver bullet for anything we desire. In John Chapter 5, Jesus healed the man at the pool of Bethesda even though he showed no faith whatsoever. And every day in this world men and women of strong faith pray for their children's lives to be spared after a tragic accident; they pray for their parents to survive life threatening cancer; they pray for financial relief to stop foreclosure of their homes; and they pray for a lost friend to come to know salvation through Jesus Christ. Sometimes God answers "yes"; but sometimes the answer is "no" or "not now". God will not be manipulated. He alone decides who to heal and who not to heal and He alone decides who is blessed with wealth and who will struggle financially.

But some in the Word of Faith movement seem convinced that if we just have enough faith and proclaim it loudly enough, every desire of our heart will be fulfilled. Some are convinced that sickness or even death has no power over us if we just have enough faith. Of course they cannot explain why eventually every one of us gets sick and I am quite certain every one of us will die unless the rapture occurs in our life-time. But hey, why quibble over details.

Rhonda Byrne wrote a best selling book called "The Secret"[14]. While some Christians read and actually embraced the book, once you study it thoroughly through the lens of scripture, it is clearly a promotion of New Age theology and beliefs. Byrne's message is when you send positive thoughts into the expanse of the universe, it reciprocates by sending positive things your way. So health, wealth and prosperity are the results of positive thoughts, or "good vibrations".

Byrne lists her success formula in three easy steps:

- First you must get clear about exactly what you want, and then you need to make a command to the universe.
- Second, you must believe that you have received. You must know that what you want is yours the moment you ask for it. You must have complete and utter faith.
- Third, to receive what you believe "You have to feel it!"

If life were only that simple and easy; and there is only one serious problem in Byrne's beliefs: They are completely contradictory to the Bible, even though Byrne has referred to herself as a "Christian". Well if it is so simple and consistent with Biblical teachings, why wasn't Paul, who had tremendous faith, rich and healthy? Why did he have to make tents to support his travels in spreading the gospel throughout Asia?

Rhonda Byrne is promoted and supported by Oprah Winfrey, and that should be a shock to no one. She is obviously a New Age proponent who believes "god" can be manipulated for our own personal gain. But just how closely are the teachings and beliefs of Rhonda Byrne lining up with some Christian Word of Faith leaders?

Kenneth Hagin

Kenneth Hagin, considered the "Father of the Word Faith Movement" seemed to tap in to this mystic teaching long before Byrne discovered it. In his book titled *"How to Write Your Own Ticket With God"*[15,] Hagin says that Jesus appeared to him personally and gave him the formula for faith. Hagin writes that Jesus told him:

> *"If anybody, anywhere will take these four steps or put these four principles into operation, he will always receive whatever he wants from Me or from God the Father. Say it. Do it. Receive it. Tell it so others may believe it."*

Whenever someone tells you they received a personal visit from Jesus, go see what the Word of God says:

> *"So if anyone tells you 'There he is in the desert', do not go out there or 'Here he is in the inner rooms', do not believe it. For as lightening that comes from the east is visible even in the west, so will be the coming of the Son of Man."*
> Matthew 24:26-27

When Jesus appears again, He will not just appear to Kenneth Hagin or Todd Bentley; everyone will witness his return in glory.

Another quote from Kenneth Hagin should cause you to question him and the movement he spawned: *"Man was created on terms of equality with God, and he could stand in God's presence without any consciousness of inferiority."*[16]

Scripture tells us over and over again that God is far superior to man. Do Hagin and those who follow him violate the first commandment by claiming man is not inferior to God? Is this not worshipping our selves as equal to God?

Hagin tells a bizarre story about a time when Jesus once again appeared to him and they were deep in conversation. Hagin claims that suddenly a "demon monkey" jumped between them and began to shout down Jesus yelling *"Yakety, yack, yack, yack!"* Hagin said he took control by telling the demon monkey to *"shut up in the name of Jesus!"* According to Hagin, Jesus told him *"If you hadn't done something about that, I couldn't have."*[16]

Are you kidding me? Jesus, who cast out demons while he walked the earth, was powerless to shut up a demon monkey, but Kenneth Hagin could with his words? Don't be too surprised because as we will see later, Kenneth Copeland, a Hagin disciple, also believes Jesus is not very powerful and needs our help to accomplish anything.

According to Hank Hanegraaff in his book *"Christianity in Crisis"*, Hagin claimed that one time while preaching, he was transported into the past, finding himself in the back seat of a car, watching a woman in his church committing adultery with the driver. Hagin says the experience lasted about fifteen minutes and suddenly he found himself back in church, leading his congregation in prayer. This alleged ability to travel between dimensions is common-place in "signs and wonders" theology, and is taught in New Age circles.

Hagin claimed to have died three times, only to be resurrected each time. In one of these occurrences he claimed to experience heat "from the fires of hell".[17]

Hagin also claimed that Jesus appeared to him in 1950, giving him a special anointing to heal the sick. He arrogantly proclaimed that God told him if pastors did not accept Hagin's teachings, many would drop dead right in their pulpits.[17]

Hagin wasn't the first Word of Faith teacher but he was arguably the most influential, spawning many disciples who are all over Christian television these days. We will touch on a few of them. There are several excellent books including Hank Hanegraaff's *"Christianity in Crisis"* that go into greater depth on this issue.

Hagin's *"The Word of Faith"* magazine reaches almost four-hundred-thousand homes, and his influence lives on through many other extreme Word of Faith teachers today.

One more point to consider on people like Kenneth Hagin and what they represent. Several times Hagin stated that his faith was so strong he never once experienced a headache. Yet he had to undergo five heart surgeries and finally died. Does anyone see any inconsistency here?

Kenneth Copeland

Ken and Gloria Copeland are on several Christian television networks including TBN and The Word Network. They are successful and quite wealthy, with reports stating their personal mansion is worth several millions of dollars and that they have a private fleet of jets to travel around the world. Are they building their wealth by their tremendous faith or on the backs of gullible followers?

> *"I was shocked when I found out who the biggest failure in the Bible actually is . . . the biggest one is God! . . . I mean he lost his top ranking, most anointed angel; the first man he ever created; the first woman he ever created; the whole earth and all the fullness therein; a third of the angels, at least. That's a big loss man . . . Now the reason you don't think of God as a failure is he never said he's a failure. And you're not a failure till you say you're one."*[18]

I can hear it now–"You're misunderstanding Copeland and taking him out of context!" Even if we were to concede that point, the arrogance, even in jest, of calling God a loser is disrespectful at best and disgusting and vile at worst. It gets worse; much worse.

Copeland taught that Adam in the Garden of Eden was God manifested in the flesh. This is exactly what the early Mormon Church taught, that "Adam is our Father and our God." Also, according to Copeland, Satan conquered Jesus on the cross and Jesus descended into hell after his death and before his resurrection as an *"emancipated, poured out, little wormy spirit"*[19] and wrestled the keys to heaven away from Satan. The Bible tells us Jesus' last words before his death on the cross were *"It is finished"*, meaning the sacrifice was complete. A rudimentary study of the original Greek words used in the New Testament along with reading and studying corresponding scriptures clearly dispel this false teaching. The Greek words *"sheol"* and *"hades"* refer to the resting place of the dead, not the permanent place of hell where Satan resides.

Just before Jesus died on the cross he said *"Father into your hands I commend my spirit."* (Luke 23:46) It was finished and the battle against Satan was won. But not according to Copeland. First Jesus had to go to hell as an *"emancipated, poured out, wormy little spirit"* to continue the battle against Satan. Is Copeland teaching a false gospel of salvation, denying the power of the cross?

Copeland also seems to be in tune with new age theology when he says *"Any image that you can get down on the inside of you that is so vivid when you close your eyes you see it, it'll come to pass."*

Copeland buys into the New Age teaching of "visualization", that teaches if you can envision something clearly in your mind, you can actually create it. He tells his followers they have the power to create an eighty-two foot yacht. First, they clearly are to see it in their mind; claim it through the scriptures; and speak it by faith. He says their words are mysteriously carried into the Holy of Holies, where it becomes real.

He teaches the same techniques to followers to abolish sickness in their lives. You envision your healing with enough faith, your vision enters the Holy of Holies, and presto--you leap out of your wheelchair![20]

His wife, Gloria, goes as far as to discredit the faith of the apostle Paul. In 2 Corinthians 12, Paul writes about the thorn in his flesh. Three times he asks God to remove it, but God refuses, saying *"My grace is sufficient"*. But Gloria Copeland demeans Paul, claiming he had the power to heal himself, but could not because of his lack of faith.[21]

Benny Hinn

> *"When you were born again the Word was made flesh in you. And you became flesh of his flesh and bone of his bone. You are everything he was and everything he is and everything he ever shall be."*[22]

Benny Hinn

There it is folks. You are not being transformed into the ***image*** of Jesus–you ***are*** Jesus. What more needs to be said about Benny Hinn? Sadly, much more.

Hinn has made outlandish statements which he claims were revealed to him when Jesus personally visited him: For one, women were originally designed to give birth out of their sides.

Hinn predicted that instead of people burying their dead relatives and friends, they would one day sit them in a chair as they watched TBN for 24 hours and they would be resurrected from the dead.[23] I'm sure Paul and Jan Crouch of TBN would love that as they promote the same foolish thoughts frequently on air.

Hinn told his followers that Jesus would personally appear at one of his events in 2000.[24] No Jesus.

Hinn has made several outrageous predictions he claims as prophecies he received from God. He "prophesied" that Cuba's dictator, Fidel Castro, would die in the 1990s. He claimed God told him He would destroy the homosexual community in America in the same decade. If a man claims to be a prophet of God, yet is continually wrong, are we not to doubt his words and teachings?

He also frequently visited the grave sites of mystics like Kathryn Kuhlman so he could "get the anointing from their bones."[25] Deuteronomy 18:11 explicitly forbids God's people from necromancy, calling forth the spirits of the dead and in verse 12 God states that *"Anyone who does these things is detestable to the Lord . . ."*

> *"I'm sick and tired of hearing about streets of gold. I don't need gold in heaven, I gotta have it now!"*[26]

Compare this quote from Hinn with Jesus' message about the folly of pursuing treasures on earth compared to heaven. Bennie Hinn is capitalizing on the growing sense of entitlement many Christians have these days.

In 1991, ABC News produced a documentary that exposed Hinn in a critical light, questioning many claims made of miraculous healings at his events. Hinn responded by threatening anyone who dared claim he was a false teacher:

> *"I'm pointing my finger with the mighty power of God on me. You hear this: there are men and women in Southern California attacking me. I will tell you under the anointing now; you'll reap it in your children unless you stop."*[27]

As with many questionable Christian leaders, Hinn evokes the "don't you dare speak against God's anointed" defense. This is nothing short of an attempt at intimidating anyone willing to question outrageous teachings. We must never succumb to these threats of intimidation because no leader should ever be above reproach.

Benny Hinn is so outrageous and ridiculous you wonder how anyone can take him seriously. But millions do, watching him on television, as he continues to line his pockets. P.T. Barnum was certainly right about a sucker being born every minute. But Hinn is not the only televangelist preaching the "name it, claim it" absurdity.

Another example of how these teachers of health, wealth and prosperity diminish God and elevate man: Jesse Duplantis--the lovable, jovial Ragin' Cajun. Duplantis must think God is really stupid. He teaches that when God created the animals He didn't know what they were, so he brought them to Adam. Adam then named them and spoke life into them.[28] I suppose after that Adam had to tell God what God was.

Many Word of Faith televangelists regularly broadcast their teachings on two Christian television networks--The WORD Network, and Trinity Broadcast Network (TBN). When I have watched the WORD Network, I rarely see anything except programs telling Christians how to acquire wealth through the power of the spoken word.

TBN does have some worthwhile programming, but it is also littered with extreme Word of Faith theology, appealing to the desires of the flesh. TBN has been rocked by several accusations and scandals over the past fifteen years, but it now appears the lid is about to be blown off this television ministry.

Lawsuits have been filed by Brittany Koper, the granddaughter of TBN founders Paul and Jan Crouch, claiming fifty millions dollars of listener contributions have been used for personal gain by TBN leadership[29]. Allegations of multiple massive mansions for the Crouch family, multiple private jets and extremely extravagant lifestyles are now in court.

If these allegations prove true, expect proposals for massive government oversight of non-profit organizations throughout the country. Oversight and accountability should always be welcomed by non-profit organizations that deal with integrity and are transparent. However, I am concerned that the growing hatred of God and His Word will cause many excellent ministries to undergo intense, costly scrutiny that will diminish their resources, forcing many to close their doors.

The extreme Word of Faith preachers are doing immense damage to many of their gullible followers, but if their irresponsible actions now force intense, over-reaching intrusion and oversight from the government, many fine ministries may be forced to end their work, driving American Christianity closer to the brink of death. Some of these leaders love to challenge anyone who questions their teachings or actions, insisting they are anointed by God, and that the accusers will be held accountable by God for their cynicism. Well, will God hold these teachers accountable if their greed causes many excellent Christian ministries to shut down because of the scrutiny these teachers are ushering in with their lavish lifestyles?

The list of participants in the Word of Faith movement include Creflo Dollar, Marilyn Hickey, T.D. Jakes, Paul Crouch of TBN, Joel Osteen, Rod Parsley, Frederick Price, and Mike Murdock. Parsley and Murdock are big into "prayer cloths", claiming that they have a special anointing they can pass on through them, available of course, for a generous gift to their organizations.

Many of these teachers do share some solid teachings from time to time, but they also share in the spreading of the prosperity gospel as our ticket to health, wealth and prosperity. A common belief among them is that all that is needed to acquire anything you want is enough faith. Arguably, the apostle Paul had more faith than any man who ever lived, and his faith in Jesus was not shaken no matter what circumstances he faced. Perhaps if Paul had access to the teachings of these televangelists he might have escaped a life of poverty and that "thorn in his side" would have been removed, even though God told him he would not remove it. To many Word of Faith teachers, our faith can even override the will and final decision of God.

This, plain and simple, is an insult to God when a teacher claims that our will and faith can create things and override God's perfect will for our lives. This is putting ourselves on equal footing with God, or even worse, elevating us over God. Well, so much for the First Commandment.

There is nothing wrong with asking God to provide us with physical health or financial blessings, but when these desires become an obsessive part of being a Christian, something is wrong. Jesus never once told us to pursue treasure on earth. In fact, He taught us it is futile. Instead He taught us to store up treasures in heaven where moths or thieves could not take them from us.

Most of these televangelists live in multi-million dollar homes, living a life of luxury. Many of them own several private jets and stay in luxurious hotels as they travel. They are accumulating tremendous wealth on the backs of deceived poor and middle-class Christians who want to tap into the power of the prosperity gospel. You may disagree, but I think this is nothing short of stealing.

Whether the "Signs and Wonders Movement" or the "Word of Faith Movement", we must recognize that many sincere Christians follow these men. They are genuine, loving people and born-again believers who will be joining us in heaven. They are not the problem; they are being deceived by teachers who are abusing scripture for personal gain.

It is one thing to over-exaggerate how our faith can manipulate God for our personal benefit, as if that isn't bad enough. But when these leaders claim personal visits from Jesus, and that Jesus had to go to hell to complete his victory over Satan, or that God cannot accomplish what He desires without our help, that is crossing the line. These claims clearly conflict with the Bible and define God as less than holy, perfect and all powerful. Many are falling into this trap, and if they do not wake up and see the deception at hand, they are in for a big fall, either in this life or for eternity.

Religious Syncretism

I realize every generation since the Book of Acts was written probably thought they would witness the return of Jesus. But when the Jews were returned to their land by God in 1948, the stage was set for the rapture and the return of our Lord. It could happen this year or two-hundred years from now, but it is a real possibility, perhaps a probability that some of us will be around for the end of the age.

The Bible warns us of the Antichrist rising to power in the end times, accompanied by the false prophet, but world domination cannot occur without religious capitulation. The false prophet will thus succeed in leading the final great deception, somehow bringing many or all faiths into harmony.

This seems implausible given the diverse beliefs of hundreds of religions, but it is not as difficult as one might think as the early seeds are already beginning to sprout. So who are the participants, whether willful or ignorant, in this "end of the age drama"?

The Bible speaks of a great falling away from the faith among Christians as the end of the age approaches. 2 Thessalonians warns of God sending a powerful delusion to those who do not trust in the absolute truth of God's Word and I believe we are experiencing that falling away and God's powerful delusion right now. When you look at the perversion of Christianity being taught by many of our influential teachers and leaders, and the number of pastors and Christians who are blindly following them, it seems obvious to me that many are under a great delusion.

The false prophet spoken of in Revelation will then unite world religions while antichrist starts to gather political, economic and military power. There is little doubt the United Nations will play a pivotal role as it has grown to where it has infiltrated every nation to some extent. Many of the social justice programs Christians fall for, including Rick Warren's P.E.A.C.E. Plan, work directly with the United Nations. The United Nations is an organization bent on world domination and intent on promoting secular humanism.

Many of the world's religions are comparatively small with little influence beyond their small group of members. Some larger religions like Mormonism are based on New Age and universalism principles already, so they will be easy prey. Buddhism and Hinduism are more philosophical than religious and also fit well into the growing New Age culture.

Only Christianity, Judaism and Islam stand as strong, influential monotheistic religions. Sadly, most Jews are more cultural Jews than religious, and even the religious ones deny Jesus as Messiah. They might well fall for a false god who shows miracles, signs and wonders, thinking he is their long-awaited messiah. So Islam and Christianity probably stand as the greatest obstacles to a world united on religion.

Allow me to speculate a little. Islam may be damaged severely by a nuclear war in the Middle East, perhaps the battle prophesied in Ezekiel

38. With Iran obtaining nuclear weapons and vowing to use them on Israel, war could break out in the Middle East any day. This war, which might include nuclear weapons, could decimate the nations that are strongholds for Islam. We know that while Israel will certainly suffer heavy losses in that war, God will ultimately protect a remnant. If this speculative scenario occurs, Islam will be largely neutralized as a major religion.

Regardless of whether Islam will be severely damaged or not, the movement of Chrislam is making serious inroads to bridging a gap between deceptive Muslim leaders and naive Christian leaders like Hybels, McLaren, Wallis and Warren. When watchmen like Chris Rosebrough, Warren Smith, Gary Kah and yours truly sound a warning about Chrislam, we are largely ignored or dismissed as hateful. So be it.

If Muslim leaders can continue to deceive naive Christian leaders, these two religions might come to look very similar in the eyes of deceived or careless Christians, especially as biblical illiteracy continues to become a greater epidemic.

A recent study showed that fifty-seven percent of Evangelical Christians now believe Jesus is not the only way to heaven. The great deception is well under way and it soon may swallow up almost all of American Christianity.

We can blame Islam, world leaders or anyone we want for this coming apostasy, but it is we Christians who will be held accountable by God when literally all hell breaks loose on earth. We have the Bible and the Holy Spirit to teach and guide us, but we are choosing to ignore them at an increasingly alarming rate.

The movement of Chrislam is leading naive Christians into religious syncretism with Islam, a religion of antichrist. The social justice movement led by people like Jim Wallis and Rick Warren preach the need for interfaith cooperation on issues of poverty and environmental issues. Evangelism takes a back seat to trying to solve the problems of human depravity by using human efforts and plans. Rarely if ever will you hear any of these leaders calling out another religion as false. Syncretism for the sake of human efforts of peace is replacing the sharing of the gospel to the lost.

The Emergent church movement is building bridges between Christianity and Islam, secular humanists, Hinduism, Buddhism and universalism religions. Nothing, including the Word of God, is sacred to these people.

The Catholic Church and the Pope are always the usual suspects when it comes to ecumenism and social justice secularism, and no doubt the Catholic Church will play a huge role in the global spiritualization movement. In recent years the Vatican has made several overtures and statements that show a proclivity to embrace Islam as a true religion that worships the God of Christianity. But every denomination of Christianity is starting to embrace this apostasy.

The Vatican will be a player. Rick Warren is a player. And the growing social justice and emergent church movements are also players. Are these the players in the final act or just part of the warm up before the big performance? Time will tell but I think we are rapidly running out of time.

The clock is ticking. The game is winding down. It is what athletes call "crunch time"; the time when the cream is supposed to rise to the top. We know who wins the war. We think we are on His side, but with wicked and deceitful human hearts are we fooling ourselves? Could we really be pawns of the enemy instead of warriors for God? This is a question worthy of prayer and internal assessment.

Footnotes

1) http://standupforthetruth.com/2011/12/signs-and-wonders-movement-exposed/
2) http://www.youtube.com/watch?v=FOPQ9Cxz5So
3) "Conversations With God", Neale Donald Walsch, 1996, Hampton Roads Publishing
4) Wikipedia.org
5) Freshfire.ca
6) www.crossroad.to/articles2/08/discernment/6-21-bentley-music-hypnotism.htm; http://livingpower.tumblr.com/post/99465058/angelic-hosts-part-1-by-todd-bentley

7) "Kingdom Rising: Make the Kingdom Real in Your Life", Todd Bentley. 2008, Destiny Image Publishing; christianresearchsefvice.com

8) http://www.crossroad.to/articles2/08/bentley.htm

9) http://www.youtube.com/watch?v=9zMRChoojZo

10) www.crossroad.to/articles2/08/discernment/6-21-bentley-music-hypnotism.htm

11) Fightingforthefaith.com,   http://www.youtube.com/watch?v=kSlt0_8HwMk

12) http://www.youtube.com/watch?v=pLv6C7b6m88&feature=youtube_gdata_player

13) https://www.freshfireusa.com/download-store/mp3-downloadssets/heavenly-courts-divine-council-by-todd-bentley.html

14) "The Secret", Rhonda Byrne. Simon & Schuster

15) "How to Write Your Own Ticket With God', Kenneth Hagin. 1997, Faith Library Productions

16) "Zoe: The God-kind of Life", Kenneth Hagin. 1981, ISBN#13978-1-60616-775-5

17) Kenneth Hagin "I Believe in Visions"

18) "Praise the Lord", TBN telethon, 1998

19) "Holy Bible: Kenneth Copeland Reference edition, 1991

20) "Inner Image of the Covenant", Kenneth Copeland Ministries. Audiotape #01-4406

21) Gloria Copeland, "Paul's Thorn in the Flesh", Believer's Voice of Victory, November, 1983

22) Benny Hinn, "Our Position in Christ". Orlando Christian Center, audiotape #A031190-2

23) Benny Hinn, "Praise the Lord", TBN, October 19, 1999

24) Benny Hinn, "This is Your Day", TBN, April 2, 2000

25) Bennie Hinn, "Double Portion Anointing", Orlando Christian Center. Audiotape #A031791-3, aired on TBN April 7, 1991

26) "Praise the Lord" broadcast, TBN, November, 1990

27) "Miracle Invasion Event", Anaheim Convention Center, November, 1991

28) http://www.youtube.com/watch?v=DDYyym5tD20

29) Businessweek.com--   http://www.businessweek.com/ap/2012-03/D9TLNK001.htm

CHAPTER TEN

REDEFINING GOD IN OUR OWN IMAGE

We discussed earlier that inept leadership, combined with followers who care more about what they want instead of the truth, are a toxic combination. They create a vicious cycle with self-centered followers breeding weak leadership, breeding more self-centered followers. Our growing love of money, comfort and individualized morality has led us to the edge of spiritual death.

In the preceding chapters, we took a hard look at some Christian leaders and explored their beliefs, methods and motives. I realize what we covered was tough, but a tough critique of Christian leadership is necessary in the midst of a growing apathy within American Christianity. If leaders are not willing to be open, transparent and accountable, they are unfit to lead. But we must also be open to a tough, honest critique of our own hearts as people who follow these leaders. These leaders seem to represent the values and character that we desire in our leaders. If not, we would not be following and elevating them.

The qualities we most want in our leadership these days seem to be cultural trendiness, charisma and a compromising spirit. These characteristics are what have led us into this mess. What is needed now is strong, principled leadership that is uncompromising on the Word of God. We will not witness this from our leaders until we who follow them truly desire it. If we do not we are every bit as much to blame for the slow death of American Christianity. As Christians who have received the Holy Spirit, we will not be able to blame leadership when we stand before a holy God one day and every thought, word and action will be judged.

Unless every Christian, leader and follower, allows God to reveal the deception in our hearts, it may be only a matter of time before God completely removes His hand of protection over the American church. Our hearts have grown cold to God's truth and unchanging nature as we slowly attempt to modify God to fit into our desired perception of Him.

The dangerous beliefs, selfish attitudes and spiritual apathy that have infiltrated our hearts and minds are slowly killing us spiritually. We look at the world and feel sorrow or disgust over their beliefs and behaviors, but ours seem to be only marginally better at times. The behavior of the world is not surprising since they have not received the Holy Spirit, but we have the Spirit of the Lord and have been charged with being light and salt to this world. We must once again become a people set-apart from secular culture, totally committed to God and His ways. We must stop worrying about being popular with secular culture and start acting like committed Christians once again.

Too many Christians attempt to mold God into our desired image of Him, instead of allowing the Holy Spirit to mold us into the image of Jesus. This is, simply put, idolatry—worshipping a false God. I submit that this is no better than the Muslim or Hindu who worships a false god; in fact it might be worse. We have the Word of God and the Holy Spirit in us and we should know better.

This abominable action is at the root of every problem we face as Christians, individually and as a body. We are continually violating the first and second commandments of God and as a result our own efforts to obey the remaining commandments are futile.

It's not that we are building and worshipping a physical golden calf like the Israelites did in Exodus, but in our minds and hearts we are doing something every bit as wrong and dangerous. We are picking and choosing the characteristics of God we like, and dismissing those parts of His stated character and nature that we want no part of. That simply will not suffice. We either acknowledge the complete character and nature of God, worshipping Him, or we worship a type of false god more to our liking.

Let's look at the subtle ways we attempt to recreate God more to our liking. As we explore, we need to be reflective, looking in the mirror. Every one of us is guilty of refashioning God to our desired image to some extent. You and I are part of the problem, not just "the rest of those Christians". As we discuss these topics, be in prayer, asking God to reveal what he sees in your heart, as David did:

> "Search me O God, and know my heart; test me and know
> my anxious thoughts. See if there is any offensive way in me, and
> lead me in the way of the everlasting.
>
> Psalm 139:23-24

"I Believe in Jesus"

We are taught as Christians that spiritual death is avoided when we believe in Jesus. I want to challenge that belief.

What we believe about Jesus and *who* we believe Him to be is the crucial issue, not just that we believe in a shallow, indiscriminate way. In the book of James the author challenges shallow believers. James states in 2:19: *"You believe that God is one; you do well. Even the demons believe--and shudder."*

James refers to God as "one", a tribute of faith to the mystery of a Triune God--Father, Son and Holy Spirit. One God manifested in Father, Son and Holy Spirit is a difficult concept for humans but we simply, by faith, choose to believe.

James says the demons also believe, so are they saved? No, because while they believe God exists they do not believe in Him as perfect love and justice, ruler of all created things. They do not accept His perfect nature and character as final authority over the entire universe and lord over their being.

Today too many Christians "believe" in a Jesus they do not understand, or they believe in a Jesus they are attempting to mold into their image and likeness. A "Buddy Jesus" who is their best friend, but not their Lord and King. A "Jesus" who would never judge or condemn anyone; a "Jesus" who accepts you just as you are--a filthy sinner deserving of eternal death--with no requirement to turn away from your sinful nature and desires. This is not Jesus. It is a poor human substitute and an act of arrogance. To think we can worship God as we think He should be in lieu of worshipping God for who He is, is the height of arrogance and rebellion.

This "false god" is the god of this world. He is a god who serves us and conforms to our desires, and a god whom we judge instead of Him judging us. We are worshipping the created instead of the Creator, an image of God we create out of convenience or greed because of our pride, self-righteousness and extreme hubris. Will this lead us to eternal death? Perhaps it will because God will not be mocked or minimized.

There is only one true God and our attempts to modify or change Him will not work. He is the same yesterday, today and tomorrow and no attempt to modify Him for our convenience will work. We will all fall short of knowing His perfect holiness until we stand before Him in his glory, but if we attempt to modify His character and nature or substitute our own beliefs to create a god we prefer to worship, are we risking our eternal fate?

God is a "God of Love"

There can be no doubt that God is perfect love. As Paul said in the famous "love chapter" of 1 Corinthians 13, love is patient, kind, not easily angered and keeps no record of wrongs. These are certainly some of the characteristics of the perfect God we worship. But are we forgetting that in addition to being perfect love that God is also perfectly just?

Human beings have difficulty accepting things we do not completely understand. We may say we accept certain concepts, but deep down we continue to struggle with them. Perfect love and perfect justice are a tough combination for us to understand.

God is perfect in every way and His perfect nature means He cannot tolerate sin. Scripture is very clear that unrepentant sin is an abomination to God and that people who choose a life of unrepentant sin will face the most severe of consequences--eternal separation from God. The fact that God is perfect love and perfectly just can cause confusion in the minds and hearts of people because as humans we cannot understand either concept.

Our love is flawed, imperfect, and often self-serving. We often perform acts of kindness for those we know or love out of hopes that somehow we may also benefit. And when we love someone we usually hope we will be loved reciprocally. This makes many of the ways we express love conditional, as we hope to receive something in return. If over time our love does not bring us rewards, our love usually fades or disappears all together.

Similarly, our idea of justice is often flawed, usually affected by our personal opinions and values. We have two issues within us that prevent us from understanding that God is perfect justice along with perfect love. The first is that as humans, we want to escape real justice so we are free to behave as we desire without consequences. Secondly, we do not understand the concept of perfect justice since we will always judge others harsher than we judge ourselves. So selfishness and ignorance combine to prevent us from understanding how God can be perfect justice.

You see an example of this when you attend a sporting event of a team you follow. The referee is in charge of making calls on fouls--handing out just penalties for infractions. Yet on almost every call made that is not clear cut, both sets of fans see the call differently. If a close call goes against our team, our human reaction is to think the official either missed the call or he has an agenda to cheat the team we follow. When a close call favors our team, the opponents' fans react in the same way. So fans generally act out from ignorance of the rules, or their view of justice is tainted by their own personal desires. As a High School official for twenty years, I have seen this scenario play out hundreds of times.

A growing number of Christians seem to believe God is not a just God. They may believe God is perfect love, but they erroneously believe that His perfect love precludes Him from being just. This is clearly refuted by the Bible, but because our view of justice is ignorant or perverted by our personal desires, too many cannot accept that God is perfectly just and that His justice demands that He judge evil.

This should cause us to ask a serious question: Would we want our eternal fate decided by a God who is not just? How could we have any eternal assurance if we were to be randomly judged by a god who is imperfect in how he dispenses reward or punishment?

God has clearly shown us how we can be assured of eternal life: Commit our life to Jesus Christ as our Savior **and Lord**. This and this alone overturns our guilt as sinners, allowing God to welcome us into His Kingdom as His children. But when we share a gospel with the lost that is void of God demanding justice, are we leading the lost astray? And if we worship a god we believe does not demand justice, are we worshipping YHWH or a false god of our own making?

God will not tolerate any man's attempts to change His perfect nature, and that nature consists of perfect love and perfect justice. You can't have one without the other.

Obeying God? Or Loving God?

True love fosters obedience, but obedience does not necessarily foster true love.

When I was a child, my father assigned my brother and me to clean the basement as one of our regular duties. At first we approached our assignment enthusiastically to show our love and dedication to him, along with showing him we could live up to his expectations. But no matter how meticulously we would clean, dad would always find some fault. We could never clean it to his standards, even though we spent hours cleaning instead of playing baseball or football.

So after a year of busting our humps and missing a lot of time with our friends, we decide to go into "obedience mode". We would spend just a few minutes working on the basement, doing a mediocre job, so we could spend more time playing. Hey, we figured dad wouldn't be satisfied either way, so we might as well have more play time. There were no significant rewards or punishments based on our performance.

What we failed to realize was that dad had our best interests in mind when he pointed out ways we could clean the basement better. He was trying to build a strong work ethic in us, preparing us for life as adults. Now he certainly could have handled it better, encouraging while he challenged us to become excellent workers, but he was well-intentioned.

It is important that we look into our hearts and check to see if our relationship with God is "obedience-based" or truly "love-based", and here is why: In our human nature, we are rebellious and we always seek to serve ourselves over anyone else. Obedience does not come naturally to fallen man and even when we do obey, it is usually self-motivated. We obey in hopes of being rewarded.

Obedience also becomes conditional at times. If we do not see a sufficient reward for our obedience, resentment builds up. If we obey our employer but begin to believe there is little chance for the reward we think we deserve--better pay, a promotion or recognition--we begin to rebel. We start giving less than our best effort because we see no incentive to work as hard as we did when we saw the possibility of greater reward.

This is what ultimately leads to the failure of every Communist nation. Workers are told where they will work and what the state will pay them. There is little or no chance for greater reward so workers become unproductive since they have nothing to gain from dedicated, obedient behavior. This is the attitude my brother and I developed with my father. We approached our relationship with our father from obedience, not love. As long as we did a decent job there would be no punishment, so why expend any more effort than necessary?

These are the results of "obedience-based" relationships. We do what we have to do to avoid negative consequences, but never fully commit to the job at hand.

Is this "obedience mode" infecting us as Christians? Our reward of heaven is secure by the blood of Jesus, so what further incentive is there for good behavior? Our works do not save us and neither does our strict obedience to the Law, so why obey? This is what living in "obedience mode" does to us. If we cannot see a reward for our obedience, or severe consequences for disobedience, we tend to discount its importance.

When we get beyond "obedience mode" and enter "love mode", everything changes. We no longer obey out of obligation or with selfish motives; rather we obey out of perfect love. Our love for God propels us to new heights of obedience because we have no selfish human motive. We obey because we truly and deeply love God and want above all to express that deep love. While I have by no means made the complete transition from obedience to love, I find that when I am in "love mode", obedience is much easier. I obey God because I deeply love him and do not want to disappoint him.

When Christian men, ordained by God as the leaders of our families, foster a culture of obedience instead of love in our homes, our wives and children act in similar manners. Their motivation is avoiding negative consequences, maybe even verbal or physical abuse. But husbands and fathers who lead from love, and foster a culture of love, usually receive love in return and find the obedience of our wives and children naturally occur out of that love.

As scripture tells us, perfect love (not perfect obedience) casts out all fear, freeing us from guilt, shame and our self-made prisons. Obedience can tend to be fear-based, keeping us trapped in a perpetual state of ups and downs. Obedience mode leads us to look at things selfishly, believing that if we obey we will be rewarded. But perfect love seeks no reward and gives of itself willingly and completely. When we enter into a state of perfect love of God, He frees us from the desires of our flesh.

As humans we are incapable of obeying one-hundred percent of the time. Our self-serving human nature will prevail at times, even in the best of us. God knows this. As our High Priest and the sacrifice for our sins, Jesus knew every temptation we could ever face yet He is perfect and we are flawed.

Paul eloquently expressed this in Romans 7, one of the most beautiful and telling writings in the Bible. Paul knew we are incapable of perfectly obeying God. That is why Jesus took human form and became the perfect, necessary sacrifice to fulfill the justice of a perfect God.

If our relationship with God is based on obedience instead of a burning, passionate love, it cannot work the way God wants it to work. Since we cannot perfectly obey God, we will continually fail Him. God knows this and sent Jesus so perfect obedience to the Law would no longer be the requirement for eternal life with Him. While God no longer requires perfect obedience, he asks for perfect love. He has removed the penalty of eternal death as a payment for disobedience. Since He has done this we no longer "have to" obey Him, but as His children we should want to.

While we are no longer under the penalty of a law we cannot live up to, nonetheless our perfect love of God should inspire us to obey His laws. Our love should propel us to a new level of obedience we were incapable of attaining when we worshipped God out of a mindset of obedience. In turn, worshipping God out of love rather than obligation will propel us to greater intimacy with Him and bring us to a higher level of living in His Spirit.

In order to find deeper intimacy with God, we must change the focus of our relationship from one of obedience to one of total love. Obedience does not perpetuate love, but love does perpetuate obedience. When we can change our approach to God from obedience-based to one of total love, everything changes. The human desire to sin becomes overwhelmed by our desire to avoid sin because we love God. We are no longer fear-based, obeying to avoid punishment or negative consequences. Our total love of God leads to a more perfect obedience of Him.

To Know Him Is To Love Him

Remember the first time you fell in love? Not just a youthful infatuation, but a deep burning love. You wanted to spend every waking moment with your new love, learn everything about him or her, hanging on every word they spoke.

Almost every one of us has experienced this euphoric state, and there is nothing quite like falling in love. The only thing better is staying in love, but too often that burning love fades and dies. Many a relationship that starts fast fizzles, as we begin to see that there is more to the person than we first realized.

We are exposed to the other side of that person, a darker side, starting with character traits that we didn't notice early on. Maybe we were just blinded by our early feelings, but often it is the result of the other person putting on a front, hiding characteristics and behaviors they thought would turn us off. We begin to see anger or selfish attitudes that we did not see early on, and these behaviors become annoying as our illusion of a perfect mate is destroyed.

Resentment starts to set in and perhaps we feel like we were victims of a "bait and switch." We feel we were deceived, thinking we were getting the perfect mate when in reality we got a flawed human, and our love fades with our lofty unmet expectations.

The best marriages are those where God is at the center of everything, but also where both parties really know each other, flaws and all, before they commit to marriage. When we are honest about our character, nature and behaviors before a commitment, the chances of a successful marriage increase dramatically. No one wants to feel they have been a victim of "bait and switch".

One of the reasons Nancy and I have such a strong marriage is we know and admit our own flaws and accept the flaws in each other. She knows I usually do not wipe off the cupboard or stove after I cook dinner. When I do she is pleasantly surprised but has no illusion that this will become habitual. Nancy is a packrat and throws nothing away. This used to irritate the snot out of me until I realized this was so trivial compared to the wonderful characteristics she displays every day as my wife and friend. We have learned to accept each other, flaws and all, and even find humor in them. We constantly joke that we are a perfect match because no one else would want either one of us.

We knew these things about one another going in to our marriage, so there was no "bait and switch" involved that would lead to disillusion or resentment. But is American Christianity offering a "bait and switch" presentation to the lost about the character and nature of the God we are trying to lead them to?

How did you first come to know God? How was He presented to you? Did you respond to a weak altar call where Jesus was presented as a friend or a solution to every problem you faced at the time, or was He presented as a fire-breathing God waiting to consume you the moment you stepped out of line?

Christians who are raised early on to have an unhealthy fear of God—a fear that He is just waiting to punish us every time we mess up--often lead lives where they never really learn to love God because they do not understand His perfect nature and character. They may never understand the depth of His love and His willingness to forgive when we repent of our sin. They remain in a perpetual state of defeat.

But Christians who responded to a Jesus presented as a ticket to earthly happiness with no responsibilities or trials, are being set up for disappointment as problems continue and sometimes mount after they become Christians. When they are led to believe that Jesus accepts them just the way they are with no expectation of transformation, they become frustrated as the Holy Spirit begins to confront and convict them of lingering sin. When they are led to a Jesus who is more like their butler than their Lord, they grow disappointed and bitter as their financial problems linger or other problems in their lives do not instantly vanish.

Both of these sets of believers often go through life without really knowing the God they claim to love, and that is such a tragedy. The "fire and brimstone" Christians never experience the perfect love and mercy of

God; the "feel good" Christians never experience the beauty of a God who draws you nearer to Him through suffering and by the convicting power of his Spirit. Is American Christianity participating in a tragic "bait and switch" trick on new Christians? We must present the complete character and nature of God to those who are seeking Him. They must understand just who they are worshipping and what they can expect. They can expect the God who loves us unconditionally in spite of our flaws; the God who is always willing to forgive when we ask forgiveness, and the God who will never forsake or abandon us.

But we must also present the God who insists on spiritual transformation and rebirth; the God who will not tolerate habitual sin in our lives and allows consequences for that sin; the God who is not a butler, but rather our Lord and King; and the God who loves us too much to allow us to continue to flirt with the enemy at the risk of eternal damnation.

This is the God we must fully disclose to seeking people. Any other God is a misrepresentation that will lead people to disillusionment and frustration, stunting or even threatening their growth as true disciples of Jesus Christ. They must understand that God demands real change, and gives us His Spirit to facilitate that change. Is this the God new seekers hear of these days? Or do they hear about a god who is more of an addition to their lives to "complete" their happiness?

God never lies, as it is impossible, given His perfect nature. When He calls us to faith in Jesus and life as His disciples, there is no "bait and switch" going on. He is totally honest about His nature, character and behavior, and His Word clearly spells it out. But do we take the time to really know Him before we say "I do"? Or are we like love-starved teens seeing just what we want to see, setting ourselves up for disappointment, and ultimately adultery, toward Him?

When we only divulge part of God's nature to new Christians, we are setting them up for failure in their walk with Him. Many become disillusioned as promises of earthly happiness or wealth go unfulfilled. "Buyer's remorse" settles in and they either leave the church or never seek God deeper because they feel betrayed.

Our view of God as a church is really confused these days. We fail to know, understand or accept several aspects of His nature and character, picking and choosing which of His characteristics to accept, and which to disregard. The result is one day we will be disappointed, either in this life or eternity. We do not truly know God these days--we "know" a god of our own choosing, molded to fit our selfish agenda, and this is killing us as a church.

God Is "Tolerant". Really?

We have come to believe that God tolerates sin. Nothing could be further from the truth--He hates sin. God cannot stand to be in the presence of sin because it is adultery against Him, as His bride is once again unfaithful, having an affair with the world.

> *"There are six things the Lord hates, seven that are detestable to Him: haughty eyes, a lying tongue, hands that shed innocent blood, a heart that devises wicked schemes, feet that are quick to rush into evil, a false witness who pours out lies and a man who stirs up dissension among his brothers.*
>
> Proverbs 6:16-19

The blood of the new covenant does not change this proclamation from God. We find forgiveness and restoration by the sacrifice of Jesus, but God still detests these sins.

When we sin, we are cheating on God with his nemesis, Satan, rejecting God's love and faithfulness for our short term pleasure. But that is not how American Christianity as a whole portrays it. We are taught we are free from the law and can live as we choose to live, so why worry?

What did Jesus free us from on the cross? Freedom from God's Law? Freedom from responsibility? Freedom to do as we choose? No, He died to free us from the power of sin in our lives. Satan no longer has power over us and our sins are totally voluntary, but we choose to commit them even though we should know better. The acceptance of sin has become the trademark of American Christianity. We don't talk or preach about sin anymore because it's become all about our happiness and having our "best life now". We do not confront one another with blatant, unrepentant sin because we fear we will also be held accountable for our sins.

The Apostle Paul gave the church the model of how to react to unrepentant sinners. It is a chilling teaching that cuts to the heart about how destructive sin is to the Body of Christ.

> *"It has been reported that there is sexual immorality among you, and of a kind that does not occur even among pagans: A man has his father's wife. And you are proud! Shouldn't you rather have been filled with grief and have put out of your fellowship the man who did this? Even though I am not physically present, I am with you in spirit. And I have already passed judgment on the one who did this, just as if I were present. When you are assembled in the name of our Lord Jesus Christ and I am with you in spirit, and the power of our Lord Jesus Christ is present, hand this man over to Satan, so that the sinful nature may be destroyed and his spirit saved on the day of the Lord"*
>
> 1 Corinthians 5:1-5

I always wondered why I had never once heard these scriptures taught in church, or even discussed by a single pastor I know. Slowly read and pray over these verses, as they are problematic for American Christianity on several fronts.

First, note that Paul chastises the church for accepting this sinner, even boasting about their tolerance of him. Unrepentant sin is widely tolerated in many churches these days.

Second, note that Paul **judged this man**. We have been told over and over again that we are not to judge others, but this is nothing more than laziness or corrupt theology. God alone is qualified to judge the eternal destiny of men, but we are clearly to judge sinners within the Body of Christ. We will discuss in what and *how* we are to judge others a little later.

The third potential problem, or at least something that should lead us to search the scriptures more carefully, is when Paul instructs the church to throw this man into the hands of Satan so his sinful nature might be destroyed and his *"spirit saved on the day of the Lord"*. Does this potentially conflict with our strong certainty that a man can never lose his salvation? I think it certainly warrants a closer look at this subject in the scriptures.

One thing this scripture confirms to me is this: God is patient, but not tolerant of sin, and His patience might well be wearing thin with American Christianity. Sin has consequences—God loves us too much to allow sin to grow in our lives, separating us from Him.

"God Doesn't Judge Us." Says Who?

This heresy is spreading through the church compliments of leaders like McLaren, Bell, Wallis and others. The arrogance of claiming that God accepts all men to eternity without condition is nothing short of a slap in the face to God. It attempts to minimize, even disqualify, the painful sacrifice and death of the Son of God on a cross nearly two thousand years ago.

This false teaching is arrogant and nothing short of calling God a liar. The Old and New Testament speak clearly of the death of Jesus as the only acceptable atonement for man to become righteous with God, and that this righteousness requires real faith in Jesus Christ as the Son of God. This is the essential cornerstone of Christianity. Scripture also teaches that God will judge all men when they stand before him.

God has judged in the past and He will judge every man in the future when the Lord returns to reclaim His faithful people and usher in an eternity of true love and peace. How anyone claiming to be a Christian can read Matthew 25 or Revelation and come to a conclusion that God does not judge is totally beyond me. It can only be the result of biblical illiteracy or extreme arrogance.

Did He not judge Sodom and Gomorrah? What about Jericho? And as stated clearly in the New Testament, He will judge again. I have seen tricky attempts by McLaren, Bell and others to confuse young Christians by misleading or lying about "errors in translation". But if you take any amount of time with a Hebrew and Greek dictionary and study scripture, you see their arguments are flawed and deceitful.

The growing lie that God does not judge might spring from several potential motives:

- A desire to justify our own sin
- A sincere, but destructive desire to appeal gently to the lost since the true gospel is a "tough sell"
- A blatant agenda to deceive Christians

None of these reasons or excuses will hold water when we stand in judgment before a perfect, holy God. Jesus taught that no one comes to the Father except through Him, and that we cannot know the Father unless you know Jesus. And He said this in Matthew 7:21-23:

> *"Not everyone who says to me 'Lord, Lord' will enter the kingdom of heaven, but only he who does the will of my Father who is in heaven. Many will say to me that day 'Lord, Lord did we not prophesy in your name and in your name drive out demons and perform many miracles? Then I will tell them plainly 'I never knew you. Away from me you evil doers!"*

The Bible is full of scriptures telling us God is a God who will judge us.

> *"In the presence of God and of Christ Jesus, who will judge the living and the dead . . ."*
> 2 Timothy 4:1

> *"But they will have to give account to him who is ready to judge the living and the dead."*
> 1 Peter 4:5

"Marriage should be honored by all, and the marriage bed kept pure, for God will judge the adulterer and all the sexually immoral."

Hebrews 13:4

In Revelation 11:18 we are told that God will destroy those who destroy the earth:

"The nations were angry; and your wrath has come. The time has come for judging the dead, and for rewarding your servants the prophets and your saints and those who reverence your name, both small and great— and for destroying those who destroy the earth."

In Hebrews 9:27 we are reminded that we only get one life (no reincarnation) and after that we face judgment:

"Just as man is destined to die once, and after that to face judgment"

For our Red Letter Christian friends, what about Jesus? When did He ever say He would judge anyone?

"If your right eye causes you to sin, gouge it out and throw it away. It is better for you to lose one part of your body than for your whole body to be thrown into hell."

Matthew 5:29

"You snakes! You brood of vipers! How will you escape being condemned to hell?"

Matthew 23:33

"But I will show you whom you should fear: Fear Him who, after the killing of the body, has power to throw you into hell. Yes, I tell you, fear Him."

Luke 12:5

The Bible consistently tells us that a judgment is coming. In John 3:36 it says this:

> *"Whoever believes in the Son has eternal life, but whoever rejects the Son will not see life, for God's wrath remains on him."*

This dismissal of the clear teaching that God will judge all men one day is watering down Christianity to where it looks more like Unitarianism than Christianity. It is a clear distortion of the nature and character of God and serves to place us as our own judges of what is right or wrong. In essence we become our own god.

Brothers and sisters, we can *know of* God, but still not *know* God. Satan and the demons know of God but do not know Him as the final authority of all creation. American Christianity claims to know God, but is increasingly denying His clearly-stated nature, character and attributes. We can know of God, but if we try to redefine Him to fit our desires do we really *know* Him? When we attempt to modify God to fit our wishes, how can we claim to know a God who says He never changes; that He is the same yesterday, today and tomorrow?

To know Him is to love Him. To attempt to change Him is to deny Him. We either love all of God, or we choose to hate Him. Which will we choose to do?

The Scourge of Biblical Illiteracy

In my previous career I was responsible for hiring dozens of people, and when our team was looking for new employees we would often receive hundreds of resumes. On one Friday afternoon a couple of us were winding down the work week and we indulged in some humor at the expense of others. We grabbed a handful of resumes from college graduates and marveled at the poor grammar, misspellings and overall effects of what college education seemed to have taught the younger generation.

One I recall vividly. A young man, a recent college graduate, sent in his resume and under "Professional Goal" he wrote this:

*"Seeking a proffessional organation where I can use my skills
and education to advance within a dynamic company."*

Obviously this young man either didn't know of or turned off the "spell check" feature on his computer.

Our public schools, in spite of incredible federal spending, have failed America. While I meet some young people who are still bright and can actually articulate a sentence without a string of "ahs" and "likes", many are almost illiterate if too many words have multiple syllables. They seem to lack basic reading and communication skills far too many times. This renders them functionally illiterate, and for the effect it has on everything from business to elections, it is killing this country.

It seems to be no better in the church as biblical illiteracy is killing American Christianity. As noted earlier, George Barna Research[1] found only one in three self-professed born-again Christians believe the bible is absolute truth. This biblical illiteracy has led to an appalling lack of knowledge on many core teachings and beliefs of Christianity. And even if we know the core teachings we are increasingly unable to articulate them to a world that desperately needs to know the truth of the bible.

Rob Bell, as we discovered earlier, was the latest in a line of Christian leaders who could not answer a simple question of why there is suffering and death in the world. When we cannot explain the basic beliefs of our faith, the world laughs at us and rejects the message they desperately need.

When we can not authoritatively articulate the very basics of our faith, just what does that say of our real love of God? If we do not take the time to really know Him and His story, I think it says that God is but a means to an end for us. He is our ticket to heaven, our "Get out of Jail Free" card, and our "911 god" when we find ourselves in trouble once again. Just how pathetic is it when we have a chance to explain why there is evil and death in the world, along with God's solution, and we cannot articulate it? But time after time Christian leaders drop the ball when given the opportunity to be God's instrument to release the scales from the eyes of the spiritually blind. What a sorry lot we have become.

"The Christian body in America is immersed in a crisis of biblical illiteracy," warns researcher George Barna. *"How else can you describe matters when most churchgoing adults reject the accuracy of the Bible, reject the existence of Satan, claim that Jesus sinned, see no need to evangelize, believe that good works are one of the keys to persuading God to forgive their sins, and describe their commitment to Christianity as moderate or even less firm?"*

Other disturbing findings by Barna document an overall lack of knowledge among churchgoing Christians include the following:

- The most widely known Bible verse among adult and teen believers is "God helps those who help themselves", which is not in the Bible and actually conflicts with the basic message of Scripture.
- Less than one out of every ten believers possesses a biblical worldview as the basis for his or her decision-making or behavior.
- When given thirteen basic teachings from the Bible, only one percent of adult believers firmly embraced all thirteen as being biblical perspectives.

Author David Wells puts the problem bluntly in his book "No Place for Truth":[2]

> *"I have watched with growing disbelief as the evangelical church has cheerfully plunged into astounding theological illiteracy."*

A major reason for biblical illiteracy and shallow theology today is the tremendous influence that unbiblical philosophies and worldviews are having on American Christianity. Liberal theology has questioned the authority of scripture, assigning its teachings more to man than to God. Truth has become subjective, leading to abuse in biblical translation and interpretation.

Human emotions and feelings cause people to look internally for spirituality and truth, instead of looking up to God through Scripture.

The Postmodern culture we live in has convinced Christians to abandon the belief in absolute truth, leading an alarming number of Christians to seek "truth" in religious syncretism, picking and choosing beliefs from numerous religions to cobble together a "truth" that matches their desires and personal agenda. One needs to look no further than the Emergent Church movement to see this in action. Since traditional Christianity seems unwilling or unable to respond to the increase of this "cobblestone religion", we are losing many younger Christians to a dangerous form of Christian Universalism that abandons the truth of the bible for a religion of convenience and selfishness.

In 2 Timothy 3:16, the apostle Paul writes:

> *"All scripture is God-breathed and is useful for teaching, rebuking, correcting and training in righteousness, so that the man of God may be thoroughly equipped for every good work."*

Only one in three born-again believers now believes that to be true. This puts bible-believing Christians in the extreme minority when compared to millions who refer to themselves as "Christians" in our nation. Experts fear the percentage will continue to decrease with each passing year, bringing American Christianity closer still to death.

I feel so sorry for people who do not think the Bible is absolute truth. Sure, you can survive without that anchor of truth when things are going well, but what happens when the world around us, to which we have become accustomed, starts to unravel? Where does one turn if not to the Bible when our nice little world starts to fall apart?

Once we are comfortable abandoning the Bible as the anchor of truth in our lives, it is a quick journey to sin and even apostasy. When we are the judges of our own morality we are headed off the spiritual cliff at breakneck speed. It leads to many of the ills we now see regularly in American Christianity.

Matthew 7:1 Christianity

"Do not judge lest you be judged". This is a powerful message from Jesus, but its meaning has been twisted and has in essence served to nullify the remainder of the New Testament in the minds of illiterate, misled Christians.

Matthew 7:1 Christianity has become the newest denomination of Christianity. It is a fast growing cult, no less dangerous than Mormonism, Jehovah's Witnesses or Chrislam.

Don't worry about the rest of what the Bible teaches, even the remainder of that very chapter where Jesus goes on to tell us how to judge the fruits of another; or that He tells us the path to salvation is narrow but the road to destruction wide. That's just too harsh for most Christians. In reality, Jesus is teaching about the dangers of hypocrisy. We are not to condemn a brother for a sin we are also guilty of committing.

Churches are filled with Matthew 7:1 Christians claiming their love and compassion for others, but the truth is they only hope to deflect attention from their own sin. They hope that if they do not have to hold a fellow Christian accountable for his life, no one will be looking to hold them accountable for their lives.

Matthew 7:1 Christians are cowards. Relationships and love involve risk. We risk that the one we love may not feel the same way about us. We risk our hearts, our reputations, and we risk losing a friend when we have to confront their destructive behaviors. And Matthew 7:1 Christians are afraid of risk. They would rather live and let live. And God forbid you should ever confront them on their sinful behavior! If you have the courage and love to do so, you will be made to feel like an unloving, ungrateful friend. "Hey, I am tolerant and understanding of you and you repay me by judging me? You're nothing but a legalistic Pharisee!"

Matthew 7:1 Christians are also enablers. They are no better than a friend who encourages an alcoholic to go out drinking or a friend who justifies his friend's physical abuse of his spouse. When a man is involved in a pattern of destructive behavior that will jeopardize his life, a real friend intervenes any way possible. He simply will not allow his friend to continue to behave in a way that could lead to his demise, doing whatever it takes for as long as it takes to straighten his friend out.

Might some Matthew 7:1 Christians one day be found guilty of manslaughter? Manslaughter can be defined as contributing directly or indirectly to the death of another by one's actions or inaction. If I supply the illegal drugs that my friend dies from through an overdose, I could be charged with and found guilty of manslaughter.

Some states now have what are called "Good Samaritan Laws" named after the story Jesus told in the Bible. Some of these laws permit charges to be brought if a person refuses to help someone in danger and it leads to serious injury or death. Can an argument be made that Matthew 7:1 Christians could be found guilty of spiritual manslaughter when they stand before God?

Matthew 7:1 Christians consider themselves loving people, but I would argue many are more hateful and selfish than they are loving. If we see a friend on a ledge ready to jump into a spiritual abyss and do not try to talk him off the ledge, is that loving or hateful? It may be the most hateful thing we can do to refuse to confront another with his sins. Just like God warned Ezekiel in his role as a watchman, if you do not warn the people and they die, their blood is on the watchman's hands.

Matthew 7:1 Christianity is spreading like wild fire, infiltrating every denomination of American Christianity. This new movement comes across as loving and caring, but it is actually lazy, self-centered and cowardly.

Seeker-Friendly Christianity--Loving or Ashamed of the Gospel?

> *"I am not ashamed of the gospel, because it is the power of God for the salvation of everyone who believes; first for the Jew, then for the gentile."*
>
> Romans 1:16

The gospel is the power of God for salvation--not our fancy words, our marketing prowess or our ability to relate to others. But American

Christianity doesn't seem to think the gospel is sufficient any more. We seem to think the gospel is losing power and needs an infusion of postmodern relativity to bring it back to life. We believe that God can't reach the lost on his own any more and needs our help. What arrogance and foolishness!

The truth is all we can do is diminish the power of the gospel when we try to add our earthly wisdom to it. Every time we open our mouths or act on our own strength we add nothing, but risk diminishing the power of the gospel, as we confuse its message.

In the early church it was the power of the Holy Spirit that added to the numbers of the body, not the wisdom of man or cute marketing strategies. Paul witnessed the power of God on the road to Damascus and realized the folly of human efforts to apply the Word of God by human efforts in a way we think is correct. As Proverbs 14:12 teaches *"There is a way that seems right to a man, but in the end it leads to death."*

Paul's letter to the Galatians gives us insight to one of the first recorded attempts at trying to be "relevant" instead of standing on the power of the gospel alone.

> *"When Peter came to Antioch, I opposed him to his face, because he was clearly in the wrong. Before certain men came from James, he used to eat with the Gentiles. But when they arrived, he began to draw back and separate himself from the Gentiles because he was afraid of those who belonged to the circumcision group. The other Jews joined him in this hypocrisy, so that by their hypocrisy even Barnabas was led astray. When I saw that they were not acting in line with the truth of the gospel, I said to Peter in front of them all 'You are a Jew, yet you live like a Gentile and not like a Jew'".*
>
> Galatians 2:11-14

Peter was guilty of hypocrisy by acting differently in front of Jews and Gentiles, depending on who he was with at the time. He was trying to be "culturally relevant" to the Gentiles, yet reverted to his legalistic behaviors when he was with the Jews, causing confusion for the Galatians. This also confused Barnabas, leading him to join in Peter's hypocrisy. Peter, the man who told Jesus he would follow Him to the cross only to later deny he even knew Him, was at it again, giving in to pressure to be seen as loving and relevant to the Gentiles and righteous to the Jews. This confusion was destructive then, and it is equally destructive now, as we try to bounce between Christian teachings and being relevant to the secular culture. The gospel, not our words, has the power to change lives.

Paul was not interested in being relevant to the cultural norms. He spoke out boldly against them, standing firmly on the truth of the gospel. Greeks and Romans in those days openly embraced homosexuality as acceptable behavior, yet Paul warned them they would need to stop it or not inherit the kingdom of God.

When the Galatians started to stray from the purity of the gospel, Paul got right in their faces, calling them foolish. Paul would never make it in the church today as he would be branded as uncaring, unloving, even a hater.

Are we ashamed of the simple truth of the gospel and believe it is powerless, needing our wisdom and marketing plans to succeed?

A few years back a couple of Christian friends asked me to help with an attempt to reach the un-churched. They put together a survey they wanted to mail to families who did not attend church, seeking to understand why these families were not attending. These are solid men of God, one a pastor and the other very active in the Lord's work in the Green Bay area.

As I sat with them reviewing the survey, I saw a pattern of questions to determine why the recipients were turned-off by religion. We would be asking these people to be honest about what bothered them about the church, hoping to get insight as to why they disliked the church experience. I asked a simple question: "So after we gather this information, what do we do about it?" My concern was that it might lead us down the dangerous road of compromising with the desires of the culture at the expense of the gospel. What if respondents said they were turned off by teachings on sin? Would we change the message to be more accepting of sin?

I cannot overstate the importance of the church and Christians taking this to heart: When we seek compromise with the culture, we lose! Nothing good can come from this unholy matrimony. When two diametrically opposed institutions like biblical Christianity and secular culture try to find common ground, all that can be accomplished is the watering down of the gospel because of our human nature.

Look again at Galatians 2:11-14, Peter's attempt to bridge the gap between Jews and Gentiles. The only things that were accomplished were the Galatians were confused and Barnabas was led astray into Peter's hypocrisy.

Seeker-friendly Christianity as defined these days is a joke---a very dangerous joke. Secular culture and its humanist beliefs are totally incompatible with Biblical Christianity. They are the two Sumo wrestlers we discussed earlier, intent on knocking each other out of the battle circle. The problem is the secular Sumo knows that's its purpose, but the Christian Sumo seems to believe dialogue will attain a mutually satisfactory compromise. The Christian combatant believes if we just talk and seek common ground, we can learn to coexist.

The Seeker-Friendly disease has grown worse and worse. Progressive Christians refuse to acknowledge that abortion is murder and homosexuality is a sin because those words are just too harsh and condemning, and preaching on the depravity of man is just so belligerent and turns sinners off. Americans just want to feel better about ourselves, and want assurance that we are a good people and that God loves us just the way we are. Well God does love us, but He does not want us to stay just the way we are. He wants us to be transformed from our sinful nature to live a life of holiness and righteousness.

Jesus accepts us as sinners, but He demands a real change in us by the power of the Holy Spirit. If there is no transformation in our lives, how dare we claim to be Christians? This is an insult to a holy God, rejecting His power to transform us into the image of Jesus and rejecting His lordship over our lives.

The pure gospel is the *real* seeker-friendly message. A message of real hope in that man can be made righteous before God by the power of the sacrifice of Jesus; that all a man must do is repent and turn away from his sinful nature, ask forgiveness and accept that Jesus is the Son of God, his Lord and Savior. Friends it doesn't get any more seeker-friendly than that!

But that's just not simple enough these days. Admitting we are sinners is just too much pride to swallow, and asking forgiveness is impossible unless you first admit you are a sinner. Oh, we want this Jesus to rescue us, but at what price? By admitting we are filthy, worthless sinners? Well that's just too high a price to pay for a growing number of prideful men and too harsh a message for the church to deliver to the lost.

Not to worry, it's "Seeker-Friendly Christianity" to the rescue! Don't want to face your own human depravity? No problem, Jesus accepts you just as you are. Just ask Jesus into your heart and you are good to go. He is a loving, non-intrusive God who doesn't mind sharing space in your heart with evil and sin. He's just happy you've made Him a part of your life. You get all this for just saying a simple, non-binding sinner's prayer.

And in a tribute to every other irritating infomercial out there, "But wait, there's more! Invite Jesus into your heart in the next fifteen minutes and we'll include this permanent 'Get out of Jail Free Card' with your prayer. This card comes in handy when the Holy Spirit gets a little irritating, convicting you of sin in your life. So when the Spirit of the Lord beckons you to turn your back on sin just sin anyway and flash your 'Get out of Jail Free Card'--it's that simple.

So you get the instant, non-intrusive Jesus and the magical 'Get out of Jail Free' card all for one simple sinner's prayer! But act now and we'll throw in a set of non-judgmental, accepting Christian friends to make sure guilt or shame never become a factor in your life. A great addition to the spiritually dead life you've chosen."

If you don't think this is commonplace in American Christianity these days, wake up and smell the coffee. We are pandering to lost people by not confronting them on their sins, and if we do summon the courage to risk our friendship with them to share the gospel, it is a humanistic gospel that we are sharing; one that leads nowhere good at all.

God detests sin and we better start to recognize that fact. If we do sin and repent, He is faithful to forgive, but this requires us to acknowledge we are sinners in the first place. But, as Joel Osteen says, "sinner" is just too harsh a word today, and American Christianity is too weak, uncaring, and cowardly to speak the truth of the gospel these days.

Truth be told, which is not done enough these days, there is another reason we don't confront people and their sins these days---a selfish reason that hits too close to home. If we dare confront people and their sins, we open ourselves up to scrutiny about the sin in our lives, and few of us want to go there.

Have you ever wondered why pornography is rarely, if ever, addressed from the pulpit, and why so few churches offer any small group discipleship and accountability systems for men struggling with it? And even if they do, will you find a pastor involved in the accountability system? A recent survey found that more than half of pastors view pornography regularly.[3] Perhaps discussing the stronghold pornography has on Christian men hits a little too close to home.

One of the Bible verses eliminated by the Matthew 7:1 Christian cult is in the very same chapter of Matthew:

> *"Why do you look at the speck in your brother's eye and pay no attention to the plank in your own eye? How can you say to your brother 'Let me take the speck out of your eye' when all the time there is a plank in your own eye? You hypocrite, first take the plank out of your own eye, and then you will see clearly to remove the speck from your brother's eye."*
>
> Matthew 7:3-5

We have no authority to speak to the sin in another's life if we also struggle with it, unless we are willing to admit to and repent of our own sin. If we do confess our sin we can be in position to be mutually accountable to one another, helping each other out of our sin by the power of the Holy Spirit.

Until our pastors and elders are willing to admit to and confess their own sin, they lack the moral or spiritual authority to shepherd the flock. Until we as followers also admit to our own sin, we are powerless to help our brother out of his sinful state.

We must take equal responsibility for this sad state of affairs. How many pastors feel comfortable coming to their elders or congregation and confessing their sins without the worry that they will be fired? And who are we as followers to condemn a man for the same sin we struggle with? Matthew 7:3-5 works both ways folks!

We are in a deep mess that we cannot get out of on our own. Only God can rescue American Christianity before we kill ourselves. The solution is simple, but not easy. Simple in that all it requires is true repentance and a commitment to worship the one true God we see in the Bible, instead of the selfish piecemeal god we have manufactured in our minds and deceitful hearts. Not easy from the view that this will require real humility and spiritual brokenness, and this is something we have not shown a proclivity for over the past couple decades.

In athletic competition it often comes down to desire--who wants victory more? Well pardon my pessimism, but it sure seems the enemy wants spiritual chaos much more than we want spiritual purity and clarity these days. I hope I'm proven wrong.

"I'm a Christian"

There was a time when words actually had clear and precise meanings. When a man or woman said "I'm a Christian", we knew what they meant.

They believed in God, and that Jesus Christ is God's only begotten Son. They believed that Jesus took human form and died on the cross for our sins. They believed that if we put our faith in Jesus and lived as He taught us, that one day we would live for eternity in the presence of God.

They believed that hell was a real place, reserved for those who rejected Jesus.

They also believed that the Bible was one-hundred percent inspired by God and was His written Word and absolute truth. Finally, they believed we were called to lead a life of holiness, abandoning our sinful nature for a new and better spiritual life.

Every day I get to meet new people in my role as General Manager at Q90 FM. In the past when they would identify themselves as a Christian, no further questions were needed. These days, I am forced to poke and prod a little deeper when someone calls themselves a Christian.

"Exactly what does that mean—you're a Christian?"

That question alone is often met with a blank look as many people struggle to explain why they identify themselves as Christians.

"Well, I believe in God". I point out what it says in James—that so do the demons and they shudder in fear.

"I believe in Jesus." Which Jesus? A great teacher, a great man, or the only Son of God? Is Jesus Lord and Savior, or just Savior?

Assuming they survive these initial questions, I hit them with the big one: *"What happens when Jesus returns at the end of the age?"*

It is amazing how many Christians have not taken the time to see what God tells us about the final days of this world. Both the Old and New Testament are packed with biblical prophecy that has been proven to be one-hundred percent accurate every time. Many of these prophesies have been fulfilled, but some await us. The Book of Revelation spells out the final years of this life, yet so many Christians ignore it or get confused, choosing to just set it aside. God is laying out His final battle plan, where He comes to rescue His children from a life of sin and death.

It is also amazing how many progressive Christians choose to read something into Revelation that just isn't there. Many believe that man will rescue the earth and that when we conquer evil and bring forth "justice", then Jesus will return and assume control of a world we have conquered for Him. People on both sides of the theological divide—conservative and progressive dominionists—actually believe we can change the outcome of biblical prophecy, in spite of its one-hundred percent accuracy over the past several thousand years.

Saying "I'm a Christian" used to be self-explanatory. We knew what was meant and took it at face value. We can no longer afford to do this, as we have lost our cohesive identity as Christians and must return to the basics. Bear with me through one more football analogy:

In the sixties the Green Bay Packers were a dynasty. Winning championships was expected and losing a game was just plain unacceptable to their coach, Vince Lombardi. After a loss where the team was fundamentally beaten at every turn by the opponent, Lombardi called the players together the next day and announced "Gentlemen we stunk yesterday. We didn't block, tackle, catch the ball or do anything well. We're going to return to the basics today." He held up a football, "Gentlemen, this is a football."

Max McGee, the class clown on the team quipped "Slow down coach, you're going too fast". This is a funny story but one that probably rings true when we look at American Christianity these days. Our leaders go on television and are thrown softballs like "Why doesn't God stop evil" or "Why do bad things happen to good people?" They are given an opportunity to share the story of creation, man's fall and his salvation available through Jesus Christ, and they stumble and fumble through an answer one might expect from a ten-year old, but not a leader of the church.

I was at Power of One, a Christian music event in 2011, meeting youth and parents. Six nice young ladies around the age of thirteen came to our booth and starting rattling off the names of their favorite Christian bands and telling us how much they enjoyed the music Q90 FM played. I felt an urging of the Holy Spirit to ask them a very unusual set of questions.

"Are you girls Christians?" They all said yes. *"Do you attend church?"* They all attended the same church every Sunday and were participants in the youth ministry.

"Do you read the bible regularly?" They all answered in the affirmative.

"One more question: What was Jesus' last name?" One said she didn't know; four answered "Christ'; one said she didn't think they had last names in those days--they were identified by their father and ancestors. So only one in six knew the correct answer, and these were young ladies who attend church and participate in their youth group.

Now before we blurt out "kids these days", how many adult Christians would know the answer to that question? And even if they did, are we taking the time to teach our children about Jesus and our faith? Are we equipping them for a Christian life in a world more hostile to God every day? Are we teaching them the foundations of our Christian faith or leading them to slaughter at the hands of an enemy who seeks to kill and destroy?

The Narrow Path

> *"Enter through the narrow gate. For wide is the gate and broad is the road that leads to destruction, and many enter through it. But small is the gate and narrow the road that leads to life and only a few find it."*

> Matthew 7:13-14

Jesus gives us a very stern warning here. The road to eternal life is narrow and few find it. A warning like this from our Lord and Savior should cause us to sit up and pay attention. He didn't say most or many would enter through the narrow gate, He said **few.**

I am fascinated with thinking and praying on this verse. Just how narrow is the road to eternal life? Do twenty percent make it? Ten percent? Five percent? None of us knows, as God alone is qualified to judge the eternal destiny of each man. But we should not quickly gloss over this verse where Jesus says few find the narrow road to eternal life. It should cause us to analyze the depth of our faith and question whether our works reflect real faith and commitment to Him as Lord and Savior; or if our words and actions reflect a faith of convenience and mediocrity.

Narrow roads we drive on present challenges to us. They allow very little room for mistake as a momentary lapse in concentration can send us into a ditch. When I drive through a construction zone with a concrete barrier on one side and a ditch on the other, I am forced to concentrate on the road and my driving instead of being enamored with changing channels on my car radio or talking on my cell phone. I realize that a short lapse in concentration or letting my eyes wander can create a serious problem--I either crash my car or end up in a ditch.

Without getting into a discussion of whether or not we can lose our salvation, I wonder if we incorrectly think that the road to salvation is an eight lane super highway where we can coast, instead of this narrow road Jesus mentions. We just put ourselves on cruise control and pay little attention to the traffic and conditions around us as our eyes wander to signs along the road or over to other drivers we encounter.

We set ourselves up for a very dangerous situation when we do not take these words of Jesus to heart. Narrow means narrow! Only a few find the road to eternal life. Is a simple "believing in God" enough? Not according to the book of James. Is a simple belief in Jesus enough? That depends what we believe **about** Jesus. Acts Chapter 19 tells a fascinating story about certain creatures who knew Jesus:

> *"Some Jews who went around driving out evil spirits tried to invoke the name of the Lord Jesus over those who were demon possessed. They would say 'In the name of Jesus who Paul preaches, I command you to come out'. Seven sons of Sceva, a Jewish chief priest, were doing this. One day the evil spirit answered them, 'Jesus I know, and I know about Paul, but who are you?' Then the man who had the evil spirit jumped on them and overpowered them all. He gave them such a beating that they ran out of the house naked and bleeding."*

These demons acknowledged knowing Jesus, so were the demons saved? No, because while they knew who Jesus was they did not submit to Him as Lord. Simply knowing Jesus is not enough for salvation--He must also be Lord and master over our lives. How many times a day do we not submit to His lordship in our lives? How many times do we willfully sin knowing we should not, as it is an affront to God? Is He really Lord over our lives? Is He Lord of every thought, word and action?

We must take this to heart the next time we offer a bland altar call and a sinner's prayer. ***What*** we believe about Jesus is equally as important as believing He is the Son of God. I think this is what Romans 10:9 refers to when it says if we confess with our mouth and ***believe in our heart.*** Head knowledge of who Jesus is will not be enough. When we truly believe in our hearts, it is something deep, personal and intimate. He becomes the sole object of our love and affection, not just an intellectual acknowledgment.

We are not taking our relationship with Jesus seriously enough as Christians. We stop at salvation, deciding we are good to go, when Jesus said if we loved Him we would obey all He commanded. Jesus tells us that many who call Him Lord will be rebuffed with His words of *"I never knew you"*. How sad for those who hear those words when they stand before Him in judgment.

Let us not stop short of where God calls us to be as Christians. Jesus must be something more than an intellectual belief; He must reside in our hearts and rule us from there. Are we fooling ourselves with a type of "phony salvation"? Or do we truly belong to Jesus?

Are we leading ourselves and others to a pot of "fool's gold"? Being led to something that looks shiny and valuable, but is worthless and meaningless? If our commitment to Jesus never goes beyond a sinner's prayer followed by a life without any fundamental change, let alone transformation, how will God judge us when we stand before Him?

These are the tough questions we must ask ourselves as American Christians. Questions like these lead to thought, prayer and seeking God intimately. They lead to repentance when we realize we've been lulled to sleep by a faith that is shallow and deceptive, and they lead to revival in each of us and the church as a whole.

We must stop trying to redefine God into an image that He is not; an image that suits the selfish lifestyles of our flesh. God is the same yesterday, today and tomorrow. We must see Him as the Apostles saw Him—many of whom gave their lives up for Him. When each of us can do that we will see transformation, revival and a moving of the Holy Spirit. Until that time it will be "business as usual" and American Christianity will continue to decay.

Footnotes

1) barna.org
2) "No Place for Truth", David F. Wells, 1993, Wm. B. Eerdmans Publishing
3) crosswalk.com/church/pastors-or-leadership/how-many-porn-addiction

CHAPTER ELEVEN

THE SPIRITUAL ABUSE OF OUR CHILDREN

Training Tomorrow's Church Leaders—But For What?

I have breaking news for adult Christians: We will grow old and die one day.

More breaking news: Today's Christian children will grow up to assume the mantle of leadership in the church over the next couple decades. How are we preparing them?

One of the primary responsibilities of a leader is to groom successors. An organization never faces a more critical time than during a transition in leadership. An institution as large and diverse as American Christianity faces an added challenge in grooming new leadership, in comparison to a corporation.

A corporation will often see its key leadership responsibilities functioning in the hands of a relatively small group of centralized leaders. American Christianity, with its size and diversity, is a different animal. Leadership is not centralized; rather it is fragmented and spread out among literally thousands of smaller entities known as denominations and churches.

This creates a unique challenge for the Church. Leadership transition comes in smaller steps with subtle, incremental changes often not easily noticeable. No one leader, no matter how potentially dangerous or destructive, has complete influence so they are easier to initially dismiss as more of a nuisance than a threat. But eventually a critical mass forms where enough potentially dangerous leaders come into power and become a real threat to the whole organization, American Christianity.

For example, a few decades ago, one or two smaller Christian denominations came out and challenged the traditional teaching of homosexuality as a sin. Because they were insignificant in number when compared to the total number of leaders and denominations, they were easily dismissed as a fringe element. But look around today and the lie that homosexuality is not a sin has infiltrated virtually every denomination of Christianity with varying degrees of success. Because we did not act swiftly to counter the lies of these leaders and take appropriate actions, their camp began to grow.

Satan is evil, a liar and the one who accuses the brethren. What he is not, is stupid. He was the most brilliant angel created, the "morning star". He is smart, crafty, scheming and patient. He realized a full-frontal assault on Christian leadership would fail, so he bides his time, lulling us to sleep as he claims small, incremental victories that seem insignificant at the time. But a lot of small victories eventually lead to a huge, decisive victory, and Satan is in position to gain victory over American Christianity. Satan has come to the brink of victory so subtly that most Christians do not even realize it.

When you look at the landscape of leadership in American Christianity these days, you find that most of the leaders who stand on the principles of absolute biblical truth are advancing in years, while a growing majority of young leaders are far more liberal in their views about absolute truth. The elderly leaders are principled, but the younger ones are much more pragmatic. Elderly leaders view Christianity and God as consistent and never changing while the younger leaders view God and Christianity as flexible to accommodate a postmodern culture's desires and dreams.

These younger leaders shun the belief of their predecessors that absolute truth exists. Absolute truth has become subjective truth—a "truth" that is subject to individual interpretation based on how a person feels. Experiences and emotions have replaced absolute truth as the guiding principle for this next generation of Christian leaders, and as this dangerous teaching spreads and becomes more accepted, we will soon be ruled and led by our human emotions rather than the truth of God. Once this happens there will no longer be any core doctrine that guides American Christianity. It will become a cobblestone of individual beliefs driven by how each individual feels about God, morality and truth.

Well fasten your seat belts because the "Young Guns" are just about ready to take control of the steering wheel that drives American Christianity, and the place they will drive the church is right into a ditch of secular humanism.

Satan has been working hard in the fields of media and education, both secular and Christian, to lay the foundation for this transition in leadership. He has succeeded in taking over the curriculum in our public schools over the past fifty years and is now making great inroads into some Christian educational institutions, promoting Christianity as subject to our individual feelings and beliefs. As this continues to grow, American Christianity will begin to look more and more like the secular culture that seeks to destroy us. We will take in more and more poison until the body shuts down, with only a remnant remaining.

"But I Send My Kids to Christian School"

We know that secular education in the public schools is anti-Christian in its views and in the curriculum it shoves down the throats of our children. The NEA believes it has a responsibility to rescue youth from the "archaic" beliefs children learn from religion and their parents. As we noted earlier, this was shared by an NEA Spokeswoman at the United Nations in 2011 as she appealed for mandatory sex education for children as young as six years old.

In Wisconsin and around the nation, the NEA has successfully lobbied progressive politicians into blocking the expansion of Christian education at every turn. Through our tax codes, the government has made Christian education a financial burden for parents who prefer a godly curriculum to one of secular humanism. The percentage of children attending public schools is at an all-time high and if the teachers' unions have their way, Christian education might soon be extinct.

But the battle for the souls of our future leaders is not just being waged in public educational institutions; it is also occurring in Christian schools. Over the past fifty years there has been a dangerous trend showing that far too often Christian education is emulating and embracing the secular values and beliefs of public education.

Here in Green Bay, a close friend was shocked when his daughter told him the teacher who teaches religion class in her parochial school taught that the flood in Noah's time was just a fable, not an actual historic event. He confronted the teacher and met with her and the school's Principal. The Principal backed up the teacher, telling my friend that our children needed to expand their thought process and embrace "other views".

Wheaton College, an esteemed Christian University, consistently brings in pro-homosexual lecturers and social justice activists like Jim Wallis to lecture. They have also hosted homosexual activist Harry Knox to teach and speak. Knox, an avowed homosexual, calls his sexual orientation *"an unchangeable gift from God for which I am very grateful. And it would fly in the face of my respect for God to give that gift back."*[1] Please try to square that up with biblical teaching and ask yourself why Wheaton College is committed to presenting views like this as Christian education. Knox has now joined president Obama's faith-based panel of experts, joining Jim Wallis and other progressive Christians and non-believers.

Several Wheaton professors are involved with anti-Israeli rallies like "Christ at the Checkpoint"[2], where the Palestinian cause is promoted and Israel is demonized as an aggressor in the conflict.

Richard Mouw and Fuller Theological Seminary

Richard Mouw is President of Fuller Theological Seminary[3]. Many Christians believe Fuller left the camp of sound Christian doctrine a long time ago, and Richard Mouw has confirmed their beliefs on his own blog, written on March 15, 2011:

> *"I told the USA TODAY reporter that Rob Bell's newly released 'Love Wins' is a fine book and that I basically agree with his theology. I knew that the book was being widely criticized for having crossed the theological bridge from evangelical orthodoxy into universalism. Not true, I told the reporter. Rob Bell is calling us away from a stingy orthodoxy to a generous orthodoxy."*[4]

Note the "generous orthodoxy" reference, a tip of the hat to Mouw's friend Brian McLaren, who wrote a book with the same title. Mouw is considered a darling of the Emergent Church and social justice movements, and is making sure his faculty teaches these dangerous doctrines to Christian youth.

In a blog he wrote for CNN, Mouw disagreed with Christian leaders who called Mormonism a cult:

> *"We evangelicals and our Mormon counterparts disagree about some important theological questions," Mouw continued. "But we have also found that on some matters we are not as far apart as we thought we were."*[5]

There are *some* similarities in Christian and Mormon beliefs, but there are huge stumbling blocks to finding common spiritual communion between Christians and Mormons.

Mormons believe that God has not always been the supreme being of the universe, but attained that status through righteous living and persistent effort. They believe God the Father has a "body of flesh and bones as tangible as man's." Though abandoned by modern Mormon leaders, Brigham Young taught that Adam actually was God and the father of Jesus Christ.

Mormon leaders have taught that Jesus' incarnation was the result of a sexual relationship between God the Father and Mary. Mormons believe Jesus is a god, but that any human can also become a god.

So Richard Mouw, the President of Fuller Theological Seminary, apparently thinks these core disagreements do not disqualify Mormons as Christians. Are you seeing a trend here? Mouw also signed on to the "Common Word Between Us" heresy a few years earlier that places Islam and Christianity on the same level. Now he is promoting Mormonism and Christianity as having common beliefs. Richard Mouw gives every indication that he is a Universalist, and it is logical that he would hire faculty that reflects and teaches those same beliefs.

Plainly stated, Mormonism is not Christianity. Mouw seems to be promoting another attempt at universalism and religious syncretism.

These are just a couple short examples of how Christian education is being corrupted these days. Our next generation of Christian leaders and pastors are being trained to embrace dangerous movements that conflict with the teachings of the Bible, and soon they may comprise a majority of Christian leaders in this nation.

I am praying about writing a future book to solely address the abomination that secular and Christian education are becoming in this nation. In the interim I encourage you to do your own research using multiple sites and finding first hand quotes whenever possible. I also want to stress that by no means have all Christian schools left the farm; some are holding on to sound Biblical doctrine in their education programs. If you are a parent who will be sending your child into Christian education, I urge you to research the schools you consider very carefully. Thoroughly check into their curriculum and research the personal and religious views of the faculty that will be teaching and training your children. Many of them have personal blogs and Facebook pages, and also write and post on other sites as well. Thoroughly investigate every aspect of their public life, along with their beliefs and opinions. You will be paying a very high price to send your children to Christian colleges, so do all you can to make sure you understand exactly what you are paying for.

Children and the Church

As education begins to systematically distort biblical doctrine, our churches must make sure they are teaching the Word of God to our children, establishing a strong biblical foundation for them at a very early age. It is crucial that our children learn the fundamental beliefs of Christianity as taught in the Bible to give them a fighting chance to survive the onslaught of secular beliefs they will be exposed to in our education system and in society as a whole.

Unfortunately our children do not seem to be a high priority in many of our churches these days. Instead of educating them we seem to be coddling, or even dismissing them.

Throughout Jewish history, boys were often required to deeply know, even memorize the Torah by the age of thirteen. We hope by thirteen our children have recited a shallow sinner's prayer. When a Jewish boy became a Bar Mitzvah (son of commandment) he was given greater authority to make certain decisions, subject to the Minion, a group of relatives and adults who guided him and taught him. We give our youth over to a youth leader who may be more interested in entertaining them instead of teaching them the bible. And if your church has a Youth Pastor who has been trained at a Christian College, this may be an additional danger to your children as we discovered earlier.

Jewish children sat at the feet of their parents and teachers, learning about the glory and commandments of God. Christian children spend countless hours on the Internet and Facebook. Their education is usually outsourced to a public school system which fights Christianity wherever it can.

A former commentator in our local paper composed a cartoon about twenty years ago that was more prophetic than he could have imagined at the time. A mom and dad were dropping their child off at kindergarten and told the teacher "Educate him, feed him, entertain him, challenge him and teach him morals and values; we'll pick him up when he's eighteen."

The Children Are Dismissed

Every Sunday our local church starts off service with three songs; then we make church and community announcements, followed by taking an offering. As the offering is completed another announcement is made: "The children are dismissed."

Sadly, there may be more truth to this statement than we realize. Are we dismissing our children, our future leaders, more and more these days? We send them off to children's church instead of having them listen to the sermon, learning the Word of God with their parents. We may do this for a variety of reasons that we have convinced ourselves are worthy motives. We think they will be disruptive as children may get antsy and bored, interrupting the pastor. Or heaven forbid our children might ask us a question about something the pastor said.

Sadly we tend to treat our children as inconveniences sometimes. As parents, there are days when we just hope to survive until they become adults and are on their own. And the church, in spite of some dedicated teachers and youth leaders, often sends the same message to our youth. At a time when our youth need to learn the foundations of Christianity the most, we seem to be dismissing them as children, failing to recognize them as the future leaders of Christianity. Satan has a dangerous agenda in mind for them, and we must recognize that fact and begin to lay a strong foundation in the minds and hearts of our children. Are we doing that?

I am quite sure that this is not the intention of most pastors and church teachers. They genuinely love and care for our children. But this status quo of how we are raising our children as Christians is leading the church down a dangerous road, because there are dangers out there to our children. Dangerous education systems, a treacherous culture and even some dangerous Christian teachers who are appealing to our youth as we subconsciously dismiss them. That is ultimately why our ministry said we would not support the appearance of Jim Wallis speaking to youth at Lifest. He preaches a dangerously incomplete and false gospel, and there are enough enemies out there dismantling traditional Christian teachings these days without our youth hearing more from misleading Christian teachers.

What Are Christian Youth Learning These Days?

We know what our children are being taught in public education--that God is an illusion and that their only hope for happiness, even survival, is to embrace global citizenship. The secular culture is telling them that their only path to happiness lies in sex, substance abuse and narcissistic behavior.

As we unintentionally dismiss our children at home and in church, there are predatory wolves out there waiting to destroy them. Satan has a dangerous agenda in mind for them and his tools include a secular American culture, a humanist education system, and the entertainment world of the internet, television and music that will destroy our youth if we do not counter their destructive messages.

We are tempted to just throw up our hands and give up, wondering how we could ever compete with these forces vying for the attention of our youth. All around us the world vies for the attention and allegiance of our children, so Christian parents turn to the church in hopes that their children will receive a solid foundation of biblical teaching to give them a fighting chance against a ruthless enemy bent on their destruction.

We know what our children are learning from the culture, but what are they learning in church? Many Christian parents drop their children off on Wednesday evenings for "youth group", hoping their children will learn about their Christian faith from a youth leader who will help reinforce the Christian values parents try to live out at home. Youth group is seen as a safe haven from the depravity of culture our youth are immersed in throughout the week. But just what *is* your child learning in youth group? Are they learning the Word of God? Or something every bit as dangerous as the culture they are immersed in throughout the week?

On Stand Up For the Truth, a regular guest, Todd Friel of Wretched Radio, shared a website that listed the top ways Christian youth leaders are entertaining our children these days. Among the most popular activities listed and used were:

- The youth leader smears peanut butter in his armpits and the girls lick it out.[6]
- The students drink coca cola through each other's dirty socks.
- The youth leader has the boys dress in female clothes and makeup, with the girls judging which one is prettiest.
- The girls then dress up as boys, with the boys judging which one is the most handsome.

Pardon my strong language but literally what in God's name is going on here? Is this what constitutes youth group these days? What about teaching them the Word of God? What about talking about the difficult choices our youth face these days—sex, drugs and peer pressure—and what the Word of God has to say to encourage them to make the right choices? Is this what our children really need—an enforcement of the secular culture they see all week with maybe just a little "Jesus" sprinkled in on occasion? These activities aimed at entertaining our children and showing them that our youth leaders can "relate" to the culture are very dangerous and destructive. They tend to reinforce the values of the very culture we are to disown as Christians.

Parents, I strongly urge you to find out what goes on in your church's youth group. If it is anything like this, you'd better find another church! Take the time to talk with your pastor and interview your child's youth leader, asking him tough questions about his Christian beliefs and hold those stated beliefs up against the Word of God. Find out which Christian leaders and pastors he admires. Failure to do so may result in you doing more damage to your children by sending them to youth group. We must hold our church leaders accountable for everything that is taught or reinforced within the church.

Our children's most influential teachers are not public school teachers or youth group leaders. The most influential people in the life of a child are right at home—their parents. The world will tell you that your children find you boring and stupid, and that they do not care what you believe or teach them. Nothing could be further from the truth. Study after study shows that overwhelmingly, youth identify their parents as the most influential people in their lives. They may not express that overtly, but trust me, they are watching and listening, and they crave your attention and input as parents.

Research and studies conducted show that the average father spends less than four minutes per day having real conversations with their children. Four minutes a day, when they spend seven hours a day in public school being indoctrinated into humanism and they spend an average of five hours a day immersed in media.

Our children are the most precious investment we have as parents. God has given us the responsibility to raise and teach them, grooming them to be the next generation of leaders in society and in the church. Is four minutes a day a worthwhile investment in the future of our nation and church?

I say this not out of judgment, and from a confession that I fell far short of being the involved father I should have been in the lives of my children. I was guilty of working long hours, coming home tired and watching television, missing so many opportunities to invest in my own children. Just a little more effort and a little less selfishness would have gone a long way. I thank God that our children have turned out great, but this is somewhat in spite of me. I missed so many opportunities to invest in them, wasting so much time on my meaningless hobbies and preoccupations.

Now that I have committed my life to God, I see the errors of my ways and hope I can help others who are raising children to avoid the mistakes I made. I encourage you to take the time to really invest in the future of your children and insist that your church does the same. Our children are the future leaders of America, and more importantly, American Christianity. Every moment we invest in them today will pay huge dividends in the future. And every moment we ignore or dismiss them will be regretted if we see them become immersed into secular culture, walking away from the hope of Jesus Christ.

We are running out of time. We cannot continue doing what we have been doing. If we as parents, along with the church, are unwilling to make a significant investment in our children as our future leaders, we deserve whatever happens to us. We will have only ourselves to blame, and only God to answer to.

Footnotes

1) http://www.onenewsnow.com/Politics/Default.aspx?id=480990
2) www.christatthecheckpoint.com
3) www.fuller.edu
4) http://www.netbloghost.com/mouw/?p=188
5) http://religion.blogs.cnn.com/2011/10/09/my-take-this-evangelical-says-mormonism-isnt-a-cult/
6) www.folioweekly.com/documents/main092909_001.pdf

CHAPTER TWELVE

A SPIRITUALLY POWERLESS AND DYSFUNCTIONAL CHURCH

I ask you to read this chapter with an open mind and an open heart because I will be painting a very bleak picture of the American Church. Some or all of it may or may not apply to the particular church you attend and I am offering no indictment of any particular church or denomination. I am merely pointing out what seems to be happening in churches around our nation.

The odds are things are not as bad in your church as I point out in this chapter. More likely the church you attend suffers from parts of what we will cover next. But please do not put blinders on as you read what I am about to share, thinking none of this could be happening in your church.

I hope you will also ask God to speak to your heart about what we discuss in this chapter. Every one of us is part of a dysfunctional church because we and our leaders are human. But as a church we are called to be a pure, spotless bride, and light and salt to the world we live in. And if you belong to a church that is spiritually powerless and dysfunctional, who is to blame? We can blame our leaders or we can look into our own hearts and ask God to reveal the ways we are contributing to a decaying church.

If you read this chapter and can honestly say none of this applies to you or the church you attend, then you are truly blessed. But do not allow the enemy to deceive you. Satan wants what is happening in our churches to continue and he will constantly seek to convince us that we are "good to go" personally and that your church is doing a great job.

Why Are You Here?

I am blessed by having occasional opportunities to preach at various churches. When I was a young Christian, I was being taught by a pastor who remains a close friend. He is a gifted teacher with sermons based solidly on God's Word.

I asked him how he was able to keep his sermons challenging and interesting, and he said that the best teachings were about subjects that he has personally experienced, or still struggles with. He finds his mind sharpest and delivery most effective when he is passionate about the subject he is teaching on. Sage advice as we are most knowledgeable and passionate about the areas in God's Word where we are personally challenged the most.

A few months ago I was asked to preach at a local church and given six weeks' notice to prepare. With less than two weeks to go, I still had not heard clearly from God as to what He wanted me to teach on. As I sat in my home church one Sunday, I heard that small still voice in my head ask a question: "Why are you here?"

Interesting question and as I pondered my response I felt the leading not only to answer God's question of me, but also to challenge the congregation I was to teach the following Sunday. Why are we here in this place we call church?

Usually I really enjoy heading to church to worship God, learn from his Word and enjoy great fellowship with other believers. I admit there are days, however, where I just want to stay home and curl up in my recliner with the Bible and seek God's voice. But God was challenging me this

Sunday, forcing me to do some self-assessment on my Sunday ritual of coming to church.

Over the next few days, I came to realize that my progression from a child to a Christian adult and the reasons why I came to church were probably similar to most Christians. Let me throw my thoughts out there and let you chew on them a little.

When I was a child, I came to church out of obligation. Mom and Dad just told us we were going to church and that was that. Church was not optional and my reaction in church showed that. I would come up with little mind games to help pass the time until we could return home and get on with life.

As I became a teen, I attended out of habit. I had become accustomed to just going to church on Sunday and so I continued to do so. Still not much more than passing time, but I was there none the less.

When I became a Christian, going to church became an act of obedience to God. That's just what Christians do--we go to church because we love God and want to worship Him. Now at least it became something more than habit, and I was there out of love rather than obligation. And there were times when listening to the Word was exciting as I sought to know more about God and His will for my life.

But I still approached church in a selfish sort of way. Church became a way for me to "fill my spiritual tank". My hope was that I would get enough Jesus to get me by and perhaps find some special message or experience that would propel me through the following week of going to work and living the daily grind. Now this can be a valuable benefit to attending church, but is it any attitude to have when we enter into corporate worship of God with our brothers and sisters? Should we have an attitude of "gimme" or one of thanks, expressing the great love of God? Is attending church about me---or about God?

I also noticed a pattern of behavior in me and my Christian brothers and sisters. When we were together at church on Sunday all of life was wonderful, at least if you listened to us talk. *"God is good. Doing great!*

Praise God!" We were filled with joy, or so it seemed. You would think that our life was just one victory after another.

But as I would meet with these fellow believers in a small group setting, I heard stories of struggles, failures and at times downright depression. Life was hard and there were many more setbacks than victories, and I was no different. The unbridled, but often phony joy expressed on Sunday, was just a mask to hide the pain and struggles of every day life. But we didn't dare be totally honest about our weeklong struggles when we met on Sunday because we just didn't do that at church. Something was wrong—seriously wrong.

I hoped church would fill up my spiritual gas tank and get me through the week. At times it did, but other times I was out of gas by Tuesday morning. The rest of the week would be a struggle to just survive spiritually, hoping I could hold on until Sunday, when it was time to refuel the tank again. I began to realize that, in a way, going to church had become a detriment to my faith. I had come to depend on church to feed me spiritually, and it would for a short period, only to leave me high and dry by mid-week.

Going to church had become my identity and badge of honor as a Christian. I searched the scriptures and found nowhere that God identified his followers as people who attended church once a week. I looked in the Book of Acts and found no requirement or teaching that instructed us to attend church every week. What I did see was that the first century believers met daily, gathering for dinner and giving thanks and glory to God. They served one another, offering all they owned to help others. They shared all the great things God was doing in their lives and celebrated their new found freedom from the punishment of sin and its power in their lives.

We drag ourselves to church for one hour a week while they gathered daily, not out of obligation, but out of joy and wonder. Folks we have it all wrong. Going to church identifies us as Christians, but the early believers *were* the church. I picture the early believers working throughout the day, eagerly anticipating their time together that night. They would spend time thinking about the sacrifice of Jesus, thanking and praising Him for all He had done for them. They were **filling** their spiritual tanks throughout the day, and came spiritually filled up for their time together as a family. We stop in for a quick fill up on Sunday and watch helplessly as our tanks get drained throughout the week.

Once I realized how I had been looking at church as a crutch to lean on and get me through the next week, something started to change in me. I realized that every day, even the tough ones, were a cause for thanks and celebration. I started praying constantly throughout the day while I worked, thanking God for every circumstance that came my way. I realized that seeking fuel on Sunday that would be used up by Tuesday was an exercise in futility. God had given me a renewable energy source that could continually fill me up and power me through the week, and I didn't have to run on fumes, hoping I could just chug and sputter into the gas station on Sunday. He gave me His Word and the privilege of approaching His throne in prayer. I could actually have a conversation with God and He would take as much time as I needed to teach and encourage me. I didn't have to wait until Sunday and hope in one hour I could get what I needed to survive the next week.

Sunday church service should be a time for family to gather in a celebration; a time to share the Word of God and all He is doing in our lives and a time to encourage and challenge one another to elevate our relationship with God to new heights.

Too often these days our churches look more like a meeting of the walking dead instead of Christians overflowing with joy and thanks that Jesus has delivered us from the punishment for sin, and is working in us to deliver us from the power of sin in our lives. In a sense we have developed an unhealthy dependence on church. It has become a house of escape from life instead of a house of worship where we celebrate life--a life of salvation and victory.

Imagine what would happen if a local church would bring families together that were overflowing with joy and victory—I mean real joy, not the fake joy we Christians often express. Imagine how the power of the

Holy Spirit would be unleashed through us if we came to church filled with love, joy, peace and real faith. We might see healings, salvations and miracles on a regular basis, and we might just witness the power of the Holy Spirit as we read about in the Book of Acts.

Please don't misunderstand when I say we seem to have developed an unhealthy dependency on church. The church is God's instrument of bringing His people together in praise, worship, prayer and celebration. But sadly that doesn't look like the church in America these days.

The church should have fewer wounded soldiers and more victorious conquerors. When we come to know Jesus as Lord and Savior, we come already having been wounded by the enemy, and now face a battle to overcome sin in our lives. We need healing from our past wounds before we can be effective in that next battle, where we will surely receive more wounds. But too many soldiers are not being healed because they are not being treated with the truth of God's Word, or they choose to ignore His Word. They come to church, get a dose of Jesus, and go back into the world where that dose starts to wear off and they face more defeat. This occurs for one of two reasons: Either they are not being mentored properly, or deep down they choose to remain wounded, ignoring the cure. Neither reason is acceptable and must be addressed to foster a healthy church.

But this would involve a major paradigm shift in how we view success as a church. The lust for "nickels and noses" would have to be replaced by a passion for spiritually deep disciples. We might have to look for ways to shrink our numbers in the short term, allowing God to prune us for greater future growth. We would need to feel free to be open, honest and transparent about our sins. We would need to give each other sincere permission to examine our lives at home and work, not just the facade we put up when we attend church.

Do we have the courage and faith in God to ask Him to have His way in our lives and within our churches? Do we believe everything we proclaim from the pulpit, that God is in control and we need to surrender to His will for our lives? It may be time to put up or shut up. We either do "church" God's way, or continue to die a slow death as sin and hypocrisy expand their foothold in our Church, eating away at her foundation.

We can continue to do things our way and hope things will change, or we can become the church God intends us to be. We can become a place where victorious warriors mentor wounded soldiers who want to join the ranks of the victorious, fighting side by side. A place that is always welcome to wounded soldiers who really want to be healed, but will not tolerate soldiers who continually fall into defeat because they will not allow themselves to be healed by the Word of God and his Spirit.

What is a Successful Church?

"Pastor, tell me about your church . . ." When you invite a pastor to tell you about the church he leads, he will probably begin with one of two responses:

- "We're a _____ denomination", or
- "We have about 125 members . . ."

Consciously or subconsciously we determine our identity and success by our denominational quirks, or how many people attend our church. Is this really what it should all be about?

So just what does constitute a successful church? Attendance? The size of our building? The weekly collection amount? Our outreach events? Or the depth of spiritual maturity the members exhibit, not just at church, but in their daily lives?

Let's be honest, America is the land of bigger is better, gauging our success on numbers and size. We live in large houses more like shrines to our own achievements than functional homes of comfort, joy and peace. Men often gauge our success on our salaries or work titles, and the family with the most toys is viewed as more successful than the family who lives a modest lifestyle.

We expect such superficial thinking from the world, but should we not expect better from ourselves as Christians? In reality we are no better than the world, as the church with the largest attendance is envied by other pastors and held up as the gold standard in the community. Church members love to attend big churches because we feel we are a part of something big and important.

Pastors are just as human as you and me, suffering from envy and pride like all of us. How many times have we seen our neighbor or friend bring home a new car or boat and we secretly envied him? Pastors are no different and in spite of their denials, many desire a larger church, bigger collections and greater influence. And even if they don't, the ruling elders probably will put pressure on them to define the church's success in these superficial terms.

Jesus invested three years of his life and only mentored twelve disciples---one of them betrayed Him, another denied he ever knew Him when he was confronted, and the remainder hid in fear after His death, probably thinking they bet on the wrong horse. By today's church standards, Jesus would be branded a miserable failure and a poor teacher who didn't know how to "relate" to people. He would have been fired and they would have fought His unemployment claim; and good luck when He tried to find another church to lead with that track record!

Jesus knew that God's plan would be better carried out by a small group of committed disciples rather than by a large group who were only really focused on themselves. When Jesus said they must eat His flesh and drink His blood if they wanted eternal life, He knew the ranks of his followers would diminish significantly. All that would be left were those truly committed to Him. Do we fear losing church members for far less radical statements than that? Do we fear if we actually preach on the conviction of sin in our lives that members will find a gentler church? I say preach boldly and let them leave, and start trusting in God, not man, to grow the church. God can do more with 11 committed disciples than any man can do with five-hundred self-righteous people who need to be coddled.

Sadly we have bought into the lie that success in the church equates to "nickels and noses", and buying in to the "If you build it they will come" mentality. Oh, that might work if you want to attract a large group of superficial believers who are dazzled by the newest and best building, but you will probably lose them to the next "newest and best" church building that pops up in your community.

Before Jesus ascended into heaven in the Gospel of Matthew, He gave us our orders: *"Go make disciples"*. He didn't tell us to attract superficial church members. God doesn't care about the size of our church; He cares about the size of the hearts and spiritual condition of people who belong to our church. He is into evangelists who grieve for the lost, not catchy outreach programs. And I am quite certain our Lord is more pleased with a church of fifty strong disciples than He is with a church of five hundred shallow Christians.

But those standards are just not good enough for American Christianity these days. We need more people occupying our seats on Sunday to feel successful. We need bigger offerings to fuel God's work. And to accomplish those goals and better relate to the culture these days, we are going to need a catchy slogan and a slick marketing plan.

We feel the need to meet the physical and emotional needs of the people, so we have to figure out what they look for in a church and overcome their objections to attending church. We need to craft a series of messages that will appeal to them and we need to let them know Jesus accepts them just the way they are. In other words we need to sell out to the world.

We discussed earlier the tremendous influence Peter Drucker had on pastors like Bill Hybels, Robert Schuller and Rick Warren. Drucker convinced these men that a church needed to function more like a corporation, being sensitive to the desires of their "customers". Look what this got us—large, spiritually-dead churches surrendering to secular culture instead of influencing it. And now many smaller churches are emulating this formula, thinking it leads to success, when in reality it leads to a spiritually dysfunctional church.

Look, I understand the pressure to grow in numbers and finances. I lead a Christian ministry; I get it. While my performance review is partially contingent upon our audience growth and financial stability, the day those become the overriding judgment on my performance, I will move on. My primary job as a leader is to challenge and encourage those I lead to draw closer to God, pursuing righteousness and holiness. If we can do that, everything else will fall into place. As a ministry we will be equipped by the Holy Spirit to accomplish what He wants accomplished.

I have been asked if we know how many people listen to Stand Up For the Truth every day. Because of limited resources and an inaccurate measuring tool utilized by the industry, I honestly cannot tell. And to be honest, I don't worry about it. Our job is to love and obey God by boldly standing on the absolute truth of His Word and challenging Christians to go back to reading the Bible. Our job is to obey what God commands and the end results are up to Him.

At the risk of sounding arrogant, I wish more church leaders would come to understand the freedom we receive when we stop worrying about results and just do what God wants us to do. It takes the pressure off, freeing you from undue stress and self-imposed performance standards. God asks for love that leads to obedience. When we love and obey Him, He takes care of the results according to His perfect plan.

Finding a Proper Balance

The saved and the lost, disciples and superficial Christians, and victorious warriors and defeated soldiers--the church has any number of combinations of all these members. A church is like a quilt, a patchwork of patterns and designs woven together into one blanket.

The church is also like a classroom of students. Some are more intelligent and advanced, wanting to be challenged with greater depth and knowledge, while others need the basics and would get lost if we jumped right to advanced studies. Imagine for a moment you are putting together the curriculum for the coming school year for incoming freshmen in high school, and since Math is a required course to get a high school diploma, you list available classes for students but you simply list it as "Math".

Students sign up and come to class on the first day, where you lay out the year-long agenda and goals. Some are expecting basic math studies; others algebra; still others advanced trigonometry. They all are expecting one thing that fits their needs and agenda.

So you announce the class as advanced trigonometry, and ninety percent of the students gasp in horror. They have not even mastered the basics of math and they are being thrown into advanced trigonometry, and they fear they may not survive the course.

Or you announce that the study will be basic math—addition, subtraction, multiplication and division—the bare essentials. Some are shocked and saddened, already knowing these basics, and they want something more challenging so they can grow in their understanding and preparation for college, and life beyond. They sit in class, bored stiff, as the other students learn what these advanced students knew eight years earlier.

Either of these scenarios leads to a dysfunctional class with some interested students and some who have checked out emotionally and intellectually.

Welcome to the church in America. A patchwork of biblical students at varying levels of knowledge and wisdom. Some can memorize entire chapters from the bible while others don't know the first thing about terms like justification and sanctification. Some read the Book of Revelation and God is revealing wisdom and blessings, and others give up reading it after the first attempt because their head is spinning.

Some come to church needing milk—the basics of our faith; others desire meat—the pursuit of righteousness and holiness.

But the only class posted on the sign is "church", and church means a lot of different things to different people. To some it is a place to come out of obligation, and to others it is a place to worship and glorify God. Some come to give and others come to take. Some come to serve and others come to be served. Some come for the basics while others come for advanced studies.

And "church" as a whole is just not working. We seem confused on what to preach, what to teach, how to train up children and what to do with a diverse blend of mature and young Christians. If a pastor preaches on basics of the faith, many sit back bored and unchallenged. If he preaches on advanced issues of the faith he might lose about eighty percent of the people by speaking over their heads.

If he preaches on sin and hell, look out! Someone might be offended and leave the church, affecting our "nickels and noses". If he continually feeds milk to the congregation, Christians wanting to learn about righteousness and holiness become bored and consider moving to a place where they can be challenged to go deeper in their faith. What is the solution to this difficult problem? It may be easier than you think if we are willing to set aside our paradigms about what constitutes a successful church, and concentrate on making disciples, not just "members", for Jesus.

Surviving Algebra Class

I was one of the students described earlier who expected my freshman studies of math to be more elementary. Quite frankly, I came in looking for three easy credits as simple math always came naturally to me. Then I signed up for algebra class.

I quickly realized I was in over my head. All the "x" and "y" symbols and calculations just shut down when they entered my brain. I started to fall behind the class and failure became a real option, and I began to think I should just drop out and take an easier class. But my friend and next-door neighbor stepped in and helped. He would sit with me and explain things in a way that, while they still didn't make a lot of sense to me, would at least get me through with a passing grade. I made it through class and ended up passing Algebra.

As I think back, I probably felt about algebra like a lot of new Christians feel about the Word of God—confused by the advanced studies and feeling like I could never understand it. But a friend and a mentor got me through it. New Christians may not yet realize that the Holy Spirit is ready to remove the scales from their eyes and reveal the power and beauty of the written Word to us, perhaps because we just don't teach a lot about the Holy Spirit these days. It's all about Jesus and the sacrifice on the cross. Now certainly the cross is the central teaching of Christianity, but as the Book of Hebrews states, it is the "milk" we start off with in our journey as Christians. We need to teach more on the solid food of righteousness and holiness, and the role the Holy Spirit wants to play in our journey as a Christian.

So imagine a new Christian, sitting in a sermon or small group, hearing the meat of the gospel, but feeling lost. Many either just shut down, or bluff their way through it, pretending to understand the power and teachings of the Bible. But deep down, they just don't get it and are restricted to a life of defeat and mediocrity.

So is the answer to dumb-down the gospel message and just stick to the basics of the cross, salvation and the resurrection? Will that turn things around?

> *"In fact, though by this time you ought to be teachers, you need someone to teach you the elementary truths of God's word all over again. You need milk, not solid food! Anyone who lives on milk, being still an infant, is not acquainted with the teaching about righteousness. But solid food is for the mature, who by constant use have trained themselves to distinguish good from evil.*
>
> *Therefore let us leave the elementary teachings about Christ and go on to maturity, not laying again the foundation of repentance from acts that lead to death, and of faith in God, instruction about baptisms, the laying on of hands, the resurrection of the dead, and eternal judgment. And God permitting we will do so."*
>
> Hebrews 5:12-6:3.

Ouch! If this is not an indictment of American Christianity, I don't know what is. We choose to remain on milk—good milk—but milk all the same. Notice that milk is described as the forgiveness of sins, faith, the resurrection and eternal judgment. We spend way too much time on these elementary beliefs of our faith and little or no time on the solid food—the pursuit of righteousness and holiness. We have too many children suffering from spiritual malnutrition, and then we wonder why we cannot find victory in our lives or effectively witness to the lost.

I would guess that as high as ninety percent of church members are still stuck drinking milk. So we continue to offer milk to the congregation over and over out of fear we will challenge or offend new Christians or people who want to stay in their infant stage. The members who want solid food are forced to find it in small groups or even give up and just accept mediocrity in their faith.

We need to seek holiness and righteous living instead of just accepting salvation through Jesus Christ. He will deliver us from the power of sin in our lives if we trust God and allow Him to take us where He wants us to go. However, this requires us giving up those strongholds of our flesh that we still too often desire. But in reality, we gain victory through total surrender.

Discipleship

> *"Therefore go and make disciples of all nations, baptizing them*
> *in the name of the Father and of the Son and of the Holy Spirit*
> *and teaching them to obey everything I have commanded you. And*
> *surely I am with you always, to the very end of the age."*
>
> Matthew 28:19-20

Jesus commanded us to make disciples, not members. He told us to teach them to obey everything He commanded, not just the things we feel like obeying. If we cannot get beyond the milk, how will we ever accomplish the great commission? If we pander to the fear of challenging believers to become disciples and obey everything Jesus commanded lest we lose members or offend the lost, we are stuck in neutral and simply treading water.

Now some churches do offer small group discipleship meetings for members who want to go deeper, and while that is a good thing, in some ways it is also a cop out and a surrender to seeker-friendly Christianity. Are we asking too much for all church members who claim to be Christians to become disciples instead of remaining on milk forever?

The last thing we need is more half-hearted, self-centered Christians. We need disciples who are on fire for God, and true disciples who seek holiness and righteousness, who hunger for the truth and grieve for the lost.

The church has become more of a country club than a family. A country club where we put on our best face and behavior so we can impress other members with our piety and spiritual depth; a country club where we behave well when we are in the club in order to impress those around us. But how do we behave when we are away from the club? Do our lives reflect God when we are at home, work or alone?

Setting the Bar Too Low

The church needs to become more of a family. When we host a Christmas or Thanksgiving dinner, whom do we invite? We dine with our family. On occasion we may invite friends, but they are select friends, not just strangers off the streets or casual acquaintances.

The early church was a family, not a social club. Christians came to learn more about the Word of God. They shared meals and possessions when necessary and they challenged one another, and together lifted up the corporate level of Christian spirituality. They were committed Christians, not curious strangers. They didn't send out fliers announcing cleverly disguised outreach events that are just ploys to attract new members. If you weren't serious about knowing the gospel, you stayed away. The Word was not reduced to the lowest level of common understanding, allowing the spiritually weak to drag down those who wanted to pursue holiness and righteousness.

When we join an organization or country club, we pledge to behave to the standards written. If we violate acceptable standards of behavior, we are first warned, but if we continue to behave outside the rules we are asked to leave the organization.

Not at church. Rules and behavioral expectations are just too harsh. A person can usually stay in a church as long as they show up and throw a few dollars in the offering plate. If you tithe, well you can pretty much do or say whatever you want. And if you bring a large tithe, heck you can even tell leadership any time you are offended by a message or unhappy with how something is handled within the church. Leadership will often bend over backwards to make sure you and your tithe remain a part of the church.

We have also become a Church of enablers. Struggling with sin? No problem because Jesus loves you just the way you are. No need to repent in a truly meaningful way, just say "I'm sorry" until the next time you sin.

Struggling with pornography? Just keep that to yourself mister, because we don't want to know about it. Hey, if we start to address issues like that, we will have to confront our own similar temptation and sin as leaders and members, and we aren't going there. And if a brave soul looks for help and confesses an addiction to pornography, infidelity or homosexuality, they will receive condemnation. Condemnation from the same men who watch pornography at home or nearly break their necks every time a beautiful woman walks by.

The early church in the Book of Acts was a place open to anyone seeking the complete truth of the Gospel. Sinners were welcome but they dared not get comfortable in their sinful state or accept it as normal behavior. Look at Ananias and Sapphira to understand how pride, hypocrisy and lying were handled by God within the church.

So the early church was an exclusive family, dedicated to learning the solid fruit of the gospel, seeking righteousness and holiness. They thanked and praised God for all things, and came to church with a heart and mind to worship God instead of escaping the world and its troubles. And in doing this, they attracted a visitor; a visitor of great power—the Holy Spirit. The Holy Spirit added to their numbers daily as they gathered, performing signs, wonders, healings and miracles. Many new disciples came to the Lord and the church grew in spite of persecution and vicious rumors.

Does that even remotely look like American Christianity these days? Are we a church of power or are we a powerless church eating table scraps the enemy and culture throw our way? Are we seeing lives transformed or lives that look no different than those of pagans?

If we have the courage and wisdom to believe that by setting higher standards for church membership, God will first prune, then grow the church, our churches can be like the church in the Book of Acts. Lives will be transformed, the sick might be healed and addictions broken. But if we remain content to let the enemy and culture define the membership rules, forget it. We will continue to die slowly but surely. It simply comes down to this: Will we do things God's way, or our way? But isn't that what it always comes down to?

Summary

The church is the Bride of Christ. But by any objective look we are not a spotless, beautiful bride. We are flirting with the enemy, our eyes more often on him than on our husband-to-be. We should be purifying ourselves in preparation for the blessed union, but instead we are polluting ourselves by accepting sin in the name of tolerance.

This is not just a leadership problem, nor solely a problem due to followers who want their ears tickled. Both parties are responsible. We are insulting God, just like the moneychangers in the temple, turning His house of worship into a den of inequity.

God never gives up on us. And if we turn back to Him, acknowledge our sins and repent with a commitment to never stray again, He will make us beautiful once more. We must crucify our flesh daily and purge ourselves of our delusional definitions of success as a church. It will not be easy, but then I am still searching for that verse in the gospel where Jesus promised us that being His disciples would be easy.

CHAPTER THIRTEEN

LOVING PEOPLE TO DEATH

There is no stronger emotion than love. We were created by God to love and be loved by Him. The gospel is the greatest expression of love in history, in that God loved us so much He sent Jesus to rescue us when we were totally unlovable.

But like all perfect gifts from God, man has continually perverted love, or at least that which we call love. Men have murdered in the name of love, left their wives and children in the name of love and fought wars over love. The famous battle of Troy was fought between the Greeks and Trojans over the competing love of a woman, leaving thousands dead and an empire in ruin.

The love of God is perfect while man's is far from perfect. Man cannot understand perfect, selfless love because in our human nature we are only capable of acting selfishly and loving ourselves.

When we become a new creation by accepting salvation and rebirth through Jesus Christ, we begin being transformed into the image of Jesus, and we show occasional glimpses of true love. But the Spirit in us is still in competition with our flesh, and we can easily revert back to our selfish human understanding of love.

As Christians we are commanded by Jesus to love all men, even our enemies; even men like the late Osama bin Laden and other men who act out of malice and hatred. This is not an easy thing to do.

We should have a special love in our hearts for the lost. Once we have experienced life in the light of God, we should desire to love the lost so much that we would do anything we can to share the true gospel with them. We should also have a deep love for our brothers and sisters in Christ Jesus. We are now family, united in love and purpose to support one another in any way possible.

The last two paragraphs describe the perfect love of God. Unfortunately we continually fall far short of that perfect standard. So we do the best we can to love one another, all the while trying to manage the internal battle between our new spirit and our flesh.

So given that we will all continue to fall short of perfect love in this lifetime, perhaps it is a good idea that we continually assess our human understanding of what love is and is not. We must understand that the temptation will always be there to define love selfishly, from a perspective of what is best for us in our flesh.

It is obvious that what we currently define as love in relationship to both our fellow Christians and the lost is often not really love at all. If it were, we would not be in the mess we are in as a church and there would be millions more in our ranks.

I Love You Brother, But Keep Your Problems To Yourself!

As my mother continued to poison herself with alcohol and cigarettes after surviving breast cancer, it grieved me deeply. She had been given a second chance at life but continued to slowly kill herself. Her typical breakfast was a Brandy Manhattan and a few Pall Mall cigarettes, and maybe one half piece of toast. She would nibble on food throughout the day in between downing on average a half a quart of brandy. Before bed she would consume a triple dose of NyQuil to help her fall sleep, and she would wake the next morning, continuing her cycle of slow death.

Our initial attempt at love was to meekly suggest that perhaps she needed professional help, but then she would start to cry and lay a guilt trip on us about how hard her life had been, asking why we could not understand that and just love her. We backed off and "just loved her" as she continued to slowly kill herself.

One night I received another in a series of regular calls around 10 p.m. Mom was intoxicated and crying about how sad she was over any of a series of circumstances that was depressing her that particular evening. She hinted that maybe she would be better off dead, a sentiment she had previously shared, but this time I sensed she was much more serious. I suggested that if she did not stop her pattern of self destruction, I would be forced to have her checked in to the local mental health center to get professional help.

My mother panicked and called her best friend, a true enabler and drinking buddy. This friend drove her to a secret location where we couldn't find mom, and for about three days I was worried sick. Mom would still call, drunk and depressed, asking how I could want her committed after all she had done for me over the years. I backed off my threat out of fear she would commit suicide, and she returned home to my father, who was livid at me over how I confronted her. Needless to say my parents were quite mad at me for the next few weeks.

My mother was in serious trouble and I made the decision that she needed to be confronted with the cold, hard fact that she was destroying herself, but she reacted with hurt and anger. I risked my relationship with my mother because I loved her and she needed to hear the truth--that she was killing herself physically and spiritually. It was painful and difficult to confront my mother but it was the right thing to do.

If we truly love someone who is headed off a cliff, we will risk our friendship to confront them with the truth. When we start to stray into dangerous spiritual waters, God loves us so much that He will do anything He can within the confines of our free will to warn us. When we see a fellow Christian start to stray, are we willing to be God's instrument to reel them in before they fall into the hands of the enemy? Usually not, because we have fallen into the trap of thinking love means accepting someone right where they are, even if that place is leading them to destruction. Friends, this is not love; this is closer to hatred than it is true love.

273

When I asked my pastor the hypothetical question of whether he would throw me out of the church if I admitted to having a sexual relationship outside of my marriage and was not repentant, and he answered "no", he thought he would be showing great love for me by allowing me to stay in the body. But Paul taught we should throw the unrepentant sinner out of the church and into the hands of Satan so he might see the errors of his ways and repent. Paul knew the real meaning of love while my pastor, with the right intentions, was buying into the world's definition of love. He was exhibiting tolerance and de facto acceptance of my sin.

Now we must exhibit caution and discernment when we confront a fellow Christian so we are not going on "witch hunts". There is a big difference between sinners who seek holiness but have not yet found freedom from their sinful bondages, and unrepentant sinners who refuse to admit their sinful ways and do not attempt to walk away from habitual sin. The day we decide it is best to throw every sinner out of the church is the day no one will ever enter church again. And as Jesus taught us, we must first remove the plank from our own eye before we try to remove a speck from another's eye.

But a habitual pattern of unrepentant sin must be addressed firmly for the sake of the church and the individual. We must again preach the full gospel. Not a gospel where we tell people Jesus accepts you as you are with no requirement to walk away from habitual sin, but a gospel of confession of sin, sincere repentance and a desire powered by the Holy Spirit to lead a life of righteousness and holiness.

To me it is funny and sad how Christians will hammer on a person who still smokes or has an occasional drink as "defiling the temple of the Holy Spirit", yet they will not confront people on the serious sins of pride, gossip, sexual sin, gluttony and a hardened heart. Of course, smoking or excessive alcohol is not good for you, but to condemn a Christian for smoking while allowing serious sins to go unchallenged within the church is the height of hypocrisy. We love to point to people who have an occasional beer or glass of wine as "causing others to stumble", but think nothing of how we cause others to stumble when we gossip or ignore sexual sin, pride and gluttony. Which do you think defiles the temple of the Holy Spirit more—a Christian who is honest, sexually pure, kind, loving and generous but who still smokes cigarettes? Or a non-smoker who is a gossip, addicted to pornography, stingy and spiteful?

Gluttony, in particular, is a sin that is affecting virtually every Christian in America. We just cannot get enough of the latest gadgets, clothes or trendy items that we desire in our flesh, yet an alarmingly small percentage of Christians tithe or give any significant amount of their income to God's work. We have become slaves to our desires of the flesh, ignoring the blessing God wants us to be to others.

How we show love to our Christian brothers and sisters these days looks more like enablement and cowardice than it does true love. We fail to understand that loving someone often involves risk. We risk being called judgmental when we confront another on their sins; we risk our reputation as a kind, loving person when we take the time to confront them with disturbing things we see them doing; and we risk being branded as a Pharisee when we talk about the need for us to pursue a life that is holy and pleasing to God. And if we do not back down once we have confronted them and been rebuffed, we risk losing a friend.

A close friend of mine stopped in to see me about two years ago, distraught and feeling the need to get something off his chest. He had fallen into the habit of frequenting local strip clubs without his wife's knowledge. One isolated stop at a strip club when he was on a business trip had opened the door for his flesh to again seek pleasure in looking at naked women. When he returned home the attraction to strip clubs became greater and greater until he gave in and visited a local establishment. It grew into a habit and he was now visiting them once or twice a week. He had managed to hide this from his wife and friends but the guilt and shame were now welling up and he had to confess to someone, and he chose me.

I listened as he cried and expressed the shame he felt over the addiction he had fallen into. He was truly sorry for opening that door in his life and didn't know what to do. I asked if he was willing to repent of his sin, and when he answered yes, we prayed together asking for God's forgiveness and restoration. I then asked him if he was willing to confess this to his wife and ask her forgiveness. "No, that would be horribly painful for her and me!" As he left I gave him my cell phone number and told him he could call me anytime he felt the temptation again so we could meet and pray.

A couple weeks later he came back, having fallen again to the same addiction. We prayed together again asking God to forgive and release him from this terrible addiction. This time when we finished, I told him he needed to confess this to his wife, asking for her forgiveness and help. He refused to go there, so I took a risk. I risked our friendship by telling him that if he did not confess this to his wife within twenty-four hours, I would tell her.

The look on his face was one of feeling betrayed by a close friend and of inquiring how I could claim to be a friend and be so cruel and heartless. He shot back "You wouldn't do that", but I assured him I would if he did not talk to his wife. He promised he would summon the courage to do it and tell her to call me so I could also support and encourage her by telling her that I understood the addiction he was fighting and would walk by his side to help him any way I could. She called me the next day and was hurt, but appreciative. She told me she had a feeling something was going on by his behavior and his cold attitude toward her lately, and every time she asked if something was wrong, he deflected.

She loves him very much, and when she got over the initial pain, she committed to helping him, together building a stronger marriage. Was I bluffing when I told him I would talk to his wife if he didn't? Would I have really called her? I think I would have but I am not one-hundred percent sure. I may have cowered when push came to shove, but I hope not. I hope my love for him would have overpowered my fear of losing a friend or looking like a meddler.

Nancy and I have found greater trust and intimacy by opening up to one another and confessing if we felt an attraction to another. On the rare occasion it would happen, we talk about it, pray together and commit to helping each other. We try to look internally to see if we are doing something, or not doing something, that is contributing to the potential problem. Am I providing the emotional and spiritual connection she desires? Am I not taking the time to hold her hand and tell her how very much I love her? Is she taking my acts of service for granted, opening a door for resentment?

I love my wife more than anyone except God, and I thank God every day that He gave me such a wonderful wife. But when I allow my flesh to rule my heart instead of the Holy Spirit, I am susceptible to temptation and start to find my eye wandering and my neck twisting and turning to take one more look at the beautiful woman who just walked by. I am every bit as capable in my flesh of doing exactly what my friend did, and if you think you are beyond it then you do not realize the depravity of your human condition. I hope if I ever succumb to temptation and walk into a place I shouldn't that a true friend will love me enough to confront me and make sure I do the right thing.

Our churches need to become safe places once again. Places where we can be honest with one another and confess the temptations we face before they turn into sin. We need to develop real friendships with Christians we can trust; Christians who will not enable, but correct and rebuke when necessary. There is, of course, a difference between temptation and sin.

> "Therefore, since we have a great high priest who has gone through the heavens, Jesus the Son of God, let us hold firmly to the faith we profess. For we do not have a high priest who is unable to sympathize with our weaknesses, but we have one who has been tempted in every way, just as we are—yet was without sin. Let us then approach the throne of grace with confidence, so that we may receive mercy and find grace to help us in our time of need."
>
> Hebrews 4:14-16

Jesus was tempted in every way that we are, but His connection with the Father was so strong He was able to remain sinless. We as humans do not yet have that perfect connection to the Father as we face the civil war in our hearts between the Spirit and our flesh. We need Christian brothers and sisters who love us enough to not let us continue in a state of destructive sin; friends who are willing to risk much for us—respect, reputation and friendship. If we are not willing to put ourselves at risk for another, are we truly a friend?

When we find the courage and love to be at risk to confront a brother in sin, we do more than just help them—we also strengthen the local church. Our relationship with God is personal and corporate, and just as Paul wrote in 1 Corinthians 5:6, a little yeast infects all the dough. When one of us is in a state of unrepentant sin, it also damages our corporate relationship with God as a church, and the power of the local body is diminished. But when we seek individual and corporate holiness and will not tolerate unrepentant sin that God hates, He will bless us individually and as a church. We will see greater strength, and yes maybe even greater numbers, witnessing the power of the Holy Spirit. We might just see more healings and more miracles, and we will certainly see more joy and peace as together we form a bond that just will not allow a brother or sister to walk through this world of temptation and sin alone.

We have a choice as the church. We can continue doing what we are doing and expect different results (the definition of insanity by the way), or we can choose this day to be a body that is committed to real fellowship, true love and corporate strength. I guess it comes down to asking ourselves one question: Are we satisfied with the direction and power we see in our church today?

Loving the Lost—Right To the Gates of Hell

Jaye and I rose from our knees at the conclusion of the prayer. Along with about a dozen other Christians we had prayed, asking God's blessing as we prepared to head in to the festival. We were preparing to be a witness to about four-hundred hundred people gathered for what has become an annual event in Green Bay—The "Pride Alive" event. It was a public gathering of homosexuals and their friends, proclaiming their pride in the lifestyle they had chosen.

As Jaye and I walked together approaching the festival, a lady caught up to us and asked why we were going in. We told her we were here to share the gospel with some lost people. She started into a three minute tirade, chastising us for being un-accepting and intolerant of others. She told us her church accepts homosexuals as part of the church because Jesus taught us to love all men, and because Jesus "told us we were not to judge another".

I told her I agreed with her that we are to love all men, but I asked her to define the word "love". She said it was "accepting people just as they are". I asked if that was what she was taught in church and she said yes, that message was taught constantly.

This is a lady who attends one of the larger churches in our area. If what she said is accurate, that the church teaches that love is accepting people just as they are, she and the church could not be more misguided or more wrong. Love is quite the opposite in most instances. Love is not being willing to accept people just as they are if they are headed into the abyss of eternal destruction. However when I gave her my definition of love, "a willingness to be at risk for another", she just waved her arms at me in disgust and walked away.

Jaye and I continued in and entered the Pride Alive event. I must say that I saw no blatant sexual acts or perversion committed. A few couples were holding hands and would share an occasional short kiss, but that was the extent of it. What I did see were a number of local and national companies who had paid money to be sponsors of the event, supporting gay rights and gay marriage. I saw vendors selling beer, soda, snacks and crafts. One vendor was a man who is a Christian, yet chose to attend the event as a paid vendor. I approached him and asked if he felt he was doing anything wrong in supporting a movement that was clearly sinful in God's eyes. His answer was short and simple: "No. I'm just here to make some money".

We continued on through the grounds, stopping at various booths and asking a few questions of people regarding their beliefs and attitudes about

God. Some told me they didn't believe there is a God; others would say they believed in a god who accepts all people just as they are.

We approached a church booth of a national congregation, asking a man why they were there and his response was to support equal rights for all people. When Jaye asked him some questions about God and the Bible, the man said "Let me bring my life partner over—he can better answer your questions." He brought the man over—a liberal priest complete with the priest collar. Jaye asked him to please square up his beliefs on homosexuality with the Bible and the man tried to tap dance around the questions, continually citing a few select verses many Christians use to exonerate and justify their beliefs on homosexuality.

Jaye kept pressing but kept getting the same tired old response—that God loves all men and accepts them just as they are. The man started to get a little irritated but kept his composure.

I went to a booth manned by the Unitarian Universalist Church. They had this catchy banner with a quote that read: "Don't place a period where God intended a comma." This was an obvious reference to how they believed man had twisted God's beliefs and writings. I asked the two men if they attended the church and they said they did. I asked them just where in the Bible we had replaced God's comma with a period. They looked at each other and one said "I don't read the bible". The other nodded in affirmation. I asked why not, and his response was "Because it isn't important; we know what we believe".

It was quite a day. No "conversions" that I know of and no sinner's prayer recitals. But it gave me a little more insight into the world of homosexual beliefs and the attitude of too many Christians like the lady who approached us—that love is all about just accepting people, even if they are headed over a cliff. That love means never having to say "You're wrong". That love means just letting people live as they see best regardless of what the Bible says. How very sad that love has been twisted into such an attitude of covert hatred.

It is not just homosexuality that Christians take a "live and let live" approach about. It is virtually every sin and cultural behavior that exists these days. Abortion? Just "love on people". Adulterers? "Who are we to judge?" Greed and selfishness? "Hey, it's my money and I'll spend it as I want."

The sad truth is that deep down, most Christians don't give a darn about the lost. Hey, we've got our salvation, so we're good to go! Our actions, or rather inaction, define love as selfish, uncaring and tolerant of just about anything, and that is a cowardly love. We just can't handle the rejection of being seen as unloving or intolerant, and would rather watch countless millions go to their eternal deaths than risk being seen as intolerant or "bible thumpers". Whether we admit it or not, we act ashamed of the gospel.

Ashamed of the gospel: What does that say about the depth of our love of God? We are like a man who says he loves his wife but never takes her out of the house because other men might think she is ugly. We tell her she's pretty, but our actions belie those words.

If we truly loved God and the gospel, we would not be able to contain our joy or our ability to share it with everyone we know. If we truly loved the lost we would do anything we could to share the gospel with them.

Hanging On For Dear Life

We have all seen the movies where a man is about to fall to his death, hanging on for dear life by his fingertips. The friend reaches out to pull him up and for a moment we are left wondering if he will be able to pull his dangling friend to safety.

Well, what would happen if the rescuer did not have a firm hold of the ground on which he stood as he attempted to rescue his friend? If he did not have one hand firmly grasping a well-anchored object while he reached out with his other hand? Both would fall to their deaths. Welcome to the seeker-friendly world of progressive American Christianity.

Organizations like Sojourners and Red Letter Christians are cowards, ashamed of the gospel. They present a façade of "love and tolerance" as the preferred means to reach out to the man hanging on by his fingertips.

They think they care for the lost, but they are like the ill-fated rescuer who is not completely anchored on a solid object that will allow him to really attempt a rescue. So they either convince themselves and the dangling man that he is not really in danger, allowing him to fall to his death, or they do something even worse. In their attempt to rescue him, they fail to remain anchored to something immovable—the Word of God—and they fall to their death just like the man they are trying to rescue.

God will not be mocked. He gave us the gospel as the sole means by which man might be rescued from eternal death. It is the power of the gospel, not our feeble, cowardly attempts at "love", that can save a man. But aren't we mocking God by saying our ways are better than His? Are we not diminishing the power of the gospel when we put our own little spin on it? Do we think that God needs to change his formula for reaching the lost in this postmodern era? That God just cannot "relate" to the world and culture as it is today?

"Seeker-friendly" Christianity as it is presented today is arrogant and ineffective. It is telling God He is less than able to reach the lost without our help and our ability to relate to the culture. God just doesn't get it, and we need to intervene. Just how foolish and arrogant is that?

Summary

Just like Vince Lombardi had to take his football team back to the basics to get them on track, we need to return as a church to a basic understanding of what love is and isn't. God's love is perfect but ours is flawed. Unless we identify love as God defines it, there is no real hope of restoring unrepentant Christian sinners or reaching the lost. We may see an occasional victory here or there, but as they say, even a broken clock is right twice a day.

Don't tell me you love someone when you lack the courage to put yourself at risk for them. And leaders, stop teaching our children that love means tolerance and unbiblical acceptance of people just as they are. Fool yourself if you desire, but stop taking our children down with you as you enter very dangerous territory.

Love is sacrifice, total commitment and a willingness to put your self at risk of harm. Love is the cross. It is not what we have come to define it.

Chapter Fourteen

The Heart of the Matter

Chrislam, New Age Christianity, and Social Justice; The Emergent Church Movement, weak leadership, mushy followers and an evil secular culture. There are plenty of battles to fight these days and no shortage of challenges facing Bible-believing Christians today. The world hates God more each day, and too many Christians are defining God and Christianity on their own terms.

But none of these opponents or challenges should be a match for the Body of Christ. We have the truth and the Holy Spirit in our corner, so any opponent should be easily vanquished. But they are not being vanquished, and they are winning the battle. We must reverse this, but how?

The first key to winning a battle is to understand that we are in a battle to begin with. Unless we realize that and understand the full scope of the battle, we are unprepared to engage the opponent.

The second key is to make sure we are an army whom an opponent would never want to fight in the first place. The greatest deterrent to an enemy attack is when the enemy fears the outcome. It is obvious that the culture does not fear American Christianity as an opponent. It views us as weak, scattered and willing to compromise rather than engage in battle, and they are correct.

Before World War II, Hitler began to annex territory and build a military force even though both were forbidden by the surrender treaty

Germany signed after the previous world war. He started testing the resolve of European leaders in small ways, and when they did not oppose him, his confidence and boldness increased. He saw weakness in his opponent and exploited it masterfully. With each additional move he made, he assured the Allied Nations it would be his last.

He signed a nonaggression treaty with his enemy to the north, Russia, effectively neutralizing the greatest single threat he might face. He continued to annex land and build his military force while his opponents continued to hope that peace could be maintained and war averted.

Then he invaded Poland and crossed a line which the Allied Nations could not excuse, so they declared war on Germany. But by this time Germany's military might was formidable. The allies declared war but their weakness resulted in a war that would leave more than fifty million dead and Europe all but destroyed.

Aggressive enemies prey on the weakness and fears of others. They use our passive attitudes and lack of commitment to our mission to exploit and manipulate us. They chip away, taking small bites out of us until we are weak and ineffective, and then they strike. If their opponent does not have a heart for battle, the enemy will prey on that weakness and gain incremental victories until they are ready for an all-out attack.

The enemy we face, Satan, is no different in his methods. He chips away at us in many ways, convincing us of lies and half-truths that weaken our position. He tells us that love means accepting all people right where they are instead of helping them out of a life of sin. He convinces us that we deserve the good things in this life even if it means compromising truth and righteousness. He convinces us that God is tolerant of our sin, and he convinces us that the sin in our life has no real consequence on us, individually or corporately as the Body of Christ.

Our sins do have consequences. They draw us away from God and take our eyes off Him, placing them on ourselves. Sin is also addicting, and once you give in to a particular sin, it becomes progressively easier. We continue down a destructive path until God intervenes by allowing the consequences of our sin to catch up to us. When that happens, it often comes with a very high price as our lives are shattered from the accumulated sin that God finally decides has gone too far. To a married man who is unfaithful to his wife, with another woman or through pornography, the price might be a severely strained relationship that takes years to restore. If this happens to a Christian leader it might also mean an end to his ministry work. Sin also gives others one more excuse to shun the Christian faith.

We must take a strong stand against the sin that has sadly become too commonplace in American Christianity. We must take a stand against the unrepentant sin of others, but most importantly we must take a strong stand against our own sin that we hide in our hearts, away from public scrutiny.

Defeating Sin in Our Lives

Have we given up trying to purge sin from our lives? It sure seems so. Righteousness and the pursuit of holiness have been replaced at the forefront of Christian teachings with less challenging messages used as excuses for our continuing to sin before a holy God.

"We're all sinners, saved by grace".

No doubt this is a true statement. There is no one who is righteous except by the grace and mercy of God through Jesus, but this true statement has morphed into a popular excuse to not walk away from sin and pursue a life of holiness.

How we view ourselves makes all the difference sometimes. If I see myself as decrepit and unlovable, I will probably start to behave that way. But if I read scripture, particularly Romans 7, I can see myself as God sees me.

Romans Chapter 7 is a perfect definition of how Christians should see themselves. We tend to look at ourselves as a singular entity, but Paul describes two entities living within himself--the Holy Spirit of God and his own flesh. These two inhabitants are in the midst of a civil war, battling every moment of our day. The Spirit within us longs to love and worship God, but the other inhabitant, our flesh, lives to serve only our sinful desires. It is very important that we see ourselves as Paul did, with two competing inhabitants fighting every moment for ultimate control of our lives and eternal destiny. If we simply look at ourselves as a "singular entity" we are setting ourselves up for trouble.

If we view ourselves as nothing more than decrepit, worthless sinners, we begin to live out that by which we define ourselves. We subconsciously give up, resigning ourselves to a life of sin, depending on the grace and mercy of God.

Conversely, if we think of ourselves as singularly holy and righteous we can become arrogant and deceitful. We start to justify our every action by the fact that we have accepted the mercy and forgiveness of Jesus, and we abandon a pursuit of holiness because we think it is unnecessary.

However, if we understand that God hates sin, and we are a dual entity--part of us hating sin and the other part loving it--we can frame up the battle in a way where we can start to fight and attain victory. We also come to understand something very crucial: That the most powerful enemy we face in restoring American Christianity resides in each of us. We must first find victory in this internal battle before we can have any real hope of defeating the enemy who seeks to discredit and destroy American Christianity.

Chrislam, New Age thought or emergent theology is a powerless threat if we could only conquer the enemy residing in each one of us, our own desires of the flesh. Once we conquer our internal enemy, the external enemies can be vanquished.

The Battle in Our Mind and Why We are Losing

There have been some excellent books written by Christian teachers on the important battle we fight daily in our minds. Good and evil fight it out in the midst of memories, thoughts and temptations, pulling us in two directions. Our flesh desires to feed its lusts and desires, while our love of God calls us to lead a life of holiness. The Apostle Paul eloquently writes of this internal civil war in Romans 7.

When we first become Christians, we carry all the baggage of our sinful past with us. We are immediately justified by our faith in Jesus, but sanctification--the pursuit of holiness--takes a long time. Years of living in the world and its influence battle against our newfound love of God that calls us to lead a pure life. We become creatures of habit in choosing sin, and our sinful human nature does not give up easily. Our mind becomes a raging battlefield where we make decisions to honor God or continue to feed our flesh. In spite of our best efforts, the old baggage we still carry often wins out and we give in to temptation and sin.

Books on the battlefields in our minds are very beneficial in our early life as a Christian. In Philippians 4:8 we are taught to think on things that are right, pure, lovely and praiseworthy to help us ward off our desires of the flesh and the enemy who seeks to steal our new love of God. Our minds are like the muscles of our body, needing to be trained and exercised to maximize their potential. When we train them properly, they become strong and fruitful.

As new Christians, we learn about receiving the Holy Spirit and allowing him to comfort us and convict us of sin in our lives, but fully understanding how to do this takes time. We receive the Holy Spirit, but our minds have not yet been weaned off our sinful habits, and past memories and experiences still have a hold on us, influencing our decisions and acting as impediments to living a life of holiness. As we continue to read the Word of God and draw nearer to Him, we slowly learn the sources of the baggage in our minds that hold us back as Christians. The many books written on the subject help us to find scriptures that teach us of being a new creation, rejecting the sin and hurt in our past that impedes our progress.

As we grow in our maturity as Christians, God exposes the dangerous programming that has infiltrated our minds, causing us to turn time and again to our sinful nature in spite of our new life in Him. This programming is similar to a virus on a computer, causing glitches and breakdowns in our mind--the computer hardware of our bodies. Books on the battle within our minds help us understand these viruses, and once we identify them, we can begin to isolate them by the power of the Holy Spirit. But while we isolate them, they are still ever present and surface time and time again. Once we know what these viruses are, we are now in position to wipe them from our minds if we understand and follow the Word of God.

Hardware, Software and Virus Firewalls

If our brain is the hardware, our hearts are the software. The heart creates an emotional reaction, feeds it to our brain where a decision is made, leading to an action. This is consistent with how computers work and the human brain is the greatest of computers, capable of millions of instinctive reactions that control every part of our body. The software tells the hardware what programs to run, and the hardware carries out the command.

The Bible mentions the heart six times more than it does the mind, identifying the heart as the proverbial source of our emotions. In 1 Timothy Chapter One, Paul encourages us to stay true to the gospel and reject sin. In verse 5 he states, *"The goal of this command is love, which comes from a pure heart and a good conscience and a sincere faith."*

However we are not born with a "pure heart". In Jeremiah 17:9 God tells us *"The heart is deceitful above all things and beyond cure."* So Paul tells us that love comes from a pure heart but in Jeremiah we are told the heart is deceitful. Obviously this presents quite a challenge for us as Christians. How do we develop a pure heart from one that is deceitful above all things? We cannot—we need a heart transplant.

> *"I will give you a new heart and put a new spirit in you. I will remove from you your heart of stone and give you a heart of flesh. And I will put my Spirit in you and move you to follow my decrees and be careful to keep my laws."*
>
> Ezekiel 36:26-27

There is your heart transplant--your new software. The old heart is gone, wiped away, and your new heart, complete with God's Spirit, now runs on the hard drive of your brain. This new heart replaces your deceitful human heart, eliminating the garbage we carried since the day we were born.

The books on the battle within our minds give us excellent information on how we can better control the emotions our deceitful heart sends to the brain, but unless we eradicate the viruses we have accumulated in our hearts and minds over many years of painful experiences, we will continually fight a losing battle in our minds. When God gives us a heart transplant, replacing our human hearts of stone with a new heart that includes his Spirit, the viruses can be wiped out. We are no longer ruled by our past failures and fears, instead we are truly a new creation--we are "born again".

In John 3:3-6, Jesus told Nicodemus *I tell you the truth, no one can see the kingdom of God unless he is born again . . . I tell you the truth, no one can enter the kingdom of God unless he is born of water and spirit. Flesh gives birth to flesh, but the Spirit gives birth to spirit."*

Unfortunately, Christians have been misled to think that saying the "sinner's prayer" equates to being born again. But until we accept the new heart God offers in Ezekiel, complete with His Spirit, we are not truly born again. We remain flesh, fighting against overwhelming odds to become holy in the eyes of a perfect God. But once we accept God's offer of a new heart **and His Spirit**, we truly *are* born again and can start living as a new creation, free from all the baggage of our old lives. Without our new heart it is virtually impossible to live holy lives, as the viruses of our previous life pollute our minds, leading to continuous sin.

Fighting the battle in our minds will produce some victories, but many more defeats, as our minds are already infected with viruses from our old heart. But when we allow God to install new software via the heart He offers, complete with His Spirit, we start clean. Our hearts, the proverbial residence of all our emotions, are now virus-free, capable of saturating our minds with a deep love of God. This gives us the power to turn our backs on our sinful nature and achieve real victory over sin.

So our brains are the hardware, and our new hearts the virus-free software installed by God. But hackers are very cunning, always looking for ways to infect computers and wreak havoc. Satan is the most cunning and brilliant of all hackers. He knows our vulnerabilities and will always seek to install new viruses on our new hearts and minds. But God has an answer for that challenge.

A Fool-Proof Firewall and Anti-Virus Protection

"When an evil spirit comes out of a man, it goes through arid places seeking rest and does not find it. Then it says 'I will return to the house I left.' When it arrives, it finds the house swept clean and put in order. Then it goes and takes seven other spirits more wicked than itself, and they go in and live there. And the final condition of that man is worse than the first."

Luke 11:24-26

Satan never gives up. Our new hearts from God are still subject to viruses that Satan will send to prod our defenses, looking for weaknesses. He is committed to disrupting and polluting the new heart God has given us, stopping at nothing in his quest to rob us of our joy and pursuit of holiness. He will redouble his efforts to infect the new heart God has given us, so we must not be lulled into a false sense of security.

Firewall and anti-virus software is critical to protecting a computer network from hackers and viruses. It is no different with our human brain, the hardware, or our new heart, the software. God provides the perfect virus protection that can detect attacks before they infiltrate our hearts and minds, causing serious problems--His written Word.

"No temptation has seized you except what is common to man. And God is faithful; he will not let you be tempted beyond what you can bear. But when you are tempted, he will also provide a way out so that you can stand up under it."

1 Corinthians 10:13

The Bible tells us a lot about the hacker and enemy we battle. It tells us Satan is like a lion, constantly prowling in search of his next victim. He is also the "father of lies" and the master of the half-truth. We just saw that when a demon is rebuked, he can return with allies to break back in if we do not securely lock our hearts and minds. However, if the anti-virus program and firewall of God's Word is properly utilized, the enemy has no entrance to gain a foothold.

With our new pure heart from God, His Spirit, and the anti-virus firewall of His Word, we can attain greater victory than we ever could by fighting the battle in our minds that have been corrupted with many years of viruses. There is a real battlefield in our minds, seeking to spoil our new life in Jesus. If we fight this battle without the new heart and virus protection of the written Word, we are bound to fail far more than we succeed. God wants us to lead lives of victory and has provided a way to do so, but this will require a real commitment from us; a commitment too few Christians seem willing to embrace in these wicked times.

The only way to successfully win the battle between our Spirit and the flesh is to wipe away the corrupted software infecting the hardware, and reinstall good software. And the only way this can be accomplished is by a spiritual heart transplant from God. When protected by the perfect firewall—the Word of God—we are now able to lead a life of victory and holiness.

Chapter Fifteen
"Now my closing thoughts . . ."

The number and ferocity of the enemies fighting American Christianity is large. But none is more destructive than the internal battle we fight every minute of every day. If we find victory personally, then corporately in the church, the remaining enemies will be powerless. Any attack they launch will break like waves on the rocks.

We as Christians are continuously making choices. We choose to love God by obeying Him or we choose to reject His perfect will for our lives, diminishing our ability to fight the external enemies dismantling the church. Every decision we make has consequences and every time we choose righteousness we strengthen ourselves and the Body of Christ. But when we choose sin, even if it goes unnoticed by anyone else, we weaken the body as a whole. Unless we gain victory internally, within our own heart and mind, we will never achieve victory against the external enemies of the church.

We are the greatest enemy we will face this day, and our human sinful nature is our greatest threat. I am as capable of doing damage to the Body of Christ as any heretical movement, weak leader or cultural cancer out there. When I choose sin I weaken not only myself, but my Christian brothers and sisters who with me compose the Body of Christ. Until each of us understands and accepts this fact, we are acting as hypocrites when we speak out against false teachers and movements. We must first remove the plank from our own eye so we have the ability and moral standing to point out the speck in our brother's eye.

Victory is ours if we have the courage to grasp it, but it will not be easy given our current state of deterioration. Do we have the courage to walk away from our sinful habits? Do we have the courage to truly love one another and risk everything to confront our brothers and sisters in their habitual sin? Do we have the courage to redefine success for the church from "nickels and noses" to an army of real disciples? Do we have the courage to respectfully challenge everything a Christian leader says or does if it seems to conflict with the Word of God? Do we have the courage to stand up to the secular culture and say "No more!"?

If we do, we can restore and renew American Christianity. If we lack the courage we will slowly die at our own hands. All that will remain of American Christianity is a remnant, and much will be lost. The choice is ours and God awaits our answer.

Can We Come Back From the Brink of Death?

The world is rapidly deteriorating into chaos because of sin. When Adam and Eve chose to know sin instead of trusting God, our Creator wound the clock and started the countdown to the end of the age. An exciting new eternal life awaits those of us who truly know Jesus as our Lord and Savior. But in the meantime we have work to do.

We cannot save our world. No source of renewable energy, no politician, no world leader and no peace treaty can stop the inevitable end of the story. We cannot stop the rise to power of the Antichrist or the false prophet. They will rule the majority of the world one day.

We cannot change biblical prophesy. No amount of social justice or dominion theology will alter the fate of this world spelled out in the Bible.

We cannot change the declining culture. It will grow more evil and hateful of God. We may be forced as church and ministry leaders to choose between our non-profit status or continuing to preach the gospel without compromise. We may face a decision one day soon to stop calling homosexuality a sin or face imprisonment for promoting hate speech.

Our public education system will never again be a place where our children hear our Christian values supported or reinforced. Instead our children will increasingly be marginalized, perhaps even bullied, for standing on their Christian beliefs.

The secular media will never again be friendly to us as Christians. It will continue to marginalize and lie about God and those of us committed to Him. Christian media will continue to slide toward mushy theology, scorning anyone who has the courage to call out false teachings and false teachers. It will begin to look more and more like the secular culture with each passing year.

Feeling depressed yet? Don't be, because I can think of no greater time to be a Christian. We might well be witnesses to the final days before our King returns to take us home, when we will see the arrogance of Satan shattered as he is defeated decisively and eternally. We are seeing history unfold right before our eyes, witnessing the time when Jesus said there would be a great falling away. We might be witnessing the strong delusion God promised to send in Romans 1 and 2 Thessalonians.

We live in a world where the harvest is great, but the workers are few. What a time to work those fields! We can be the select few who stand strong until the end no matter what the enemy sends our way, leading many to the light and hope of the true gospel.

There is work to do and all is not lost by any stretch of the imagination. We can salvage American Christianity. Perhaps our numbers will decrease, but Gideon only needed three hundred to conquer a much larger army because the Lord was with him. Moses delivered his people with nothing more than a shepherd's staff, because the Lord was with him. All we have to do is repent of our apathy and recommit ourselves to the Lord's plan for our lives. Whether we are three hundred, three thousand or three million, when has the size of an army ever mattered to God?

When the world starts to fall apart and others begin to panic, we can be God's instruments to bring the lost home to Him. We can shine the irresistible light of the risen Christ right through the darkness of this world. It can be a bright beacon for millions of lost ships. What a time to be alive!

But it will take genuine repentance and a total commitment to the Lord's agenda, abandoning our own selfish desires. It will take real love, not the phony love of cowardice and tolerance. It will take courage to speak out boldly, compassion for those in troubling times, and a willingness to abandon everything of this world that we have come to love.

We cannot do it. But the Holy Spirit can do it through us if we give Him permission and total control. That's asking a lot and Jesus told us it would not be easy. As my wife often says "Jesus asks only one thing from us--everything". Are we willing to surrender everything to Him?

I end this book with a few of my "closing thoughts" that I write and read at the end of most episodes of Stand Up For the Truth. I hope they challenge you when you read them as much as God challenged me while I was writing them. Every one of us needs to challenge our own thoughts, words and actions these days in addition to holding our leaders accountable. There are enemies everywhere looking to destroy American Christianity, but let us never forget that sometimes the greatest threat to American Christianity resides in our own depraved human hearts. These hearts fight against the new heart and Spirit that God gives each of us when we become true believers. It is an internal civil war that we must win before we can take the battle to the enemy.

Question everything except the Word of God. Become a good Berean and take everything you hear to the scriptures to validate it as truth or refute it as a lie. Paul commended the Bereans for checking everything he taught against the scriptures. If our Christian leaders are unwilling to be scrutinized in the same manner, then we must stop following them.

I sign off as I do at the end of each Stand Up For the Truth show: **Be bold, be strong; and always remember, the Lord your God is with you!**

August 8, 2011

Paul's letters to the Corinthians cover a myriad of subjects. But an overriding message is for Christians not to quarrel with one another over relatively unimportant issues--but he also encouraged them to not tolerate false teachings and false teachers within the church.

We tackle a lot of difficult issues on Stand Up For the Truth. There are many attacks from the outside from Islam, humanism and atheists who seek to discount the truth of God's Word. But the attacks from the outside do not worry me as much as the attacks from the inside. Jesus and Paul warned that in these final days there would be false teachings that tickle the ears and turn many away from the true gospel. But how do we determine which of our differences are relatively insignificant and which pose a real threat to the church? I think this is a crucial issue that our church leaders need to pray about and address.

Look, as Christians we are always going to disagree on certain issues that are relatively insignificant to our faith. Should Christians ever consume alcohol? When will the rapture of the church take place? These are issues we should discuss with one another, allowing a lot of grace and respectful disagreement. But there are some issues we need to take a stand on, particularly when the character and nature of God are called in to question.

When leaders like Rob Bell question if hell is real, we need to take a stand. When Brian McLaren calls the cross false advertising and doubts that God would send Jesus to pay the price for our sins, we need to take a stand. When Pastors and leaders are reaching out to find common ground with Islam, a religion that says Jesus is not the Son of God, we need to take a stand.

Last week a Christian I have known a long time told me there are a few local pastors who get upset at our show. They feel we are dividing the Body of Christ rather than helping to unify it. Well, just what are we supposed to unite around? If they are asking us to be accepting of the teachings of

Rob Bell, Brian Mclaren and the Chrislam movement being led by people like Rick Warren—well that's not unity, it's a sell out.

The goal of Stand Up For the Truth remains the same—to share news that affects our Christian faith and point you to the Word of God as the only source of absolute truth we can depend on. And we will continue to ruffle some feathers as we move forward. If that is what it takes to wake us up from our malaise as a church, so be it.

You know it would be nice if we could all just go on with our lives pretending that everything is just fine. But a look at today's headlines quickly wakes us up. Growing tension in the Middle East, a world possibly on the verge of economic collapse, and an increasingly lethargic church that seems too willing to accept false teachings about God are all embraced for the sake of "unity". The fact is the world is ripe for change and just looking for a hero that will usher in peace and prosperity. Does that character sound at all familiar to you as a Christian?

Many of our guests on this show comment on how few Christian radio shows are willing to tackle the tough issues these days. They seem more interested in garnering big audiences with a soft, squishy message. Well, that's just not us. We are called to be watchmen on the wall and point out danger when we see it. And we will continue to do so, always being in prayer and asking God to help us discern the difference between honest disagreements on non-crucial issues, and when to take a stand against dangerous compromise and false teaching.

So yes, we will continue to ruffle some feathers. And we welcome your feedback, positive or negative. And to those few pastors who seem to think we are off base biblically, we welcome you to come on air with us and share your opinion. Because what we need most right now is a real discussion on issues facing the church. The last thing we can afford is to continue to go on blindly thinking everything is OK. The world is changing rapidly and there is pressure on the church to change along with it. And that my friends, is a real danger!

January 9, 2012

It's important when we read the news or listen to what a leader says, that we look beyond the rhetoric and discern the real intentions of the one delivering a message to us. Watch the nightly news about what is going on in Africa these days. The secular news reports with terms like "tribal violence" or "civil war" to describe what is going on. But if they were truthful and principled, they would report it like this: Militant Muslims continue to track down and slaughter thousands of Christians and secularists in a move to eliminate anyone who does not submit to the Koran and Allah.

But you will rarely, if ever, hear that for a couple reasons: First, it would put the news networks at risk of falling out of favor with radical Muslim groups, inviting criticism and boycotts; and second it would go against their anti-Christian bias. Now what else should we expect from the world that hates Jesus and the exclusive message of the bible in these politically correct times? They are only doing what we expect the world to do.

But what about those who call themselves "Christians"? Is it too much to ask them to address these stories with honesty and courage? A case in point, our friend Jim Wallis and Sojourners: They claim to be Christians who seek justice and peace for all, but what do they have to say about the murder of innocent Christians in Africa? NOTHING! The stories covered on their website will talk about how the "99%" in this nation are being abused by wealthy Americans; about how politicians who stand up for the unborn are extreme; and how every attempt to reign in crippling spending is a fight against the poor—but nothing about the mass murder and genocide being carried out by Muslim fanatics against all who oppose Sharia Law in Africa, including Christians.

And what of those Pastors and Christian leaders who bend over backwards to accommodate Islam and seek to find common ground with a religion of the antichrist? How do they sleep at night signing on to cooperation with a religion that denies the deity of Jesus Christ and endorses the murder of millions of Christians, Jews and secularists every year? Sadly, they probably sleep quite well—because being asleep is something they do very well. And if you think my words on Islam being a religion of the anti-Christ are harsh, read 1 John Chapter 4 and see what God has to say on the subject.

How many innocent Christians and people must be murdered before Christian leaders wake up and see what is happening—and what soon might happen right under our noses? Don't expect anything to change—because these "leaders" are not men of courage; they are men who seek the approval of other men, not of God. They will not change; it is up to us as Christians to determine if we will continue to turn a blind eye to this evil and choose to continue following these men who have become our self-appointed leaders within Christianity. If we do not stand up and challenge them and their self-appointed authority, we are no better than these blind men who are leading us.

July 7, 2011

In Matthew Chapter 16 we read the story of Peter's acknowledgment of Jesus as the Son of God. Jesus asks His disciples "Who do people say I am?" They replied that some say He is John the Baptist while others say He was a reincarnated prophet like Elijah or Jeremiah. But Peter speaks up and proclaims Jesus for who He is—the Son of God and the Messiah.

Well today we're starting to see this discussion ramp up again. The New Age movement and its affiliate movements are starting to refer to Jesus once again as a great prophet or teacher, but stop short of professing him as the Son of God. And sadly, some Christian churches and leaders seem to be following suit. Just read some of the writing of emergent and social justice leaders and you will see a great emphasis on Jesus the teacher—and a lack of focus on Jesus as the Son of God. Some of their false teachings even suggest we can all become gods on a par with Jesus.

You know in the past when someone stated they were a Christian, you could take it at face value. But these days, I find I must do a little digging and questioning when I meet someone who says they are a Christian. Just what does that mean? Who exactly is Jesus: A great teacher, a prophet, or the only begotten Son of God? He is the Son of God who took on humanity to die on a cross for our sins so that those of us who truly believe in Him could become righteous in God's eyes.

Sadly, there are a lot of different versions of "Jesus" out there today. And I fully expect as we move forward you will see more and more people look at Him as a great teacher and philosopher, but deny Him as the Son of the living God. We live in the times prophesied where good would be looked at as evil, and evil as good. So we need to take the time to know God's Word so we might recognize the counterfeit when we see it. Scripture tells us many will abandon the faith for the ways of man. That path to salvation that Jesus taught about just might be a lot narrower than we have been led to believe.

May 6, 2011

In John 15, Jesus says: "If the world hates you, remember that it hated me first. If you belonged to the world, it would love you as its own. As it is, you do not belong to the world, but I have chosen you out of the world. That is why the world hates you."

This is one of the more challenging and sobering verses in the bible. As followers of Jesus Christ, we are going to be hated by the world. I think of this in light of our reaction to the death of Osama bin Laden and a protest event that happened yesterday at the National Day of Prayer Women's luncheon in Green Bay. A small group of protestors picketed the luncheon because Julaine Appling was the main speaker. Julaine and her organization are avid defenders for the rights of the unborn and the establishment of marriage as between one man and one woman. Both of these are strong biblical issues. Yet some of the world hates Julaine and what she stands for.

How does the world look at you as a Christian? Do you stick out like a sore thumb and perhaps even irritate the world at times? Or are you treated as one of their own?—blending in and being loved by the world?

Now I am not advocating we become raving maniacs spreading hateful or condemning speech, but I am asking each of us to take stock in how the world and its sinful ways look at us.

Do our neighbors even know we are disciples of Jesus Christ? Does our family even know? Or are we hoping to just fly under the radar screen so we will be loved by the world, our friends and family?

There is a strange irony in being a true disciple of Jesus Christ. We are to love all men, believers and non-believers. But by that love, the world will hate us because of our commitment to Jesus. I think it begs examination into the definition of the word love. If our neighbor is not a true Christian, do we love him enough to risk our friendship to share the gospel of salvation with him? When we attend family events with our parents or brothers and sisters who are not committed Christians, are we willing to risk our peaceful relationships with them to stand strong on God's Word and share the gospel message in word and deeds?

Strangely ironic that the best way we can love a non-believer is to be willing to risk our earthly relationship with them for the sake of the gospel. But if we truly love our neighbor, our friends and our family, we need to be willing to risk being hated by them if they reject the gospel message. 2000 years ago, Jesus Christ, the Son of God, gave up his very life because He loved us enough to risk offending us as sinners. Are we to do any less to reach our neighbors and friends for Him?

So if the world is in love with you, do not be flattered. Rather, take a good look in the mirror and drop to your knees in prayer, asking God for the boldness in love to risk being hated—all for the sake of Jesus and His message of salvation. And when the world hates us, remember it hated *Him* first.

October 5, 2011

I find it quite interesting that the Christian world and the secular world seem to be headed down different paths these days regarding the spirit world. As the New Age movement is growing, being spurred on by

Oprah Winfrey and the New Age books she endorses, Christians seem to be paying less attention to life in the spiritual realms these days.

The bible is full of references to the spiritual realm. In Leviticus and Deuteronomy God forbids us from being involved with mediums and familiar spirits. In 1 Samuel 16, verse 14 it says "the spirit of the Lord had departed from Saul, and an evil spirit of the Lord tormented him." And Ephesians is full of references to rulers, authorities and forces of evil in the heavenly realms. And of course Paul tells us our battle is not against flesh and blood, but against the powers and principalities in the spiritual realm.

The New Age Movement is all about the spiritual realm and is suggesting that all people can connect on the spiritual level and together become god. And sadly, as we will discuss in the coming weeks, many Christian leaders are openly encouraging their followers to join in this new age movement, wanting us to all become one and achieve more together—a modern day tower of Babel.

So as Christians who still believe in the absolute truth of God's Word, I think it is important we spend some serious time seeing what God has to say about life and battle in the spiritual realm. This will take discernment and the wisdom of the Holy Spirit because it can be treacherous ground.

How do we distinguish between spiritual attack and the weakness of our own flesh? When things seem to be going wrong at every turn, is it Satan fighting us? Or is it a consequence of our own poor decisions? Or is God allowing difficulties in our life to teach us and train us for greater things?

We have been so blessed as Christians living in this great country of ours. As a whole, things have been pretty easy for us compared to Christians in Asia, Africa and the Middle East. But times are changing. As the battle in the spiritual realm heats up and we approach the final days before the Lord's return, things will only get more challenging. And in my opinion, the real challenge will be this: There is a counterfeit Christian movement that is growing, luring ignorant Christians into a dangerous "New Age Christianity". Unless we are anchored in the truth of God's Word we will not recognize this counterfeit when we are confronted with it. And many will be deceived, falling for something that might look bright and shiny on the outside—but full of deceit and corruption on the inside.

Be on guard—and be in the Word of God, seeking and knowing His truth. Understand as best we can what God has to say about the battle going on in the spiritual realm. God is moving his chess pieces into position—and so is the enemy. It will be one hell of a battle—and we will have to choose what side we are on--a choice that will have eternal consequences for every one of us.

February 3, 2012

Discernment: Both David and Solomon continually asked God for discernment so they might serve Him and His people wisely. The Apostles preached about the need to be discerning regarding spirits and teachings of leaders. It is obvious God wants us to have a discerning heart when we deal with things of this world and in the spiritual realm.

Yet discernment seems to be getting a bad rap these days. When Christians discern that perhaps something might be wrong with a teaching or movement these days, they need to be very careful about addressing it. Many attempts by well intentioned Christians to question the teachings of television preachers or movements is often met with scorn and an accusation that they are being divisive or coming against one of God's prophets. Rick Warren in his "Purpose Driven Church" curriculum warns that when people question ideas like removing crosses from churches, you need to come against them and remove them from positions of leadership, so it will not cause disunity in the Body.

Now do some watchmen or discernment ministries go off the deep end, wrongly questioning or accusing leaders of heresy where there is none? Yes, and they need to repent of it and be more prayerful and discerning before they publicly accuse a fellow Christian of false teaching. But there is also a "smoke and mirrors" game going on with some churches and organizations when someone wants to question something being taught or promoted. Case in point—Rick Warren. Many discernment ministries who are increasingly concerned with Warren's teachings or leanings on The Daniel Plan, Chrislam, and Tony Blair's global spiritualization movement, attempt to contact Warren before going public with their concerns. We have done so before we air concerns about Warren—but getting them to return a call or address the concerns is stonewalled and rebuffed. So when a discernment or teaching ministry public questions what is going on, they are scolded and told they have no right to do so until they meet with the individual so we can "know their heart".

Is it sound practice to talk with an individual before you publicly question some of their teachings? Yes. But what do you do when you go to them, asking for clarification or explanation first, and the messages you leave go unanswered? If a defendant in a trial pleads his fifth-amendment rights, does the district attorney simply drop the case? Or does he move forward presenting the facts and circumstantial evidence, always giving the accused the right to respond?

We live in a world where being politically-correct and sacrificing the truth to avoid hurting peoples' feelings is rampant. And when we sacrifice truth to spare feelings, we are in deep trouble.

Look, any one of us can and does make mistakes. No pastor or teacher is above error or a misstatement. But when they refuse to explain their statements or wrap themselves in a cocoon, refusing to address the concerns of fellow believers, their teachings become fair game for discussion.

Yes, discernment and questioning church leadership seems to be getting a bad wrap these days. The motto of the church in America seems to be "unity at all costs". But biblical truth must never become a casualty of that unity.

February 28, 2012

Apathetic Christianity is a real disease infecting the Body of Christ, and it is infecting us in several ways.

First, our Christian faith has become something that is incomplete these days. We come to accept Jesus as our Savior and Lord and think the race is complete. But becoming a Christian is not the end of the race, it is the beginning. We are told by Paul to work out our salvation daily. A work out suggests exercise and commitment, not apathy and laziness. There is a powerful enemy that seeks to kill and destroy us, robbing us of joy and victory. And fat, apathetic Christians are an easy target.

Second our faith has become self-focused too often these days. I accept Jesus as Lord and Savior and I'm good to go. Our attitude toward neighbors and friends seems to be "I've got mine, but son you're on your own." Our faith should excite us so much that we want to shout it out from the roof tops and tell everyone we know about this awesome Jesus who has rescued us from eternal damnation. We should desire that everyone we know learn about the saving grace and power of Jesus Christ, the Son of the living God. Instead we horde this pearl of great price thinking if we share it with others, somehow its value will diminish in our eyes.

But I wonder if the real reason for our apathy is a lack of confidence—confidence in our ability to articulate the story of salvation to a world with scales on their eyes. Afraid if we don't explain it just the right way, people just won't get it! This might come from our own inner knowledge that we just don't know the Word of God well enough to where we are comfortable sharing it with others. We are afraid we will be exposed as shallow believers, unable to share the greatest story ever told with those we know—those who desperately need it.

We see Christian leaders like Rob Bell trip all over themselves when given an opportunity to share the good news of the gospel on national television and fear we will look just as foolish if we try. Well, here are two simple steps to overcome this fear of sharing the gospel:

First, make sure you know the story yourself. Take time to study the Word of God and understand the basics of the tragic story of man's fall and the glorious story of how God, needing the perfect sacrifice for sin, took it upon Himself to bear that sacrifice.

Second, stop placing too much value on what you bring to the table in sharing the gospel. Our job is to plant a seed; God's job is to grow it. We don't need the eloquence of a Franklin Graham or Chuck Swindoll—just share the basic story of salvation and share your heart about how God has rescued and changed you—and leave the rest to God. Check in on occasion and see if the seed is starting to sprout. If it is, start watering it gently. That's all God asks us to do—plant a seed, watch and see if it sprouts, and if it does, nurture it along gently with his Word.

If the church as a whole, made up of individual Christians, can wake up from our apathy, things can change. The church will see real revival, one soul at a time. God's family will grow and we will find a renewed zeal to share the gospel with people we know. A groundswell might just occur where our churches again become filled with strong, committed Christians willing to make disciples of all nations.

Wouldn't that be something to behold . . .

March 12, 2012

Confusion: When human beings are overloaded with varying opinions and conflicting reports we are faced with the need to take a step back and process all we are hearing and seeing. Sometimes the more we try to process all this information, the more confused we become. Eventually many people just shut down mentally and accept the easiest conclusion we can think of, hoping to move on.

But sometimes this simplistic method of coping with conflicting opinions and emotions can get us into trouble. We take the easy way out of conflict hoping to just move on and end the confusion our brains and hearts are trying to sort out.

We want leaders who will clearly articulate their values and views, but when our leaders--political, social or religious—send us conflicting messages, we get confused and internally conflicted. We want to believe the best in our leaders so we often tend to ignore facts or opinions that might cast doubt upon them. Is this happening to the millions who follow Rick Warren?

No one will deny that Rick Warren has led many people to a relationship with Jesus Christ. His "Purpose Driven Life" book has been read by millions and used in numerous Bible studies around the world. But has the success of that book and the accompanying fame changed Rick Warren? Has he become addicted to the trappings of fame and popularity at the expense of the pure gospel? Many think so as he sends out conflicting messages on Islam and homosexuality.

A question we need to ask ourselves is this: Do we judge a man on what he says? Or what he does? And please do not give me that weak, tired argument that we are not to judge anyone. While true that we are not to judge the salvation of any man, scripture clearly tells us we are to make judgments on one another as Christians, confronting one another when we see sin or false teachings. Jesus did it with the Pharisees and Paul did it with the other Apostles and the church of his time.

The Christian Church in America faces some very challenging times. She is under attack from the secular culture and media and our rights as Christians are being stripped slowly but surely by new laws and regulations. Many of our youth are leaving the church and will never return. In a time of crisis we need leaders who are strong, principled and consistent; not leaders who change their views to appease whomever they happen to be speaking to on a particular day.

Have we fallen into a devious trap set by Satan that teaches we are never to question our Christian leaders anymore? Is it in our best interest to simply blindly follow our leaders no matter what they say or do? Do we believe just because they are anointed or appointed as leaders that they are infallible? If that is indeed what we believe we are in serious, serious trouble.

Jesus spoke out boldly against the religious teachers of his day because they were hypocrites and they were leading people astray. Paul commended the Bereans for not taking anything he taught as truth and checking it against the scriptures to determine its truth and validity. But sadly these days, with biblical illiteracy at an all time high, many seem to be choosing to just accept what they are taught as truth because we are too busy to actually read what God's Word says about the issues of our time. If this continues we are in very serious trouble as a church.

No leader—political or religious—should ever be followed blindly. Every one of them must be held accountable for their words and actions. That is our duty as Christians, a duty we seem to be ignoring more and more these days—at a time when we can least afford to.

I'm Mike LeMay standing up for the truth . . .